Q&A
Torts

Routledge Questions & Answers Series

Each Routledge Q&A contains questions on topics commonly found on exam papers, with comprehensive suggested answers. The titles are written by lecturers who are also examiners, so the student gains an important insight into exactly what examiners are looking for in an answer. This makes them excellent revision and practice guides.

Titles in the series:
Q&A Company Law
Q&A Commercial Law
Q&A Contract Law
Q&A Criminal Law
Q&A Employment Law
Q&A English Legal System
Q&A Equity and Trusts
Q&A European Union Law
Q&A Evidence
Q&A Family Law
Q&A Intellectual Property Law
Q&A Jurisprudence
Q&A Land Law
Q&A Medical Law
Q&A Public Law
Q&A Torts

For a full listing, visit http://www.routledge.com/cw/revision

Q&A Torts

Birju Kotecha

Routledge
Taylor & Francis Group

LONDON AND NEW YORK

Eleventh edition published 2015
by Routledge
2 Park Square, Milton Park, Abingdon, Oxon OX14 4RN

and by Routledge
711 Third Avenue, New York, NY 10017

Routledge is an imprint of the Taylor & Francis Group, an informa business

© 2015 Birju Kotecha

First edition published by Cavendish Publishing 1993
Tenth edition published by Routledge 2013

British Library Cataloguing in Publication Data
A catalogue record for this book is available from the British Library

Library of Congress Cataloging in Publication Data
Kotecha, Birju, author.
Q&A torts / Birju Kotecha. – Eleventh edition.
    pages cm – (Routledge questions & answers series)
    Includes index.
    ISBN 978-1-138-78021-7 (pbk) – ISBN 978-1-315-77088-8 (ebk) 1. Torts–England–Examinations, questions, etc. I. Title. II. Title: Questions and answers torts.
    KD1949.6.K68 2015
    346.4203–dc23   2014025863

ISBN: 978-1-138-78021-7 (pbk)
ISBN: 978-1-315-77088-8 (ebk)

Typeset in TheSans
by Wearset Ltd, Boldon, Tyne and Wear

Printed and bound in Great Britain by
TJ International Ltd, Padstow, Cornwall

Contents

Preface

The law of tort does not stand still. Its policy and legal principles are forever being driven and re-shaped by a fast-moving common law. This book takes into account recent developments in the law, including cases such as *Coventry and Others v Lawrence and Another* (2014), *Taylor v (A) Novo UK Ltd* (2013) and *CCWS and others v Various Claimants and others* (2012), amongst others. Perhaps more unusually there has also been recent legislative reform through the **Defamation Act 2013** which has considerably transformed the law of libel and slander. This has also been updated. Otherwise, I have attempted to reflect the law as at June 2014.

As with this series, the spirit of this book is focused on providing examples of effective writing when answering both essay and problem questions. To this end, the introductory chapter is essential reading as it provides a range of tips, hints and strategies that will help sharpen and improve your written analysis. It will also allow you to read the answers in this book with critical scrutiny and help you identify where you need to focus in order to improve. New features that are in this edition are intended to provide you with further support. This includes guidance in 'how to read' questions which will highlight particular issues of concern in the question but also help you approach and plan your response. There is also greater direction provided in 'up for debate' boxes that will precede essay questions which will introduce topical academic discussions and direct you to further readings. This will help you become more self-starting and advance the academic quality of your discussion so you can fully convey the depth of your understanding and your ability to engage with critical perspectives.

I am thankful to Emma Nugent, Rebekah Jenkins and (formerly) Damian Mitchell at Routledge for their guidance in revising this edition. I am also grateful to both John Bates and William Ralston at Northumbria Law School who have frequently provided clarity of thought and insight in illuminating many principles of the law of tort. Any errors remain my own.

This book is otherwise dedicated to all those law students whose ambition and motivation to learn and achieve, makes teaching so rewarding.

Birju Kotecha
Northumbria Law School
July 2014

Table of Cases

Table of Legislation

■ EU Directives

■ Treaties and Conventions

Guide to the Companion Website

www.routledge.com/cw/revision

Visit the Law Revision website to discover a comprehensive range of resources designed to enhance your learning experience.

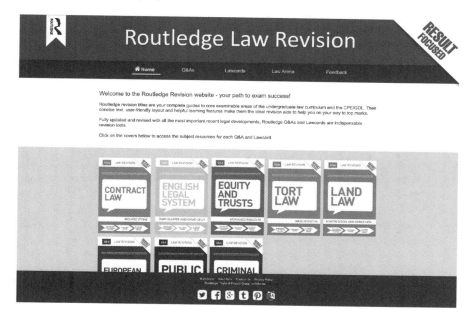

The Good, The Fair, & The Ugly

Good essays are the gateway to top marks. This interactive tutorial provides sample essays together with voice-over commentary and tips for successful exam essays, written by our Q&A authors themselves.

Multiple Choice Questions

Knowledge is the foundation of every good essay. Focusing on key examination themes, these MCQs have been written to test your knowledge and understanding of each subject in the book.

Bonus Q&As

Having studied our exam advice, put your revision into practice and test your essay writing skills with our additional online questions and answers.

Introduction to the Features of the Book

Welcome to Torts Q&A! The main purpose of this book is to support you in writing effective examination answers (or even, in some limited circumstances, written assignments). It will provide a means of consolidating your understanding of torts and enable you to improve the way in which you organise and structure your writing when answering both essay and problem questions. The book therefore is designed to provide guidance in meeting the demands of questions across tort law and will hopefully improve your confidence and your ultimate grade.

WHAT DOES THIS BOOK DO?

The book focuses on the skills of answering questions and there is a justified focus on answering tort problem questions. Solving problem questions is a skill that is acquired and honed throughout your studies and across many different areas of law. It is not an innate skill we all possess and it's something that is a unique feature of the study of law. It requires a logical and methodical application of law to a set of facts. I hope this book will support you in developing a rewarding approach to such questions and put you in the best place to achieve at the highest level. There is also due coverage of essay questions in those areas of tort that are open for critical discussion. When you have been studying you will have been considering not only what the law says, but what it does and what it is about. Its potential and its flaws and the difficulties in developing law that strike the best balance between the needs of claimants, the liability of defendants and broader concerns that are in the public interest. As a result tort law can be inconsistent and case law can be driven heavily by policy, making it potentially unfair and, at the very least, problematic. I hope that the book will help you review such critical debates and support you in better marshalling your own analysis in writing effective essays.

WHAT DOES THIS BOOK NOT DO?

However this book is not intended to teach you the subject from scratch and cannot do so. It should ideally be used with your textbooks, lectures, cases along with any further reading. Therefore this book will not replace learning tort throughout the duration of your course. Finally this book also does not provide answers that are perfect and merely require memorising. A common mistake made when using Questions & Answers books for revision is to memorise the answers provided and try to reproduce them in exams. This approach is a sure-fire pitfall, likely to result in a poor overall mark because your answer will not be specific enough to the particular question on your exam paper. There is also a danger that reproducing an answer in this way would be treated as plagiarism. You must instead be sure to read the question carefully, to identify the issues and problems it is asking you to address and to answer it directly in your exam (features such as the book's 'How to Read this Question' sections will help you with this). If you take our examiners' advice and use your Q&A to focus on your question-answering skills and understanding of the law, you will be ready for whatever your exam paper has to offer.

THE QUESTIONS

In this spirit, the book provides a range of 'typical' examination questions and provides structured suggested solutions to them. The book is arranged in a series of chapters which cover a range of topics considered on the majority of undergraduate tort courses. Not every aspect of tort law is set out here, but care has been taken to focus on areas that are particularly common and are likely to be of keen interest to examiners. Such areas will therefore be an essential part of tort law, for example common law negligence or areas that are particularly controversial and open to debate, for example psychiatric injury.

Problem questions and essay questions are fundamentally different and a different skillset and approach is required for answering them. Most tort subjects, as this book will demonstrate, are able to be assessed by either method, although some are generally seen as lending themselves to a specific format more readily. In the case of problem questions you will be presented with a set of facts and be required to discuss the liability of the relevant parties, often by being asked to advise one of those participants. For this you will be required to not only to state the relevant law, but to apply it within the context of the parties and the factual scenario you are presented with. By contrast in essay questions you will often be given a critical statement that addresses a problem that the relevant area of tort law presents. You will be asked to discuss the statement and often the extent to which you agree whether it is accurate. Thus what the answer is demanding is a greater focus on analysis and critical comment that will follow a particular argument and address the statement. More advice on both types of questions is given below.

Depending on how much you have enjoyed or closely engaged with the topic, it can often mean you will have a preference over a certain question. Don't think that one type of question (essay or problem) is inherently more difficult to achieve a higher mark in. No doubt sometimes it will be better to choose one question or the other (because it will allow you to choose one that plays to your strengths or others may appear acutely complicated or difficult). However where you have a choice, give every question due consideration and do not allow length alone to put you off. A key piece of advice is to always *plan* your answer, whether this is an essay or a problem question. Do not be rushed into beginning writing your answers even if everyone around you has begun scribbling away! They are unlikely to produce the high standard you can achieve if you follow this advice.

LENGTH OF ANSWERS

The attempt has been aimed to keep all answers to approximately 1,000 words. This is to reflect what can be expected by an informed student writing in exam-like conditions, where time can be pressing and the desire to be brief and concise is greater than the need to cover everything in exhaustive detail. The length of any examination answer will depend not only on your own knowledge and your performance on the day, but naturally the time you have available and the number of questions you are required to answer. It should be borne in mind that not everything that is worthy of credit can realistically be included and that for most essay questions, a whole book, or at least a chapter of a book, could be written on the answer. You of course could not be expected to cover everything in its maximum depth, indeed if you tried you may end up 'waffling' too long on a narrow point, are likely to run out of time and have an answer that has limited coverage of the relevant issues. By contrast in a problem question, the information you are given is 'leading you through' and 'pointing you in the direction' of your answer, so it is to be expected that certain legal elements that are staring at you should be combined with reasoned application. Therefore a balance has to be struck and this book provides samples of answers which will help you draw the type of good balance that will help your own responses. The answers in the following chapters address the questions in a way a high-achieving candidate would. What connects them all is not that they are necessarily 'perfect' but that they provide a structure, clarity, coverage and focus and adopt the typical features of a good response to the question. You may read them and think they can be sharpened and this would be a good strategy to enhance your preparation.

SUGGESTIONS FOR EXAM TECHNIQUE

Below are tips that will improve your exam technique but also warnings about common failings often found in weaker exam answers The two types of question are considered separately because as noted above, they carry different expectations. However there are also some points which apply to both and these are included at the end.

EXAM TECHNIQUE FOR PROBLEM QUESTIONS

Problem questions are the bread and butter of all law students. Law and courses like tort law are naturally about solving disputes and therefore applying your knowledge to problems and drawing conclusions is a necessary skill to develop. You will be given a problem and asked to discuss potential causes of action for the relevant claimants and the liability of the defendant(s) on the facts. In your discussion you will be expected to state the law, but of most importance is to apply it to the details of the facts and where possible draw conclusions on those facts. You may already be versed in particular approaches in solving problem scenarios. One common approach is the '**Identify–Define–Explain–Apply**' method when you tackle the writing of answers. Below are general tips and advice that in my own experience are important to appreciate when answering problem questions. You should of course heed relevant advice given by your course tutors and where any advice conflicts, follow the advice of your tutor.

(1) First, do not be deterred by a seemingly long and complicated problem question. The information in the problem will be giving you clues and hints about what to write about, and the length of the problem in many ways gives you more to work with in the answer. Read the problem carefully and highlight/annotate and circle relevant facts that will be worthy of discussion or are critical when you apply the law. Obviously one of the first things to highlight and confirm is to identify the relevant claimants and defendants. List who is bringing a claim and who is being sued. This initial activity will give you some clarity and will provide an initial structure to avoid any confusion.

(2) Where possible and if it has not been given in the question, begin your answer by identifying the general area of relevant law or the applicable statutes in a brief opening paragraph that introduces the parties.

(3) One of the most important aspects of answering a problem question is to have a very good structure. Do not jump between ideas or different aspects of liability as you are likely to miss aspects of the question and the work will appear patchy, out of sequence and therefore lacking coherence. How you organise your discussion will vary according to the number of claimants and defendants and the similarity of the law that applies to them. As a rule of thumb it is best to complete the liability of an individual claimant one by one, rather than trying to do all of the parties simultaneously. If you take the latter approach and especially where the position of the parties are substantially different, this can lead to confusion and make it harder for you to draw overall conclusions. Also, as would be the case in practice, you would deal and judge the prospects of success for a claim on an individual basis rather than judging parts of a claim for many people. It is for this reason that time spent planning a problem question answer is never wasted, so that your answer is focused and follows a clear logic; but do remember to check back with your plan when actually writing the answer. Examiners are often disappointed to see that crucial aspects of a plan have not been included in the relevant answer, and little (if any) credit for this can be given

(4) When tackling a problem question, you need to be aware of the facts and refer to them and the people within. However do not needlessly repeat the facts in your answer. Weaker candidates will do this excessively and it will be evident to an examiner that the candidate is compensating for lack of preparation. The examiner already knows the question: (s)he wrote it.

(5) Remember the main mission is to solve the problem, but this will still mean there is still space in your answer to define your terms and legal principles that you are then going to go on to apply. These are basic marks that you can earn easily, don't fall into the trap that such principles are worth omitting because they are self-evident. However do not over elaborate and over-describe. For instance paraphrase particular sections of a statute and be concise in your description of the law, referring the reader to the case names, statute sections and so on. If you over-describe the law not only will you arguably run out of time but you are likely to only have application that is too lightweight to attract higher credit.

(6) As a golden rule *never* write 'all you know' about a topic when answering a problem question – the skill you should be displaying is the ability to identify, be selective and

apply aspects of the law you have learnt that are relevant. It may help to think about how you would explain the legal position to clients – they are only going to be interested in the aspects of the law *that affect their situation*, and the strengths and weaknesses of it; not, for example, the history of the law. For example, in a case involving personal injury in negligence the examiner (or even a client) does not need to know about the development and rejection of the two stage *Anns* test; in other words a lengthy explanation of the history of the law will not be relevant. This will be the mark of a weaker candidate. Nor do you need a lengthy description of the facts of cases on a very minor point in the scenario. All of this could be occupying too much time and will not be focused on answering the problem given to you, therefore not attracting any marks. Be confident and learn to make editorial choices. Indeed, there would be little point writing down full lengthy case names if you have already referred to them previously in your answer. Likewise if you have thoroughly explained and applied a tort to an individual claimant, and are having to do it to another claimant, then focus more on the application, and the relevant conclusions without re-explaining everything again. This is especially the case when you are racing against the clock. Remember the examiner will be looking at what impression your answer is conveying, not have a checklist marking system.

(7) Having clarified the relevant law, apply the law to the facts. This means showing how the law you have stated relates to the factual scenario you have been given. This is really what marks out an answer from mediocre to something that is worthy of much higher credit. When you apply the law ensure you do this as closely as possible referring to the relevant names in the facts and any specific behaviour, actions and events that take place (without repeating it). As part of this application you can conclude whether the facts meet the requirements of the law to apply. Justify such conclusions by citing any reasons. For instance where facts of decided cases are relevant and worth mentioning is if you are drawing an analogy or a comparison with the facts of the question, and are drawing a conclusion on that point.

(8) Where you are not sure about a particular conclusion due to a lack of information, then you are entitled to cite that there is too little information, and raise those questions that need to be answered as part of your application of the law. It is often not always possible to be definitive, even at the end of your analysis so if you needed to know something more precisely, e.g. the age of a child claimant, then raise this with an explanation, because this will demonstrate that you have realised this is an important factor. (In practice, of course, you would ask your client these types of questions.) By the same token do not significantly re-word or re-imagine the facts by going off on a tangent, with several 'it would depend if … and if he had done this, or he had not done this, or it is not known whether he did but the liability would have been different etc.' Too much of this and you will straying away from the problem, which is applying the law on a given set of facts to the scenario and coming to your own judgments.

(9) Finally some tips on style. Treat your examiner as an intelligent lay person. Ask yourself, for example, who is liable, what for, how can it be established and why liability is likely or not to be made out. The process of getting to the answer, just as in a maths question, is almost as important as the answer itself. As for your writing

however never personalise, and therefore avoid 'I believe, I think, I feel and so on'. Your argument will sound weaker and it is not good practice. Rather write in the third person which will sound more academic (e.g. 'It can be concluded', 'It is likely', 'It would be possible', 'It is submitted that' or 'It is arguable that' or 'A claimant is required to prove'). Don't begin or conclude with, e.g. *X will win because* … You may well be wrong, and you will not fully consider any alternative arguments if you start from such a definite position. A better introduction would be 'For A to be liable for …, X would need to prove liability under …). Unless your tutor expressly discourages it, then I would suggest the use of sub-headings which will help in the organisation of the work, and at least you may be able include headings in the margins so you are clear on who you are talking about and why. Finally if a particular principle applies more than once (e.g. for two different parties) then once you have described it once, then it is perfectly acceptable to refer the reader to a previous part of your answer (e.g. 'see above') or simply to discuss it in very concise terms. There would be little need to re-describe the law twice in an answer, where you have already accurately done it once.

(10) Do not feel that you have to have a definite answer, but you can indicate in your con-clusion what you think is the *most likely* outcome based on the strength of your arguments in your answer. The point is to get you to demonstrate the ability of making a reasoned application of the law to the facts.

EXAM TECHNIQUE FOR ESSAY QUESTIONS

In the case of essay questions you will have been introduced to areas of controversy and legal criticism through tutorial sessions or readings recommended by your lecturers. Sometimes this is because the case law has got itself in such a complicated and inconsist-ent state, that even the judges themselves call for clarification by a higher court or Parlia-ment. Or that the law has not been able to keep up pace with new developments and there indeed has been a legislative or a Law Commission response. Such areas of tort make it more natural for a discursive essay rather than a problem question. Therefore as you are studying tort it is always worth your while gaining a thorough understanding of wider criticisms and views that challenge the current state of the law. Have a grasp of debates and some of the critical opinion which can come from judges and case law, aca-demics, theorists and even your own knowledge. You will be reminded of these when you review the answers and come across 'Up for Debate' features among many of the essay questions in this book. Generally if you address these debates where relevant and applic-able to the argument when answering the question, then you can expect to do very well. It is always worth referring to academic commentary where you can. When you review the answers here, consider where and when you might add academic opinion to develop some of the arguments raised by including reference to such secondary sources, and even your own analysis.

(1) Essay questions will ask you to do something specific, such as to criticise a proposi-tion, to analyse developments within an area of liability or to balance competing imperatives (such as privacy and freedom of expression). Make sure you do. It is a common frustration of examiners when the candidate answers their 'own' question

rather than the one set. It is not advisable to try to 'question spot' in advance and then produce your rehearsed piece for whichever question is actually asked. This is a strategy that will not pay off and lead to disappointment.

(2) As with problem questions, writing 'all you know' about a topic is not a good technique and the time spent thinking about what the question is actually asking you, and organising the information you have to fit this question, will be crucial to the mark you receive. A plan is very helpful, and you should aim to end with a conclusion that refers back to, and answers, the question set.

(3) When you read the statement, try to think of what your position is regarding the statement and the question being asked. When you have identified what your view is, try to present this in your introduction and closely follow that line of argument throughout your answer through the use of appropriate examples and analysis. By doing this early on, the examiner will know you are closely addressing the question and avoiding an essay that is too balanced and descriptive.

(4) Many essays follow an 'upside-down pyramid' approach, where the early parts of the essay define the key terms in the statement and provide the broader legal background and context of the law. This is a good strategy to adopt, as much of the early discussion will be focused on clarifying and explaining key features, such as principles and case law that affects your analysis. It is important though that this early description does not dominate the answer and you are in turn focused on analysis, criticism and arguments, which is where the pyramid is narrow and reaches a point where the analysis will be more in-depth. Too much early description and the essay will never fully develop the critique and argument you want to pursue.

(5) You should try to ensure that you integrate the analysis of leading thinkers or commentators, including, of course, judges where appropriate. Quote or paraphrase their comments and this will enhance the quality of the answer but do always attribute who is making those comments. This can be used to support your own argument, or it could be that your position differs to the argument, in which case attempt to critically engage with the comments and defend a particular position where applicable. However, do not be tempted to 'rant' or develop your own stream of consciousness. You must base arguments on established law and principles.

(6) Make sure you answer the question which is critical and ensure that your conclusion always expressly addresses the statement and question which will tie your essay off well.

(7) Tips on style: as with problem questions, adopt an impersonal style. Avoid the use of the word 'I', e.g. I think, I believe, I feel etc. A more detached style enables you to appear to be more objective, and will prompt you into using the opinions of learned commentators.

EXAM PAPERS

The typical tort paper will usually include questions on each of the principal areas of liability and it would be a very unique paper that did not contain at least one question relating to negligence. The main interests protected are the person, property and reputation, so that might include negligence, trespass to land/person, nuisance and/or *Rylands* and defamation, at a minimum. More specialist application of negligence, in say the context of psychiatric injury, product liability, pure economic loss and occupiers' liability are also all favourites with examiners, and developing areas such as privacy could always be a possibility. Ultimately it will depend on the syllabus you study. The building blocks or basic requirements of particular torts are key to their explanation: such as, for example, the requirement that there is a duty, a breach of that duty, and the defendant legally and factually caused damage, for a negligence claim. You will notice, therefore, that in the suggested answers given in this book there is some repetition of this key material in response to different questions. Certain principles such as defences, vicarious liability and rules relating to limitation periods and available remedies will apply to many areas, although there will be more specialist application in different torts as well.

GENERAL EXAMINATION ADVICE

(1) It is important to back all your assertions and statements of law with authority (i.e. a case or a statute), in both essay and problem answers. In this book, a full case name and date is given, but your memory may not be able to retain all of this information, and trying to do so may make you spend less time on the more important aspect of your revision, namely understanding legal concepts. Therefore it would not be wise committing to memory the years of the cases. The whole case name and the court where the decision was made are obviously best; but if not, one name (preferably the first) will be better than nothing, or, if you cannot remember any part of the name, a brief outline of the facts will identify it. Otherwise, as mentioned, the facts of cases are usually relatively unimportant and you can waste a lot of valuable time writing them out in details, unless the facts are very similar to your scenario *or* different in an important aspect, which means that there is room for *distinguishing* existing case law. It is the *ratio*, or legal reasoning, from the case that is important to include. However, you will need to know the facts of the cases to identify similarities etc., and in some essays, particularly in a developing area of law such as privacy, the facts of the cases will be valuable to the answer. Do note that it is not feasible or realistic to cite every single possible authority and nor is it desirable. You will not gain marks for every authority cited in isolation. Mentioning cases is not an end in itself. It is not simply a memory task either. Do not lose sight of the fact that the answer you write must convey the impression that you have a firm grasp of authority, and the legal points you make are broadly supported by them.

(2) When citing statutes, the full name and year should be given (abbreviations are acceptable thereafter if you have explained them initially, e.g. **Occupiers' Liability Act 1957 (OLA 1957)**. If you are provided with statutory material, or allowed to take it in with you to the exam, it will be even more important to cite the section/subsection accurately, so it may be worth checking. However this is where your familiarity with the statute from your preparation for workshops and seminars will pay off. However do be selective as you will be wasting valuable time if you copy out large segments of the statutory material, but you may want to include a short 'quote', e.g. referring to an independent contractor undertaking work on the premises as someone 'in the

exercise of his calling', who will therefore 'appreciate and guard against any special risks ordinarily incident to it' (**OLA 1957** s 2(3)(b)). Also do not make the common mistake of referring to this as s 3(b).

(3)   Manage your time effectively so that you always provide the required number of answers. So if, for example, the examination requires four answers, make sure you *at least attempt* four answers. Failing to do so will greatly diminish your chances of success. For example, answering only three questions if you were required to answer four will immediately lose you 25 per cent of the marks for the paper, and it is unlikely that you will be able to compensate for that loss within the other answers. It is better to provide a limited answer than none at all, as the first, basic marks, are often the easiest to earn. Including them as bullet points if you have run out of time is better than nothing.

(4)   Never leave an exam early, however tempting it may be to get out of the exam room. In fact, always allow enough time to go back over your answers when you finish, as there will almost always be small additions or amendments you can make. This will also give you the opportunity to rectify careless mistakes such as muddling up the names of the parties (rendering your advice incorrect or incoherent), which can cost you crucial marks. Examiners have to mark what is written, not what you may have intended to write, so ensure you have expressed yourself clearly and accurately (and preferably, legibly!).

(5)   Finally in the lead-up to the exam, the best advice is really to practise. Use past examination papers and time yourself. Try to simulate exam conditions by not referring to your notes or texts, as you will be best placed into achieving well.

Tort can be a challenging course but with early revision, a clear understanding of the law and a good grasp of the best way to improve your writing, then you can achieve highly. I hope this book will assist you in meeting the demands of your revision in tort, and you achieve a grade that will be a further springboard for greater success. **Good Luck!**

General Introduction

The law of tort is a fascinating and fundamental area of English law. It provides the principles which apply in many aspects of our daily lives, helping to define our legal relationships when those around cause us harm; from neighbours to employers to people whose care we rely on. The law is very fluid and constantly evolving often moulded by the desire to uphold broad policy considerations weighed against the competing demand for individual wrongs, to be remedied.

In addition to being a 'core' subject for the legal profession, a clear understanding of its principles is required for other areas as diverse as environmental, employment, media and company law. Tort illustrates, moreover, another characteristic of English law, in that it is primarily a common law area – its rules have been largely developed through the decisions of the courts rather than dominated by statutes. As a result of this, there can be a bewildering array of cases and rules, and many of you may find difficulty in deciding what information is relevant to a problem.

If you are such a student then this book attempts to help you. The book's focus is to tackle the problem faced when you need to be selective in determining what is most essential to include in an answer. It is not intended as a substitute for lectures or for using textbooks or law reports or articles. The more reading you do of lecture notes, textbooks, articles, cases and statutes, the more you can benefit from this book. The book is aimed at illustrating how to set about answering questions in the law of tort through the use of written answers. These answers are not intended to be perfect solutions, no such thing exists; rather, they are intended to demonstrate the type of well-reasoned and structured answer that would attract credit from a well-prepared student.

What the book shows is how to best present, organise and structure your knowledge so you can gain the best possible grades. In particular, emphasis has been placed on the way in which the legal principles relevant to a question should be stated and applied. Any examination problem question is designed to test your grasp of legal principles and your ability to apply those principles to the given facts. So strategies like arguing in the alternative, having a good structure and the use of authority are one of the many strategies that this book will convey. Similarly for essay questions you will see the type of focus, critique and analysis that really distinguishes good answers. It is hoped that when you read through the book, you will gain the encouragement that you can do the same.

The questions provided in this book are typical LLB examination questions, as regards both style and complexity. Broadly speaking, the cases and principles cited should be familiar to you, though this will depend on the emphasis placed on your tort course. Answering questions is not a finite exercise with marks given for the number of relevant precedents cited. The dynamic and common-law led nature of the subject will mean you may also be aware of other current precedents which may have equal application. This is absolutely fine and where possible you should keep up to date with the current movement and developments of the case law. It is how you use the case law to argue and reason which is really what matters. A careful study of the answers to the questions contained in this book should also reveal several things. You will notice how basic concepts frequently reappear across a range of topic areas. You will similarly notice how there may be a common academic tone. As you write more, you too will develop your own academic voice. You will also notice the broadly consistent and logical approaches to structure and the use of authority, which will give you greater faith and confidence in your own approach and writing style.

You may decide to dip into this book, reading answers on topic areas that you find most challenging. However if one thing only can be recommended it is that you **must read** the Introduction to the Features of the Book chapter. It is essential reading as it will not only provide information on the broad coverage of the book, but also the tips, strategies and examination advice that have inspired many of the written answers here and will help you draw on the best practice when it comes to your own writing. Writing examination-style responses in timed conditions is a skill that can definitely be improved, and the book provides examples where that skill has been mastered.

When you read the answers in the book your reaction should be 'I can do that', not, 'I could never write an answer like that.' Even where it appears that you cannot reach the level required remember that there will always be some allowance made as you are in exam conditions. Tort is an absorbing and complex area of law that always captures legal curiosity. Coupled with the confidence to solve problems and pursue critical arguments, your confidence will soon grow in the quality of your writing. With good motivation, you will soon feel comforted by the knowledge that the grade you are going to gain will reflect both interest and preparation. I wish you the best of luck.

1 Negligence – Duty of Care Generally and Economic Loss

INTRODUCTION

Please note the first four chapters are all concerned primarily with the tort of common law negligence. They are divided into chapters for the purpose of clarity with different areas emphasised. However as you will know by now the concepts of duty, breach, causation and the general defences all form key components of forming liability in the law of negligence. Therefore the coverage of the answers will, to a greater or lesser degree, be duplicated in many of the first 14 questions in this book.

Questions solely on duty of care, however, usually take the form of an essay, typically on the test for imposing a duty. It is important therefore that you are aware of the stages of its development. It is also vital to be thoroughly familiar with situations in which limits are placed on whether a duty of care will exist. This chapter will include coverage of such limitations that are found within the area of negligent misstatement and economic loss, through the form of three essay questions and two problem questions. The second chapter will consider limits posed on the existence of a duty of care when considering recovery for psychiatric injury, the liability of the emergency services as well as the policy implications of the 'compensation culture' phenomena.

Checklist

Students must be familiar with the following areas:

(a) the development of a test for ascertaining the existence of a duty of care;

(b) negligent misstatement:
- statements made to a known recipient and the special relationship;
- statements put into general circulation;

(c) economic loss:
- liability for negligent acts or statements;
- the decision in *Junior Books v Veitchi* (1983);
- the decision in *Hedley Byrne v Heller* (1964);
- the judicial retreat from *Junior Books*;
- the current position regarding economic loss.

QUESTION 1

'Although the decision of the House of Lords in *Anns v Merton London Borough Council* (1978) was welcomed as a rationalisation of the law, it is now regarded as too simplistic and the so-called "incremental" approach is now universally used to determine the existence of a duty of care.'

▶ **Discuss this statement.**

How to Read this Question

The question takes the form of a typical essay question by providing a quote which will require a critical discussion. The examiner is looking for a consideration of the development from *Anns* to the new incremental approach and whether this is more effective than the *Anns* test. There needs to be a discussion of the relationship/differences between the current incremental approach and the test in *Anns*, i.e. is *Anns* incorporated into our current approach or is the test distinct. As implied in the question, the examiner is looking for a thorough understanding of the duty of care element as it is today.

How to Answer this Question

The following points need to be discussed:

- ❖ a brief background to *Anns v Merton London Borough Council* (1978);
- ❖ the *Anns* test;
- ❖ the judicial retreat from *Anns*;
- ❖ the current approach of the courts based on *Caparo v Dickman* (1990).

Answer Structure

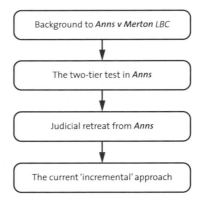

Background to **Anns v Merton** LBC

The two-tier test in **Anns**

Judicial retreat from **Anns**

The current 'incremental' approach

Up for Debate

The test in *Anns* is often taken to be a controversial development and seen as a starting point for the expansion of liability in negligence. The existence of a duty of care often reflects many of the core policy aims of tort, and many view the duty of care threshold as a control device to restrict floods of claims. This was a risk created in the era of *Anns*. Two articles that consider fundamental questions about the concept of a duty of care and the many judicial developments that have shaped its modern relevance are N McBride, 'Duties of care: do they really exist?' (2004) 24(3) Oxford Journal of Legal Studies 417 and K Stanton, 'The neighbour principle in the 21st century: yesterday's revolution' (2012) 20(2) Tort Law Review 61.

ANSWER

Although an attempt to formulate a general test or principle to decide whether, in any particular circumstances, a duty of care arose was made in *Heaven v Pender* (1883), it was not until 1932 and the judgment of Lord Atkin in *Donoghue v Stevenson* that the neighbour principle was firmly established. The courts were for some time a little hesitant in applying the neighbour test broadly until *Home Office v Dorset Yacht* (1970), where Lord Reid stated that the neighbour test was a statement of principle and should be applied as a working presumption. Proceeding from this, Lord Wilberforce, in *Anns v Merton London Borough Council* (1978), developed the principle arguing that the questions to ask are: First, is there a sufficient relationship of proximity of neighbourhood between the wrongdoer and the person who has suffered damage such that, in the reasonable contemplation of the former, carelessness on his part may cause damage to the latter, in which case a prima facie duty of care arises? Second, are there any considerations that ought to limit the scope of the duty or the class of persons to whom it is owed or the damage to which a breach of it may give rise? Thus, *Anns* neatly rationalised the law regarding the imposition of a duty of care by essentially stating that *Donoghue* applied unless there was a legal reason to disapply or modify *Donoghue*.[1]

However, the courts came to realise that the imposition of a duty of care involved more complex considerations. Thus, in *Junior Books v Veitchi* (1983), the House of Lords held that liability could arise in respect of economic loss; in *McLoughlin v O'Brian* (1983), the House limited the scope of psychiatric injury recovery. From 1985 onwards, perhaps fearing the rapid expansion of a liability culture, the courts began to retreat from *Anns* approach.[2]

The starting point was *Peabody Donation Fund v Sir Lindsay Parkinson* (1985). Lord Keith stated that the *Anns* test was not of 'a definitive character' and that, although a relationship of proximity must exist before a duty of care can arise, the existence of duty must depend on the circumstances of the case and whether it is just and reasonable to impose a duty. Further criticism was to be found in *Leigh and Sillavan v Aliakmon Shipping*, both in the Court of Appeal (1985) and the House of Lords (1988). Oliver LJ, in the Court of Appeal, stated that *Anns* did not establish a new test applicable in all cases, nor did it enable the court to determine policy in each case. The fear was that the first tier is so easily satisfied that it leaves too much to the second tier – namely, policy. The criticisms continued in

---

1   This introductory paragraph puts *Anns* in its historical context.
2   It is important to explain why the courts began to retreat or move away from the two-tier test in *Anns*, as there was a fear of unrestrained expansion.

Curran v Northern Ireland Co-Ownership Housing Association (1987) where Lord Bridge approved the judgment of Brennan J in the High Court of Australia in *Sutherland Shire Council v Heyman* (1985), in which he had held that it was preferable to develop novel categories of negligence incrementally and by analogy.

The two-tier test was again criticised in *Yuen Kun-Yeu v AG of Hong Kong* (1988) by the Privy Council and by the House of Lords in *Hill v Chief Constable of West Yorkshire* (1989) and *Murphy v Brentwood District Council* (1990). The incremental approach was finally affirmed in *Caparo Industries plc v Dickman* (1990) as involving the consideration of three factors: the loss must be reasonably foreseeable; there must be a relationship of proximity between the claimant and the defendant; it must be fair, just and reasonable to impose a duty of care. Recently, and to highlight the flexible approach the House of Lords has warned against too literal an application of the tests (*Customs & Excise v Barclays Bank* (2006)).

The first factor merely states that harm must be reasonably foreseeable, i.e. by a reasonable person in the position of the defendant. The second factor of proximity is, however, not immediately clear. The phrase was used in the *Anns* test and was considered in *Yuen Kun-Yeu*, in which Lord Keith stated that proximity was a composite test describing 'the whole concept of necessary relationship between claimant and defendant'. This factor of proximity would seem, in many circumstances, to be the policy tier of *Anns*. The third factor that it must be fair, just and reasonable to impose a duty of care also seems very similar to the policy test in *Anns*. Indeed, in *Marc Rich and Co AG v Bishop Rock Marine* (1995), Balcombe LJ doubted whether the words 'fair, just and reasonable' imposed any additional test to that of proximity. Similarly, in *Caparo*, Lord Oliver stated that the above factors were really three facets of the same thing; also supported by judicial sentiment in *Marc Rich*, where the Court of Appeal stated that the factors were helpful approaches to the pragmatic question as to whether a duty should be imposed. The broad criteria have been seen as a mask whereby courts consider the wide policy and public implications against holding a duty of care (see for example *Hill v Chief Constable of West Yorkshire* (1988) and the concern for both floods of claims and defensive practices, and this was recently affirmed in *Robinson v Chief Constable of West Yorkshire* (2014) by the Court of Appeal).

Thus, the simple two-stage test in *Anns* has been replaced with a more complex three-stage test in *Caparo* test in which the policy aspect of the court's decision has been restated in terms of proximity and whether it is fair, just and reasonable. However the courts have still been willing, where appropriate, to impose a duty of care in novel fact situations. Thus, a referee in a rugby match owes a duty of care to players to ensure that no dangerous play occurs (*Smoldon v Whitworth* (1997)). Furthermore, the police have been found to owe a duty of care to persons with suicidal tendencies, whether that person is of sound mind (*Reeves v Commissioner of Police of the Metropolis* (1998)) or of unsound mind (*Kirkham v Chief Constable of Greater Manchester* (1990)). This highlights how far the law has moved in a pragmatic direction from the unchecked and very 'loose' umbrella test that *Anns* provided.

QUESTION 2

Martin was on a train, reading a copy of the *Financial Times*. Norman, who was sitting next to him, asked Martin what his job was and Martin replied that he was a stockbroker. Norman then asked Martin for some advice on investment and Martin jokingly replied that publishing seemed to be a good area. As a result of this discussion, Norman invested his life savings in publishing shares. A few months later, the value of these shares fell dramatically and Norman lost all of his money. Depressed at being penniless, Norman then committed suicide.

▶ **Advise Norman's widow, Olivia, of any remedy she might have against Martin.**

How to Read this Question

This is a typical problem question in the area of negligent misstatement and thus will require a discussion of *Hedley Byrne v Heller* (1964) and other later relevant decisions. The examiner is looking for a clear structure and concise application that addresses any liability between Martin and Norman for the statements made on the train. It is important to note that it is Olivia who is bringing the claim against Martin and this must be reflected in your discussion to avoid confusion. The examiner will be assessing whether there are adequate definitions of the law but most critically application that makes the appropriate references to the parties and the facts.

How to Answer this Question

The following points need to be discussed:

- ❖ the duty of care between Martin and Norman considering *Hedley Byrne v Heller* (1964);
- ❖ social occasions and *Chaudry v Prabhakar* (1989);
- ❖ the developments in *Caparo v Dickman* (1990);
- ❖ Martin's liability for Norman's suicide.

Applying the Law

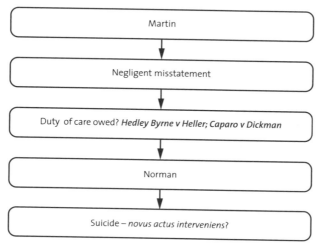

Martin

↓

Negligent misstatement

↓

Duty of care owed? *Hedley Byrne v Heller; Caparo v Dickman*

↓

Norman

↓

Suicide – *novus actus interveniens?*

ANSWER

In order to advise Olivia, we must first decide whether or not Martin owed Norman a duty of care. The traditional approach is to see whether a special relationship exists between Martin and Norman, as laid down in *Hedley Byrne v Heller* (1964). In *Hedley Byrne*, there were held to be three elements to special relationships.

First, the representor must possess a special skill. Furthermore, in *Mutual Life and Citizens Assurance v Evatt* (1971), the Privy Council held that liability would only arise when the statement was made in the course of a business. *Evatt* is a decision of the Privy Council and of persuasive authority but from which the principle is held that a prima facie duty will be owed by anyone who took it upon himself to make representations knowing that another person will reasonably rely on them. This view was later followed by the Court of Appeal in *Esso Petroleum v Mardon* (1976) and *Howard Marine v Ogden* (1976). This is often context dependent though and in *Gran Gelato v Richcliffe* (1992), it was held as unarguable that a vendor of premises did not owe a duty of care to a purchaser to take reasonable care when answering inquiries regarding the property. In *Spring v Guardian Assurance plc* (1994), Lord Goff stated that the reference to 'special skill' in *Hedley Byrne* should be understood in the broad sense and that it would include special knowledge. If this is today's approach, then Martin would satisfy this element of the test as he identified himself as a stockbroker, and was asked for investment advice by Norman.

Second, the representee must reasonably rely on the representations. In *Smith v Eric Bush* (1990), it was held to be reasonable for the purchaser of a modest house to rely on the survey carried out by the lender's surveyor, but not reasonable for a buyer with a 'buy to let' mortgage to do so, as they are deemed to have more business acumen (*Scullion v Bank of Scotland* (2011)). In *Edwards v Lee* (1991), it was held to be reasonable for the recipient of a reference provided by a solicitor concerning a client to rely on that reference. In *Royal Bank Trust (Trinidad) v Pampellonne* (1987), the Privy Council held that there was a difference between the giving of advice and the passing on of information, and that it may be more reasonable to rely on the former than the latter. Thus, the question here is whether it was reasonable for Norman to rely on Martin's statement and whether it was advice or the mere transfer of information. Here, it could be classed as passing information but it does not seem reasonable for Norman to rely on Martin as to how to invest his life savings. In *Chaudry v Prabhakar* (1989), May LJ, dissenting, stated that a duty of care would not be imposed regarding statements made on social occasions. The meeting between Martin and Norman could be described as social (an encounter on a train) and therefore, overall, it seems that Martin does not satisfy this requirement.

However, if this hurdle is overcome then the final requirement is that there must be knowledge of the type of transaction envisaged by the representee. Martin would satisfy this given the request for investment advice, and that its purpose would be to invest and make a financial commitment.

In *Caparo Industries plc v Dickman* (1990), Lord Oliver analysed *Hedley Byrne* and held that the required relationship between the representor and the representee may typically be held if (in short):

(a) the advice is required for a purpose made known to the representor when the advice is given;

(b) the representor knows that his advice will be communicated to the representee in order that it should be used by the representee for that purpose;

(c) it is known that the advice so communicated is likely to be acted upon by the representee for that purpose without independent inquiry; and

(d) it is so acted upon by the representee to his detriment.[3]

Lord Oliver emphasised that these conditions were neither conclusive nor exclusive, but that *Hedley Byrne* did not warrant any broader propositions (see also Lord Bingham in *Customs & Excise v Barclays Bank* (2006)). Considering these conditions, it seems that Martin satisfies (a), (b) and (d), but condition (c) is not satisfied and so again we conclude that Martin owes Norman no duty of care as regards the statement concerning shares. In *Hedley Byrne*, it was stated that a duty of care will arise where the representor voluntarily assumed a responsibility to the representee and it seems from the facts that Martin has not done this, as we are told he 'jokingly' recommended publishing shares in conversation. Despite the criticism of the assumption of responsibility concept by the House of Lords in *Caparo* and *Smith v Eric Bush*, recent decisions have emphasised its importance: *Spring; Henderson v Merrett Syndicates* (1994); *White v Jones* (1995) (see especially the speeches of Lord Goff). This is another factor that limits the imposition of a duty. Thus, Olivia cannot sue Martin in respect of the loss in value of the shares purchased by Norman.[4]

Even if Martin owed Norman a duty of care and was in breach of that duty, he would not be liable for Norman's subsequent suicide, as this causally may not be a reasonably foreseeable consequence of any breach (*The Wagon Mound (No 1)* (1961)). Norman's suicide could be regarded as a *novus actus interveniens* that broke the causal chain between Martin's earlier negligence (if any) and Norman's suicide. The criterion used by the courts is whether the conduct by the claimant is reasonable or not. Thus, in *McKew v Holland and Hannen and Cubitts* (1969), Lord Reid stated that 'if the injured man acts unreasonably, he cannot hold the defendant liable for injury caused by his own unreasonable conduct'. In contrast, in *Wieland v Cyril Lord Carpets* (1969), it was held that the defendants were liable for the injury as the claimant had not been unreasonable (see *Spencer v Wincanton Holdings* (2009)). As, by its nature, suicide is unreasonable conduct, it is arguable that he would not be liable for Norman's suicide, as that act may be considered to have broken the chain of causation. Norman's suicide would not allow any defences of *ex turpi causa non oritur actio* (*Kirkham v Chief Constable of Greater Manchester* (1990)), or *volenti*, as presumably Norman was of unsound mind when he committed suicide (*Kirkham*).

....

3   Here there is a potentially negligent misstatement, rather than action, and it is thus necessary to establish liability depending on the line of cases from *Hedley Byrne*. For further discussion of recovery for economic loss, as here, see Question 3.

4   Being able to attribute aspects of a leading case to the appropriate judge will add quality to your answer.

QUESTION 3

The current law relating to the existence of a duty of care in negligence for pure economic loss is so full of fine distinctions as to lack coherence and legal certainty.

▶ **Discuss this statement.**

How to Read this Question

This question provides a broad critical position requiring you to discuss the basic exception to the rule against recovery for pure economic loss in negligence, and whether the law of negligence for pure economic loss is full of fine distinctions, incoherent and uncertain. The examiner is looking for a critical discussion where you will provide evidence and examples that support or refute those labels. There will be a need for depth in your discussion, as well as broad coverage through the examples you choose, as to why pure economic loss recovery is so controversial and open to criticism.

How to Answer this Question

The following points should be discussed:

- ❖ the general exclusionary rule in negligence concerning claims;
- ❖ for pure economic loss;
- ❖ the principal exception in *Hedley Byrne*;
- ❖ the development and extension of the *Hedley Byrne* tests;
- ❖ the stretching of certain concepts, such as 'assumption of responsibility'.

Answer Structure

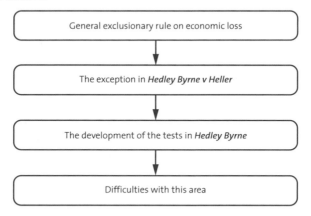

General exclusionary rule on economic loss

↓

The exception in *Hedley Byrne v Heller*

↓

The development of the tests in *Hedley Byrne*

↓

Difficulties with this area

Up for Debate

The basic exclusion imposed for the recovery for pure economic loss, provides many of the policy foundations for this area of tort law. The fact that it has been questioned repeatedly and there have been exceptions created as in *Hedley Byrne* serves as an example of how the law of tort is so choppy and inconsistent. The question remains where to draw the line on recovery and how far the *Hedley Byrne* exceptions extend. For a leading article that provides much of the early context and inconsistency then J Stapleton, 'Duty of care and economic loss: a wider agenda' (1991) 107 Law Quarterly Review 249 is a good read. For an interesting comparative perspective then P Giliker, 'Revisiting pure economic loss: lessons to be learnt from the Supreme Court of Canada' (2005) 25 Legal Studies 49 is a provoking piece that considers how claims may be classified, and what policy factors are given priority.

ANSWER

Negligence operates as a means to compensate a claimant for foreseeable losses caused by a defendant's breach of a duty of care (*Donoghue v Stevenson* (1932)). Considerations of policy have defined some extensions and contractions in the application of the duty of care, but there would appear to be some certainties, such as the rule against the recovery of pure economic loss. Loss said to be purely economic, that is, loss that was not the foreseeable consequence of physical injury to the claimant or the claimant's property,[5] is not normally recoverable in negligence for acts (*Weller & Co Ltd v Foot and Mouth Institute* (1966)). In *Spartan Steel & Alloys v Martin & Co* (1973) Lord Denning observed that the issue of recovery for economic loss was really a question of policy.

There had been a degree of expansion in negligence to embrace the potential for claims for pure economic loss. The general expansion of means of establishing a duty of care that had taken place in *Anns v Merton LBC* (1978) led to the boundaries being pushed further, until, in the case of *Junior Books v Veitchi* (1983) a 'high point' was reached in claims for pure economic loss, where it was argued that the distinction between tort and contract liability was being blurred.

Otherwise, early on, the courts had begun to develop exceptions to the general rule. In *Hedley Byrne v Heller and Partners Ltd* (1964) the House of Lords accepted that in certain circumstances a duty of care could arise where a person gave advice to another. A duty would exist where the claimant relied on a 'special relationship' with the defendant to give correct advice; second, that the defendant voluntarily assumed the risk of the provision of the advice; third, that the defendant knew or ought to have known that the claimant was in reliance; and, fourth, that it was reasonable in the circumstances for the claimant to rely on the defendant.[6] Each of these tests has been the subject of considerable qualification and evolution over time, which has increased legal complexity and decreased legal certainty.

5 Note that you are advising Norman's *widow*, who would be suing as his personal representative and/or as a dependant under the **Fatal Accidents Act 1976**.

6 There is sometimes confusion about what is meant by (pure) economic loss, but it should be remembered that loss of earnings as a result of being injured, or damage to property, though they are *monetary* losses, are *not* regarded as economic loss as they are as a result of physical injury.

Regarding the special relationship aspect, it is envisaged that the claimant will rely on the skill of the defendant in relation to the advice (*Mutual Life & Citizens' Assurance Co v Evatt* (1971); *Esso v Mardon* (1976)). This seems to indicate that the advice should be given in a business context, although the case of *Chaudry v Prabhaker* (1989) adds a degree of doubt as advice given on a social occasion was held to be sufficient, although the case is understood as being exceptional on this point. The issue of voluntary assumption of risk ties in with the special relationship. The leading contemporary case on this issue is *Henderson v Merrett Syndicates Ltd* (1994), where Lord Goff stated that if those accepting responsibility are assumed to provide a certain service and they do so negligently, they could be liable for economic losses stemming from this (see also *Lennon v Metropolitan Police Commissioner* (2004) and *Customs & Excise Commissioner v Barclays Bank* (2006)).

Due to the nature of the claimed relationship, it would often be straightforward to assume that a claimant relied on what they had been told. However, it is important that it is reasonable for the claimant to have relied on the information and this will depend on the context and the nature of the advice given. The facts of *Caparo Industries plc v Dickman* (1990) provides an illustration of this concept, where the House of Lords held that it was not reasonable for the claimant to have relied on the accounts and when information is given for one purpose, it is not reasonable for a third party to rely on the information for another purpose (see also *James McNaughton Papers Group Ltd v Hicks Anderson & Co.* (1991) and *Reeman v Department of Transport* (1997)).

In contrast to this decision was the case of *Law Society v KPMG Peat Marwick* (2000), where the Court of Appeal held it was fair, just and reasonable to impose a duty of care; it was foreseeable that incorrectly prepared accounts would lead to the fund being claimed upon, and because the Law Society was supposed to see the accounts annually, there was sufficient proximity. It would seem that the degree of connection between the maker and receiver of the statement is important.

These developments suggest a degree of extension to the original principles. Other evidence of expanding liabilities can be seen in the so-called 'wills cases' and in relation to the provision of employment references (*Spring v Guardian Assurance Ltd* (1994)). The wills cases have permitted claimants to recover in situations of pure economic loss, but in situations that do not easily fit within the general *Hedley Byrne* principles. The first of these to note was *Ross v Caunters* (1980), which involved loss to a claimant because the defendant solicitor had negligently prepared the will for his client. Clearly, the claimant had suffered pure economic loss and was in no 'special relationship' with the solicitor but what had occurred here was negligent performance of a service.

Many commentators have noted that this was quite unremarkable at the time, following on from the landmark decision in *Anns*, and thus took place within a period of expansion of the duty of care concept. The real interest comes when the reasoning was adopted in the case of *White v Jones* (1995) where Lord Goff referred to an 'impulse to do practical justice' in the case. However this laudable aim does not promote legal certainty, particularly when seen in light of a further extension in *Carr-Glynn v Frearsons* (1999).

There has been considerable development in the ability to recover for pure economic loss in negligence. Considerations of 'practical justice' have often seemed apparent, even if not always overtly expressed. While this is undoubtedly welcome for the claimant, the ability to predict which direction the law may take next is compromised. It could be concluded that the general incremental approach to the development of the duty concept in negligence has certainly found a receptive audience in relation to claims for pure economic loss.[7]

QUESTION 4

'Due to some of the difficulties of bringing an action in negligence, the tort of misfeasance in public office has recently become a popular alternative cause of action.'

▶ **Discuss the above statement, with particular reference to the scope of the tort of misfeasance in public office.**

How to Read this Question

This is an essay question, where the examiner is looking for an understanding of why the conceptual problems with the law of negligence, has made it more likely for a claimant to choose to sue in the tort of misfeasance in public office. However as the latter half of the question suggests, the examiner is looking for a good grasp of the principles of misfeasance in public office. You should only attempt this question if you are confident in the breadth of your knowledge in this tort.

How to Answer this Question

The following points need to be discussed:

❖ an outline of circumstances in which misfeasance in public office offers advantages over negligence; and

❖ a discussion of the principles of misfeasance in public office with particular reference to *Three Rivers v Bank of England* (2000) and subsequent cases.

Answer Structure

Problems with negligence

Principles of misfeasance in public office

Three Rivers v Bank of England and other cases

Advantages of misfeasance in public office

---

7 Being able to include a short quote from a leading case, and attribute it correctly, will add to the quality of your answer.

Up for Debate

There is an interesting debate about the existence of the tort of misfeasance of public office, in terms of its usefulness, its relationship to other intentional torts such as false imprisonment, and the rule on proving damage as a consequence. The Law Commission Consultation Paper 'Administrative redress: public bodies and the citizen' (LCCP 187, 2008) debated whether it should be abolished, and replaced with another fault based liability heading. However there are also policy considerations at play here in terms of public bodies protecting themselves against expensive litigation.

ANSWER

Claimants seeking to rely on the tort of negligence to recover for any loss beyond physical injury may find several difficulties in overcoming legal hurdles in establishing a successful cause of action.

In particular, they may find it difficult to establish the required degree of proximity between themselves and the defendant, which means that the claimant may be unable to establish the existence of a duty of care. Another problem might arise if the loss suffered is pure economic loss. Although recovery for pure economic loss was allowed in the House of Lords in *Junior Books v Veitchi* (1983), *Junior Books* has been heavily criticised and it is unlikely that the case will found any future actions involving pure economic loss. In such situations, the tort of misfeasance in public office may provide an alternative cause of action.

Although the tort of misfeasance in public office can be found in law reports of the seventeenth and eighteenth centuries, it was a comparatively unknown cause of action until 1985 and the case of *Bourgion SA v Ministry of Agriculture*. Here, the claimants, who were French turkey producers, had been banned by the defendants from exporting turkeys to England. The defendants admitted that the true purpose of this ban was the protection of British turkey products and that this constituted a breach of **Art 30** of the **Treaty of Rome**. Nevertheless, the defendants claimed that they were not liable for misfeasance in public office, as they had no intent to injure the claimants, but rather had the intent to protect British interests. The Court of Appeal found that malice is not an essential ingredient of the tort: it was sufficient that the defendant knew that he had acted unlawfully and that his acts would injure the claimant. As in this case the claimant had suffered only pure economic loss, an action in negligence was almost certain to fail.

In *Jones v Swansea City Council* (1990), the House of Lords held that the claimant could sue the council for misfeasance in public office if she could prove that the majority of councillors who had voted for a resolution had done so with the aim of damaging the claimant with knowledge of the unlawful nature of this act. Again, in this case, the claimant had suffered only pure economic loss.

In *Three Rivers District Council v Bank of England (No 3)* (2000),[8] the House of Lords reviewed and confirmed the tort has the following ingredients:

(a)   The defendant must be a public officer and the exercise of power must be as a public officer.

(b)   The state of mind of the defendants. A study of the case law shows two different forms of liability for the tort:

    (i)   cases in which a public power is exercised for an improper purpose with the specific intention of injuring a person or persons (the 'targeted malice' limb); and

    (ii)   cases in which a public officer acts in the knowledge that he had no power to do the act complained of and that it would probably injure the claimant (the 'illegality' limb).

(c)   Both limbs involve bad faith. In the targeted malice limb, the bad faith is the exercise of public power for an improper purpose; in the illegality limb, the bad faith is the lack of honest belief on the part of the public officer that the act is lawful. The House of Lords made it clear that for the illegality limb, reckless indifference as to the illegality and its probable consequences is sufficient to establish the required mental element. The recklessness must be subjective, so that the claimant must prove that the defendant lacked an honest belief in lawfulness of his actions, or wilfully disregarded the risk of unlawfulness. Indeed such malice broadly speaking has been determined is a requirement for the tort to be made out as established by the High Court in *Isaacs v Commissioner of Police of the Metropolis, Dunn and Carroll* (2013).

(d)   Duty to the claimant. In *Three Rivers DC* their Lordships held that the required mental element will keep the tort within reasonable bounds and that there was no need to introduce proximity as a control mechanism.

(e)   Causation is an essential ingredient of the tort.

(f)   Damage covered includes pure economic loss, but the claimant must suffer special damage – that is, loss that is specific to the claimant and not suffered in common with the general public. In *Watkins v Secretary of State for the Home Department* (2006), the House of Lords held that the tort was actionable only where the claimant had suffered loss or damage due to the defendant's tortious conduct. Lord Bingham noted that the rationale of the tort was to compensate the claimant rather than to punish the public officer. The case concerned a prisoner's complaints that his mail had been withheld and that there was no actual damage to speak of. Similarly in *Hussain v Chief Constable of West Mercia* (2008), a claimant who suffered no recognisable psychiatric injury but stress-related conditions, was classed as suffering insufficient damage for the tort.

(g)   The test for remoteness here is not reasonable foreseeability, but knowledge by the defendant that the decision would probably damage the claimant. Had *Three Rivers DC* concerned a negligence claim, the problem of pure economic loss would have caused insurmountable difficulties, including establishing the necessary proximity to found a duty of care.

---

8   The question here was about the lack of coherence and legal certainty, so it is always important to ensure some focus and direction to the question.

After *Three Rivers DC* was heard, the Court of Appeal faced a misfeasance case involving personal injury or death: *Akenzua v Secretary of State for the Home Department* (2003). It is highly likely that an action in negligence would have failed for insufficient proximity and possibly on public policy grounds: see *Hill v Chief Constable of West Yorkshire* (1989). Essentially, the Court had to decide whether the claimant had to prove (i) that the probable harm was to the claimant or a class of which the claimant was a member or (ii) only that the probable harm was to someone and that someone turned out to be the claimant. The Court held that the second requirement was the correct one and that the first requirement amounted to an attempt to introduce proximity into the tort.

From the above discussion, it can be seen that the tort of misfeasance in public office is particularly appropriate where the claimant may face problems of proximity, pure economic loss or public policy considerations that limit recovery, in negligence. However, it is of only limited application given the restrictions on the tort, as has been shown, and thus is unlikely to be 'popular' in the sense of a large number of cases.[9]

QUESTION 5

Zena and Yang have just begun a relationship. Two years ago, Yang, who had been married before, had a vasectomy operation. He tells Zena that the surgeon, Dr Ahmed, told him that the operation was 100 per cent successful and he would not be able to have more children. Zena, who does not want a family, is keen not to have to use contraception as she has had problems with some methods in the past. She therefore checks on the internet, on a site called Health-E-U, which states that this type of operation is wholly dependable. She notices a small box which states that the website does not accept liability in negligence for the information it contains. She therefore also checks with her GP, Dr Snow, who confirms that Yang's sterilisation operation renders contraception unnecessary.

Six months later, Zena finds out that she is pregnant. She subsequently discovers that recent scientific research has shown that such operations can 'spontaneously reverse'. She decides to go ahead with the birth.

▶ Advise her if she is entitled to any compensation from Drs Ahmed and Snow, and Health-E-U. Would it make any difference if you knew that the baby was born disabled?

How to Read this Question

This problem question involves considering potential liability for wrongful advice, i.e. a negligent misstatement, giving rise to economic loss in the form of bringing up a baby. As such, it covers an area known as 'wrongful birth', where the courts have restricted recovery for policy reasons. It thus gives you an opportunity to demonstrate understanding of the difference between liability for actions and words, and for physical and economic loss, plus convey an appreciation of the role of policy in some court decisions. Note the structure; you have three potential defendants, and the original involvement of Yang who had the operation with

---

9   As the sole leading case in this area, it is important to give a full account of legal details of the judgment.

Dr Ahmed, giving rise to a proximity discussion. You also have a final consideration of how your discussion may change if you knew the baby was disabled.

How to Answer this Question
You will have to consider:

❖ duty of care for economic loss;
❖ the standard of care for professionals;
❖ liability for 'wrongful birth';
❖ causation.

Applying the Law

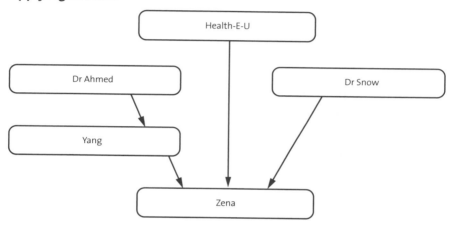

Up for Debate
Wrongful birth cases are often seen to be morally fraught as liability and damages can crudely reflect the worth of an unwanted child. It serves as a useful example where the policy aims of tort are boldly on display. This is acutely the case in *McFarlane* and the judgments are well worth reading for the varying ways in which moral theories of distributive justice are inconsistently invoked to deny the claim. For a discussion on Lord Steyn's reasoning and the case broadly see L Hoyano, 'Misconceptions about wrongful conception' (2002) 65 Modern Law Review 883, and for a discussion of the meaning of harm in such contexts see N Priaulx, 'Joy to the world: a (healthy) child is born! Reconceptualising 'harm' in wrongful conception' (2004) 13(1) Social and Legal Studies 5.

ANSWER --
Zena will have to prove that she was owed a duty of care by one or more of the defendants (here both the doctors and Health-E-U), that the duty was breached because they fell below the standard of reasonable care, and that the breach caused her loss.

As her claim is based on a statement, she will be arguing that the owed duty was based on the line of cases starting with *Hedley Byrne v Heller* (1964). In that case it was held that where there is a special relationship between the parties, and one negligently (without sufficient care) gives wrong information to the other expecting it to be acted on and which the other acts on to their detriment, then the information giver will be liable for the economic losses that flow. However, the courts have been concerned to restrict the boundaries of this duty because of the large number of potential cases and subsequent cases such as *Caparo Industries v Dickman* (1990) have referred to an 'assumption of responsibility' which the defendant must have undertaken.[10]

The standard of care required by professionals is not that of a reasonable layperson, but 'that of the standard of the ordinary skilled man exercising and professing to have that special skill' (*Bolam v Friern Hospital Management Committee* (1957)). Thus if 'a responsible body of medical men' can be found who accept the procedure as 'proper', then it will be regarded as reasonable. It does not matter if the professional is a trainee, or junior, as it is an objective standard (*Wilsher v Essex Area Health Authority* (1987)). This may seem as though the courts are allowing the professionals to set their own standards, but in the case of doctors, the House of Lords in *Bolitho v City and Hackney Health Authority* (1997) held that, exceptionally, if the professional opinion was not logically defensible, then the judges could intervene.

Causation normally falls to be decided using the 'but for' test (*Barnett v Chelsea and Kensington Hospital* (1968)).

In *Goodwill v British Pregnancy Advisory Service* (1996) it was held that a hospital did not owe a duty of care to the subsequent partners of a man who had a vasectomy due to insufficient proximity. The situation here may have been different if it had been Yang's wife who had become pregnant (*Thake v Maurice* (1986)). This would seem to rule out any liability for Dr Ahmed and it is likely he could argue that a reasonable doctor at that time would not have had the newly available research information, and thus there would have been no lack of care. He would be judged against knowledge prevailing at the time (*Roe v Minister of Health* (1954)).

Health-E-U may claim that it could not owe a duty to everyone who read its contents, as there is no special proximity. The success of this latter argument might depend on whether the website included visible recommendations from esteemed medical opinion, which might demonstrate that it was assuming responsibility to browsers. It is however unlikely. Health-E-U should be informed that any attempt to exclude liability for death or personal injury will be ineffective under s 2(1) of the **Unfair Contract Terms Act 1977**, unless it does not qualify as acting in the course of a business. It would do better to make it clear that individuals should not rely on its advice to ensure the failure of any assumption of responsibility argument.[11]

....

10 Do not get confused between the importance of *Caparo* in setting out the three-part test for the existence of a duty of care generally, and the important role it also plays in the development of liability for pure economic loss.

For Dr Snow, it is well established that a doctor owes a duty of care to patients, as shown in *Bolam* and *Bolitho*. The standard is that of the reasonably competent GP, who is not of course an expert in sterilisation procedures but would be expected to know more than a layman. The fact that Dr Snow was unaware of the latest research would suggest that she is in breach of duty, but if she can find a body of medical opinion which would have advised similarly, she may be able to satisfy the *Bolam* test (subject to *Bolitho*).

Zena would still need to prove causation, that 'but for' the doctor's advice she would not have got pregnant. This might be difficult to establish, as she has made it clear that she is wary of using contraceptives, and no contraceptive method is 100 per cent guaranteed. However, she may be able to demonstrate that on the balance of probabilities (*Hotson v East Berkshire Area Health Authority* (1987)) she would not have become pregnant.

Dr Snow might argue that the fact Zena chose to continue with the pregnancy, rather than have an abortion, might amount to a *novus actus interveniens* by the claimant themselves (*McKew v Holland and Hannen and Cubbitts* (1969)) or possible contributory negligence. In *Emeh v Kensington Area Health Authority* (1985) it was held that the claimant's failure to have an abortion was not so unreasonable as to 'eclipse the defendant's wrongdoing'.

In *McFarlane v Tayside Health Authority* (2000), the House of Lords held that the costs of raising an unwanted but healthy child were not recoverable, as the hospital did not hold a duty for such losses. Damages were limited to the discomfort of pregnancy and the pain of giving birth, i.e. personal injury. In *Rees v Darlington Memorial Hospital NHS Trust* (2003), the House of Lords said that there were policy reasons for not allowing recovery because there was 'an unwillingness to regard a child (even if unwanted) as a financial liability and nothing else, a recognition that the rewards which parenthood (even if involuntary) may or may not bring cannot be quantified'.[12] However, their Lordships felt that there should be a 'conventional award' in cases of wrongful birth over and above pain and suffering.

If the child was born disabled, the case of *Parkinson v St James Hospital* (2001) allowed for the extra costs of disability (although the hospital's negligence was not the cause of the disability). In spite of this the Court of Appeal decision stands after *Rees* and *Parkinson* was followed in *Farraj v King's Healthcare NHS Trust* (2008).[13]

....

11 Note that in the *Hedley Byrne* case, the disclaimer was effective to defeat liability. However, this was before the introduction of the **Unfair Contract Terms Act 1977**, and this demonstrates the importance of being aware of the chronology of the leading cases.

12 This quote from Lord Bingham in *Rees* clearly adds to the authority and quality of your answer. If in exam conditions it is not possible to remember quite all of it, then just paraphrase certain elements of the quote.

13 This demonstrates the importance of knowing and being able to comment on the standing of a decision and the date when it was decided.

Zena will, in all likelihood, be able to recover from Dr Snow for the pain and discomfort associated with birth and a 'conventional award' to mark that a wrong has occurred. Practically, a small sum would be weighed against the possible psychological harm the awareness of a 'wrongful birth' label may cause the child. Only if the baby is disabled will she have the possibility of claiming towards the cost of raising her child.

Aim Higher

When answering problem questions for duty of care, it will not be practically possible for you to recall every relevant precedent and seek to apply it. They may not be as important as other cases and you will only have limited time. However to enhance your understanding and to impress a reader you can demonstrate a grasp of up to date case law, from which you may want to draw a factual comparison on the given problem. Examiners will find this impressive where done well. Though the tests for the existence of a duty of care are firmly established you may want to review their application and recent Court of Appeal cases include *Robinson v Chief Constable of West Yorkshire* (2014) and *Gillian Harrison and Others v Technical Sign Limited and Others* (2013). For a consideration of how policy arguments are weighed, appraise the arguments advanced by the Ministry of Defence in arguing that they should not be held to owe a duty of care to provide adequate equipment to armed forces personnel in military and combat operations (*Smith v MOD* (2013)).

2 Negligence – Limitations on Duty

INTRODUCTION

The principles on the recovery for psychiatric injury are perhaps the most complex in the law of tort. Well known for policy restrictions, and questionable technical distinctions, much of the law depends on the tenuous criteria that make up potential primary or secondary victims. As many judges themselves have admitted it is well known that the law is in urgent need of reform. Similarly policy factors are relevant in claims against emergency services, and also within the broader social and economic shifts that tort law reflects. This is perhaps best seen in the debate surrounding whether we are living in a 'compensation culture'. This chapter reflects these discussions with two essay questions and two problem questions.

Checklist
Students need to be familiar with:
(a) psychiatric injury/nervous shock:
■ the criteria for recovery;
■ the restrictions on recovery;
■ the possible extensions of persons owed a duty of care;
(b) any special rules for the emergency services:
■ duty owed to police, fire and ambulance services;
■ restrictions on the duty;
(c) the broad social and policy debates underpinning negligence including the effect of the **Compensation Act 2006**.

QUESTION 6

Clive has a part-time job in a petrol station. He was working one evening when three rockets, part of an organised firework display, crashed into the garage forecourt. It was later discovered that the rockets' launch mechanisms had not been properly assembled by the event organiser.

Alex was filling his car with petrol when the rockets landed, causing a violent explosion. Miraculously Alex was not badly hurt but was powerless to get to his wife Katie who was trapped in the burning car. Unable to save her, he collapsed with shock.

Dave, the station manager, watched the chaos unfold on CCTV in the office behind the petrol station. Concerned for his own safety, and that of his lovingly restored vintage Bentley, which was parked on the garage forecourt, he told Clive to 'take the fire extinguisher, get outside and save my car'. He then bolted the fire door and dialled the emergency services. Clive attended to Alex, and also Jodie, who was walking her dog when the explosion happened. Jodie was otherwise unhurt, but the Bentley was completely destroyed.

▶ **Advise all of the parties as to their likely success in claiming damages for the psychiatric harm each claims to have suffered.**

How to Read this Question

This problem question involves multiple claimants, so it is important to have a clear structure in answering the question, and as mentioned in the first chapter to clearly identify the claimants in the question (in your head, if not on paper). It would be wise to classify these claimants into possible primary or secondary victims when you read the facts. To help with this look out for easy clues such as whether they were witnesses or involved in the accident, and the relationships between the main parties, e.g. were they mere bystanders or were there any family connections between the parties. Identifying such issues will help you to organise your discussion and boost the clarity of the writing.

How to Answer this Question

The following points need to be discussed:

❖ the basis of the duty for psychiatric harm;
❖ primary and secondary victims;
❖ damage to property;
❖ rescuers.

Applying the Law

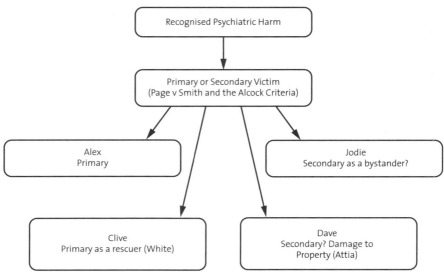

ANSWER

The scenario requires an evaluation of the law relating to the recovery of damages for psychiatric harm (PH).[1]

Liability is limited to instances of recognised mental injury meaning that temporary grief or fear is insufficient to ground a claim (*Alcock; Brice v Brown* (1984); *Vernon v Bosley* (1997)). The current law states that the PH caused by the defendant's negligence must either result in physical injury (*Bourhill v Young* (1943)), and, following the decision of the House of Lords in *Grieves v F.T. Everard & Sons and others* (2007), a claim must be based on a real, rather than imagined, injury. The burden of proving PH would fall on Alex, Clive, Dave and Jodie to show that they had such injuries.[2]

The leading case of *Alcock v Chief Constable of South Yorkshire* (1991) provides the ground-work in establishing a duty of care. Arising out of the tragic circumstances of the Hillsborough disaster, Lord Oliver distinguished primary and secondary victims, the former being those who could be identified as being involved directly or indirectly as a participant, and the latter where the claimant was (no more than) a passive and unwilling witness of the harm that had been caused to other people.[3] Primary victims are much more likely to be able to claim successfully though in *Page v Smith* (1996), recovery was restricted to people in the zone of foreseeable physical danger and those in reasonable fear of their safety. It is clear in the present situation that Alex is a primary victim: he was directly involved in a horrific incident, certainly within the zone of physical danger and likely to succeed in a claim. Dave may wish to claim that he was a primary victim, 'in the zone of danger' as the facts indicate his instructions to Clive were motivated out of a concern for his own safety. However it is unlikely this would succeed as following the decision in *McFarlane v EE Caledonia* (1994), it appears being inside meant he was safely out of harm's way.

The position is less clear when advising secondary victims. According to *Alcock* there are three considerations. A claimant now needs to prove that their relationship with a primary victim was sufficiently close, there was sufficient proximity to the incident or its immediate aftermath in time and space (see *Bourhill*) and, finally, that the claimant suffered PH through seeing or hearing the accident or its immediate aftermath to the extent that a claimant must be a witness with their own unaided senses. As for the first require-ment, the Lords referred to a relationship akin to 'a close tie of love and affection', however confusingly suggested that a mere bystander could claim if the event was par-ticularly horrific. This has not transpired, and cases such as *McFarlane v EE Caledonia Ltd* (1994) and *Robertson v Forth Road Bridge Joint Board* (1995) suggest a negative view of

1 An abbreviation such as this can be a good idea in exam situations where there is limited time; however, ensure that it is written out in full and then the chosen abbreviation put in brackets when using it for the first time.

2 Students often fail to give sufficient emphasis to the need for a genuine psychiatric illness, such as post-traumatic stress disorder, to be proved by the claimant.

3 It is essential to distinguish clearly between *primary* and *secondary* victims and cite the relevant case law where appropriate.

such a position. There has also been some judicial consideration in relation to the duration of the sudden event that has led to the PH, with authority that a slow event over a two-week period as not counting (*Sion v Hampstead Health Authority* (1994)). However there is now a sense of judges taking this requirement on a case by case basis, depending on how they classify the single traumatic event and the claimant's proximity to it (*North Glamorgan NHS Trust v Walters* (2002) and the more recent decision of *Taylor v A. Novo (UK) Ltd* (2013). The *Taylor* judgment distinguished past cases in deeming that there must be proximity to the original traumatic event, and not just a later death that was the consequence (which on the facts was three weeks later). Dave and Jodie both fall within the category of secondary victims as witnesses but both would be unable to succeed. This is because, although both were proximate in time and space to the incident, and were likely to have witnessed it directly, it cannot be shown there is a tie of close love and affection (such as a sibling or spouse) to Alex or Katie. Were it to be proved, Jodie may have a claim as she saw and heard the incident with unaided senses and whilst Dave probably heard it the dicta by Lord Keith and Oliver in *Alcock* about bystander recovery for viewing horrific events such as an oil tanker crashing into a school does not appear to have been followed. Dave viewed the rest on a CCTV screen and opted to stay in a 'safe' environment. There is only limited authority that live and unedited TV, and particularly shocking, may amount to perception through unaided senses (*Alcock*), and CCTV may satisfy this. Nonetheless the critical limitation is the apparent lack of a close relationship.[4]

Clive might be a primary victim as he had a reasonable fear of his own safety. Alternatively he could be considered a rescuer which traditionally allowed recovery of any type of injury (physical or psychiatric), for reasons of public policy (to encourage praiseworthy behaviour) (*Chadwick v British Transport Commission* (1967)).

Nonetheless this principle was blurred slightly by *White v Chief Constable of South Yorkshire Police* (1998). It was held that they were not entitled to claim as rescuers under the traditional position. The House of Lords, by a majority (see Lord Goff's dissent), held that only a rescuer who either was or believed themselves to be in danger could claim, unless they fulfilled the *Alcock* criteria. That said, a rescuer must actually be involved in a rescue, and not as in *McFarlane*, be some distance away. Clive though has placed himself in a certain amount of danger to overcome the hurdle in *White* when he tended to Alex and Jodie and, if so, the case of *Tolley v Carr* (2010) suggests that he would not have damages deducted for contributory negligence given the allowance made for emergency situations and actions motivated by the desire to rescue.

One final consideration would be the novel approach to PH adopted in *Attia v British Gas* (1988), where the claimant successfully sued for PH on the basis of having witnessed her house being destroyed by fire. Dave may claim in this regard for the destruction of his car,

---

4 As no information is given about the possible relationship between Jodie and Dave (as secondary victims) and Katie (which might suggest that none exists), it is not possible to be more definite as to whether they would succeed. However, the issue must be raised, as it is a crucial factor in determining liability to secondary victims.

but post-*Alcock* the tests may prove hard to satisfy. However on the grounds of normal negligence principles, he would be able to claim for the damage to the car as damage to property would be a foreseeable consequence of a breach of a duty of care to ensure the safety of a firework display.[5]

In conclusion, it would appear that the claimants most likely to succeed in an action for PH would be Alex, as a primary victim, and Clive as a rescuer. The remaining claims would not be likely to satisfy the current test for secondary victims.

Aim Higher

Maintain an effective structure and ensure you convey the clarity in the distinction between primary and secondary victims. Students often forget the status of the *White* decision and, therefore, coverage and analysis of where it applies will give you additional credit. Similarly an awareness of current case law such as the *Taylor v A. Novo Ltd (UK)* (2013) decision, will demonstrate that you are up to date with the law.

Common Pitfalls

The chronology and status of the cases often trips candidates up – make sure you know which case informed which subsequent decision. Applying the cases for secondary victims to primary victims will not gain you any marks, hence the importance of classifying them early on. Similarly it is very easy to over-describe in answers so be sure to take a principled approach to the application of the law to both the claimants and the facts.

QUESTION 7

'The House of Lords has stated in the clearest possible terms in *White v Chief Constable of South Yorkshire Police* (1999) that the law on nervous shock or psychiatric injury is so illogical that only Parliament can come up with a solution.'

▶ **Discuss the above statement.**

How to Read this Question

In short this is an essay question requiring you to critically discuss whether the current law on recovery for psychiatric injury is in need of reform. In so doing you need to highlight the inconsistencies, problems, policy issues and the lack of fairness that has even led to judges growing restless for reform. In so doing you can also address how the current state of the law could be improved and consider what some of those proposals are. The case of *White* highlighted in the quote will need addressing, as this is a source of much of the debate.

---

5   For more on contributory negligence, see Chapter 4.

How to Answer this Question

The following points need to be discussed:

- ❖ the criteria for liability in psychiatric injury, *Alcock v Chief Constable of South Yorkshire* (1991);
- ❖ the uncertainties as regards possible claimants – rescuers;
- ❖ intervention of third parties, lapse of time;
- ❖ the extent to which a statute may improve the current situation;
- ❖ the possible problems that a statute might bring.

Answer Structure

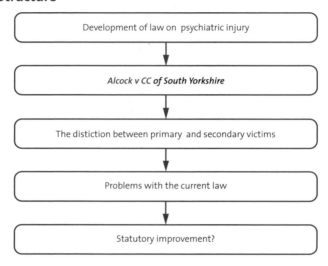

Development of law on psychiatric injury

↓

Alcock v CC of South Yorkshire

↓

The distiction between primary and secondary victims

↓

Problems with the current law

↓

Statutory improvement?

Up for Debate

In the words of Lord Steyn in *White*: 'The law on the recovery of compensation for pure psychiatric harm is a patchwork quilt of distinctions which are difficult to justify.' The decisions that have arisen out of the tragic Hillsborough disaster have been subject to the most criticism often from judges themselves as well as commentators, and much of the remaining common law has had to unsatisfactorily develop from shaky foundations. You will find many critical discussion points from your reading. Lord Goff's dissenting judgment in *White* is well worth reading, including how his criticism in applying the reasonable exposure to danger test to rescuers can be so problematic, see also S Todd, 'Psychiatric injury and rescuers' (1999) 115 Law Quarterly Review 345. A stimulating read is also provided in P Case, 'Now you see it, now you don't: black letter reflections on the legacies of White Chief Constable of South Yorkshire' (2010) 18(1) Tort Law Review 33. For an interesting and short case analysis on the recent decision in *Taylor v A. Novo (UK) Ltd (2013)* that also provides broader criticism of the Alcock landscape see K Patten, 'Patchwork quilt law' (2013) 7561 New Law Journal 24 May.

ANSWER

Initially the courts were wary of imposing liability for non-physical injuries which could not be seen (*Victorian Railway Commissioners v Coulthas* (1888)) because of the fears of fraud and the 'floodgates' argument. But as knowledge of psychiatry has developed the judiciary has been more ready to accept the existence of mental trauma and the law has developed from allowing recovery where the claimant was reasonably put in fear of his own safety (*Dulieu v White* (1901)) to allowing recovery for a wide range of persons. However, psychiatric injury must now be considered in the light of the decision in *Alcock v Chief Constable of South Yorkshire* (1991).[6]

In *Alcock*, the House of Lords adopted Lord Wilberforce's approach in *McLoughlin v O'Brien* (1983) and held that a claimant could only recover for psychiatric injury if he satisfied the test of reasonable foreseeability with the additional controls of relationship, proximity and perception of the accident or immediate aftermath through sight or sound.

Taking the first requirement, a spouse or parent will be presumed to have such close ties of love and affection, and siblings and other relatives will have to prove such ties. Presumably, it would be open to the defendant in the cases of spouses to rebut the presumption by proving (say) that the partners have separated and have not been living together for some years. This wide approach, however, is not free from difficulties. It seems that *Alcock* would allow recovery by a particularly close friend who can satisfy the criteria of love and affection, but how is a defendant to reasonably foresee the existence of such a close friend? Given the readiness of some judges to foresee a great deal and others to take a narrower view, can this approach be said to bring certainty or logic to the law? It may be just from the point of view of the secondary victim, but is it just as regards the defendant to impose such wide liability?[7] Similar moral concerns arise in both the arbitrary nature of the presumption as well as the request for 'proof' of sibling affection to someone who is deceased.

Another area that gives rise to problems of justice and uncertainty is proximity. What is meant by being close in both time and place? In *Alcock*, Lord Ackner was not prepared to allow recovery to a plaintiff who saw the body of a brother-in-law at the mortuary some eight hours after the accident, and Lord Wilberforce stated in *McLoughlin* that a two-hour delay period was at the margin of the time span for recovery. This seems to be an arbitrary timescale that would appear to suggest that a claimant, who is contacted by mobile telephone and told to attend at a hospital, having access to a fast car, may be able to recover, whereas a claimant who has to depend on public transport may not.

The problem as to just what is meant by the claimant's proximity to the event or its immediate aftermath has been rendered even more confusing by the decision of the

---

6   Though the question was confined to psychiatric injury, given the inclusion of the damage on the facts, it would demonstrate breadth of knowledge to include reference to the recovery for the property damage.

7   This introductory paragraph sets the scene and provides an overarching context. It is important not to 'over-introduce' however, and ensure you give adequate time to the critical issues. This will come with developing your exam technique through practising timed answers.

House of Lords in *W v Essex County Council* (2000) where Lord Slynn refused to strike out a claim despite claimants not being proximate to the incidents of abuse, and who only had knowledge of the abuse which caused their psychiatric illness. Hence, there would appear to be considerable uncertainty in deciding in any particular case whether or not there was sufficient proximity to the accident or its immediate aftermath in time and space.[8] Indeed as the *Taylor v A. (UK) Novo Ltd.* (2013) case highlights, defining the relevant event which the claimant has to be proximate to is important, see also *Walters v North Glamorgan NHS Trust* (2003), where the Court held that a 36-hour period constituted an event and stated that the present law permits a realistic view to be taken in each individual case.

Finally, *Alcock* retained the rule that the shock must be caused through seeing or hearing the accident or its immediate aftermath. Thus, if a mother attends a hospital to be told that her children have been burnt to death and feels unable to see the bodies, but still suffers psychiatric injury, she cannot recover. It could even be open to the defendant to argue that it was the news of the death of her children, negligently relayed by a nurse or doctor that caused the shock, rather than a much later sight of the bodies. In other words, a *novus actus interveniens*. This seems to be a most illogical and unjust result, but it follows from *Alcock*.

Two decisions of the House of Lords have attempted to clarify and make the law more coherent, but many say have done the opposite. In *Page v Smith* (1995), their Lordships held that once it can be established that a defendant is under a duty of care to avoid causing personal injury to a claimant, it is immaterial whether the injury caused is physical or psychiatric. For primary victims, the distinction between physical and psychiatric injury has been abolished.

In *White v Chief Constable of South Yorkshire Police* (1999), the House of Lords (in respect of the police officers claiming out of the Hillsborough case), held that a rescuer had to show that he had exposed himself to danger or reasonably believed he was so doing. Thus, rescuers are not to be treated as primary victims merely because they are rescuers. If they were not a primary victim, they would have to satisfy the Alcock criteria.

While *White* brings some logic to the area of psychiatric injury, in that employees are treated in an identical manner to other claimants, it has weakened the position of rescuers. The case is well known for being a decision made, more out of distributive justice, given family members in *Alcock* being unable to recover and for both Lord Hoffmann, who stated that the law was 'making distinctions which the ordinary man would find hard to understand' and Lord Steyn declaring that the best strategy for the common law was to say 'thus far and no further'. The case is seen as the height of judicial frustration on the law on psychiatric harm.

· ·

8   It is important to highlight the key debates in essays, which address the substance of the question; as in this case whether the law is drawing a fair balance. Using occasional rhetorical questions can highlight your critical instincts.

Thus, the current state of the law on psychiatric injury is illogical and uncertain in some respects. The enactment of a statute could remove some of the uncertainty, but whether this would be at the expense of justice and flexibility is a concern.[9] Should the law specify categories of relationship into which a claimant must fit to recover? Should the criteria for proximity in time and space be defined? Surely, the only limits that could be so defined are 'reasonable' proximity in time and space, but this is hardly certain. Guidance in putting together such a statute could be taken from the Law Commission Report on 'Liability for Psychiatric Illness' (1998) which suggested broadening the relationships under the 'close tie of love and affection', and in effect completely relaxing the requirements of proximity and direct perception of the event. Whether this will mitigate the risk of the floodgates opening is unclear, however the length of time passed since the reports suggests that there is little parliamentary appetite for such legislation.

QUESTION 8

A group of young people, aged between 13 and 15, were hanging around outside a parade of shops. During some light-hearted jostling, one youth, Raymond, picked up an empty plastic bottle and threw it. The bottle hit Dirk in the face and his eye began to bleed. In the general angry confusion which followed, a waste bin was set on fire. Sam, a passer-by who had some first aid training, decided not to try to help Dirk as he did not want to get involved, but he did phone for an ambulance and the fire brigade on his mobile.

When the fire brigade arrived it hosed down the bin and the surrounding area vigorously to ensure the fire was out. A stream of water from the hoses flooded into a nearby cellar, where Bilbo kept his collection of rare books, ruining many of them. On the way back to the fire station, a piece of equipment that had been insecurely attached to the fire engine fell off and injured a passing cyclist.

The ambulance took some time to arrive, and when Dirk was eventually examined in hospital, the doctor said that he would lose the sight of one eye, but if he had been treated earlier there would have been a 50/50 chance of his sight being saved.

Local residents subsequently told Dirk's mother that they had repeatedly asked the police to move the young people away because of their anti-social behaviour, but no action had been taken. She and Bilbo believe that if there had been more police patrolling the area the damage would not have occurred.

▶ **Advise Dirk, Bilbo and the cyclist as to the legal position in tort.**

How to Read this Question

This presents a negligence based problem scenario that centres on aspects of duty (especially of the emergency services) and causation which are two of the three central

---

9   The concluding paragraph of an essay question should refer back to the question and attempt to answer it directly. Avoid writing a lengthy summary, but attempt to concisely tie up the strands of the argument you have pursued in the answer.

features in a negligence action. This is one of the situations where establishing duty is not straightforward, largely for policy reasons, and gives you an opportunity to display awareness of the issues. However, it is not an essay on policy, and as there are other aspects to cover as well, your discussion of this should be kept relatively brief in the context of a problem question. As ever an effective structure that allows concise application will be required. You should have noticed causation issues in this question, and often poor medical treatment is a frequent way in which causation is made complicated and thus included on many tort examinations.

How to Answer this Question
You will need to look at:

❖ liability in negligence and trespass to the person of young people;
❖ liability for omissions;
❖ duty of care owed by emergency services;
❖ standard of care required in an emergency;
❖ causation in fact and law.

Applying the Law

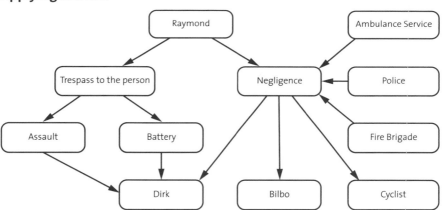

ANSWER

This question concerns aspects of duty, breach and causation.[10]

It could be argued Raymond owed a duty of care to his neighbour, Dirk, on straight-forward *Donoghue* neighbour principles. However, as we are told that Raymond is at most 15 years old, it may be that he is considered too young to foresee the consequences of his actions, as in *Mullin v Richards* (1998). In that case, the court decided that an 'ordinarily prudent and reasonable' 15-year-old would not foresee the risk of a plastic ruler breaking during a 'play fight' and was thus not liable. Although there is no set range of what is foreseeable at what age, the court will ask whether a reasonable child of the age of the defendant would foresee the risk. In *Orchard v Lee* (2009), it was held that a child would have to act with a 'very high degree of carelessness' to be found liable in negligence.[11]

Alternatively, Dirk could claim against Raymond in trespass to the person. This would involve establishing that the bottle was intended to hit someone, but it is not necessary to show that Raymond intended to apply force to Dirk specifically, if he had 'transferred intent' as in *Livingstone v Ministry of Defence* (1984). There is doubt as to whether it has to be done with a 'hostile' intent (*Wilson v Pringle* (1986)). In *Re F*, Lord Goff suggested that a 'prank that got out of hand' could be a battery, as could be said to be the case here. We are not told whether Dirk saw the bottle coming towards him, but if so, it would be an assault. If he was not looking, it would be a battery.

Sam cannot be liable for a failure to act, or his omission, as he was under no obligation to do so; as expressed by Lord Keith in *Yuen Kun-Yeu v Attorney General for Hong Kong* (1988) there is no liability in English law if someone 'sees another about to walk over a cliff with his head in the air, and forbears to shout a warning'.[12]

The courts have been reluctant to impose a duty of care on the emergency services, although one can exist in limited circumstances. This is due in large part to policy considerations, which were well rehearsed in the House of Lords in *Hill v Chief Constable of W. Yorks* (1989) and the Court of Appeal in *Capital and Counties v Hampshire Fire Brigade* (1997), as it is argued that the emergency services would act defensively and divert resources from the public generally if they had to be concerned about litigation. It is highly unlikely, following the reasoning in *Hill*, that it would be held that there was sufficient proximity between Dirk and the police to create a duty (*Robinson v Chief Constable of West Yorkshire* (2014), *Van Colle v Chief Constable of Herts* (2006) and *Smith v Chief Constable of Sussex* (2008)). The situation might have been different if the police had been aware of previous threats made by Raymond to Dirk, but this is unlikely given the known

---

10 This problem question covers a wide range of potential liability, and will need careful planning (see diagram). Time spent planning a problem question answer will not be wasted, especially when it is complex.

11 Short phrases quoted from the cases that are cited will add to the quality of the answer.

12 Being able to quote from a named judge will add to the quality of the answer.

facts and the decision of the House of Lords in *Van Colle* and *Smith*.[13] Given this, it is even less likely that Bilbo could maintain a successful claim against the police. Even if a duty was breached, the police could rely on the *novus actus interveniens* of the fire brigade (see below).

A fire brigade is not obliged to attend and will only be liable to an individual if the position is made worse by their actions (*Capital and Counties* (1997)). Bilbo may find it difficult to demonstrate that a duty was owed, but the facts seem to indicate that the firemen did not take reasonable care and thus breach could be established. The relevant causation rule here that applies to the question of whether liability extends to the valuable books, is the 'eggshell skull' rule, which means that the defendant must take the claimant as s/he finds him/her as far as their physical characteristics are concerned (*Smith v Leech Brain* (1962)). Here there is property damage to the books which the courts may take a more restrictive view and possibly hold as too remote. He therefore could struggle to recover.

The cyclist could sue the fire service in negligence as it is well established that one road user owes a duty to another (*Nettleship v Weston* (1977)). The fire service would no doubt argue that the standard of care required in an emergency is lower than normal (*Watt v Hertfordshire County Council* (1954)). However, it should be noted that the accident occurred on the way *back* from attending the emergency, so this argument may not be successful.

In the case of the ambulance, the courts have said that the position would be close to that of the NHS which owes a duty to individual patients once a specific call has been accepted (*Kent v Griffiths* (2000)). We would thus have to discover exactly what Sam said when he phoned for help – if he just gave a general request for assistance the court may hold no duty existed. If the duty was established, it would still be necessary to establish that the reason for the delay was lack of reasonable care by the ambulance driver, and not for example a justifiable reason such as, maybe, traffic congestion.

Whether Raymond and/or the ambulance service could be liable for the loss of sight is a question of causation. The normal position is the application of the 'but for' test (*Barnett v Chelsea and Kensington Hospital Management Committee* (1969)) and anything less than a 50 per cent chance would fail (*Hotson v East Berkshire Health Authority* (1987)). Therefore here, Dirk would need to establish not only that a duty was owed which was breached, but that considered medical evidence can be provided to show that it was more likely than not that but for an earlier examination he would not have lost his sight, i.e. more than a 50 per cent chance. In *Rahman v Arearose Ltd* (2001), which involved a hospital's negligence on top of an initial injury caused by another, there was an attempt to divide up liability between successive defendants, but Raymond could argue that the delay caused by the ambulance was a *novus actus interveniens* which broke the chain of

---

13 Some speculation is allowable if it can be demonstrated that it is clear how the law applies to the facts given. However do not over speculate and ponder over new facts which may or may not have occurred and would alter the liability of the parties. You can only address the given set of facts.

causation (*Knightley v Johns* (1982)). As it is unlikely that Raymond will be in a position to fulfil any award of damages made against him, even if found liable, it would be preferable for Dirk to pursue the ambulance service which would be in a position to pay him compensation.[14]

QUESTION 9

To what extent has the **Compensation Act 2006** been successful in dealing with the problems associated with the 'compensation culture'?

▶ **Discuss.**

How to Read this Question

This essay requires both a thorough understanding and explanation of what the 'compensation culture' is and the problems that it has seen to have created. Similarly you need a thorough understanding of the provisions of the **Compensation Act 2006**, and the impact or intended impact it has had on resolving those problems. You should support your explanation with appropriate evidence and case illustrations, and these can come from the range of torts that you have studied.

Up for Debate

The concept of a compensation culture is one of the most well-known phenomena that surround not only tort law, but perhaps much of the legal profession in general. Its existence has been questioned as being part media-inflated myth, but for some, the phrase also captures what many perceive to be a social trend with a reduction of personal responsibility and an increase in a 'have-a-go' culture where people shift blame in order to receive damages; a trend which many judges (e.g. Lord Hobhouse in *Tomlinson v Congleton Borough Council* (2004)) have warned against. For a thorough review of the report see K Williams, 'State of fear: Britain's "compensation culture",th>' (2005) 25 Legal Studies 499. For an important judicial perspective, Lord Dyson MR 'Compensation culture: fact or fantasy?' Holdsworth Club Lecture 15 March 2013 (available online).

How to Answer this Question

You will need to look at:

❖   the meaning of 'compensation culture';
❖   the effect of **s 1**;
❖   case law that provides context and interpretation of **s 1**;
❖   the effect of **s 2**;
❖   the implications of **part II** on the regulation of services.

---

14 The inclusion of some practical consideration like this at the end of your answer will demonstrate that you have weighed up the best course of action for the claimants, and therefore convey your grasp and understanding of the scenario to the examiner.

Answer Structure

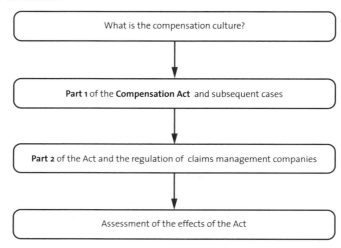

What is the compensation culture?

Part 1 of the **Compensation Act** and subsequent cases

Part 2 of the Act and the regulation of claims management companies

Assessment of the effects of the Act

ANSWER

The **Compensation Act 2006** was introduced largely to counter the perceived problems created by a compensation culture. This phenomenon has been described by the government as where 'people believe that they can seek compensation for any misfortune that befalls them, even if no one else is to blame'. It has the pejorative meaning that many of the claims are frivolous or at worst fraudulent. Evidence of the problems was produced by the government's Better Regulation Task Force report 'Better routes to redress' (2004).[15] Although the report found that the huge increase in successful claims was largely illusionary, it concluded that its imagined perception had led to 'risk averse' behaviour ranging from a decrease in school trips to a failure of businesses to invest in new products or move away from well-tested procedures.

Section 1 of the Act is targeted towards both the torts of negligence and breach of statutory duty. It is aiming to deal with the perception that organisations fearing litigation are deterring from undertaking socially beneficial activities such as organising school trips. The section is supposed to reflect the fact the basic standard of care expected in law, which is that of the reasonable person (*Blyth v Birmingham Waterworks* (1856)). What can amount to 'reasonable care' will vary due to a multitude of factors: for example, what might be required to prevent harm in one circumstance may be too much of an imposition (*Latimer v AEC Ltd* (1952)) so it is clear the section does not alter the standard of care. It does, however, present some uncertainty. The Act refers to so-called 'desirable activities' to which the courts should have regard when considering the standard of care, but is silent on the meaning of the term.

---

15 Recalling specific details such as the name and dates of official reports are not as important as conveying the details and arguments contained with them. However, if you do know them, then including them will enhance the overall impression of the answer.

There has been very little litigation directly on **s1** of the Act, the first reported case being *Hopps v Mott MacDonald & the Ministry of Defence* (2009), where it was used in a case concerning a civilian injured in Iraq. The Act was said to have retrospective effect as it simply restated existing law, and, interestingly, the 'desirable activities' in **s1** were not to be restricted to social or leisure activities but could include the reconstruction of a war damaged country. In the case of *Cole v Davis Gilbert* (2007) it was held by the Court of Appeal that there was no breach of duty as Lord Justice Scott Baker concluded: 'If the law courts were to set a higher standard of care than what is reasonable, the consequences would quickly be felt. There would be no fetes, no maypole dancing and no activities that have come to be a part of the English village green for fear of what might go wrong.' [16] Some commentators have argued that it was unnecessary and was 'legislation as PR', especially in the light of *Tomlinson v Congleton BC* (2003) where the House of Lords robustly denied compensation to a trespassing swimmer, and roundly condemned compensation culture, with Lord Hobbhouse declaring it carried 'evil consequences'.[17]

In *Perry v Harris* (2008), a child was injured accidentally by another child on a bouncy castle. The Court of Appeal found, without specifically mentioning the **2006 Act,** there was no liability on the parents who had hired the bouncy castle for their children's party. It was 'a tragic accident' that happened 'without fault', however the difficulties are evident as there was far more press coverage of the first instance decision, where the parents *were* held liable. A more recent example of the trend can be seen in *Bowen v National Trust* (2011), where the Trust were not liable for the death and injuries caused when a branch fell on child visitors, and *XVW & YZA v Gravesend Grammar Schools for Girls* (2012), where a school was not liable for the rape of pupils during an overseas trip, although again the Act was not specifically referred to in these judgments. Similarly in *Uren v Corporate Leisure* (2011), the Court of Appeal mentioned the Act but confirmed that it merely reasserted the common law position. The case however is useful in understanding that the social benefit of an activity does not automatically trump inherent risks (see also *Scout Association v Barnes* (2010)). Social utility is always balanced against the risk-taking behaviour, and in *Uren* an inadequate risk assessment that did not properly protect against the risks of head-first entry into an inflatable pool was not acceptable despite the utility of the competition.

Section 2 of the Act appears to simply restate the position that giving an apology does not amount to admitting liability. The idea behind this section was to encourage people to give apologies with research showing that many people would not be driven to pursue litigation if the defendant had apologised and/or provided an explanation. Measuring the success of such a section is therefore very difficult.

Part II of the Act led to the establishment of the Claims Management Regulation Unit under the auspices of (now) the Ministry of Justice in 2007, which assists in the registration and regulation of claims management services (or so-called 'claims farmers'), which are defined as 'advice or other services in relation to the making of a claim' (**s 4(1)**). It has

---

16 Use of an appropriate quote will strengthen and enhance the depth of your argument.

17 See Chapter 7 on Occupiers Liability and Question 24 in particular.

been clearly targeted towards the perceived mischief of proliferating merit-less claims and nearly 900 companies had been registered by 2012. This part of the Act may be said to have been more obviously successful, as it has led to a disappearance of the worst forms of marketing for 'no win–no fee' services. However, the situation is not entirely resolved, for example companies exploiting mis-sold PPI insurance have been criticised for aggressive marketing and profiting. Further measures to tackle the whiplash claim phenomena have been needed. In 2013 a range of reforms were introduced; the simplification of claims for road traffic accidents, with a reduction in fees for basic and uncontested claims, restrictions on lawyers being able to double their fees when claims succeed (to drive down the cost on insurers and defendants), the banning of incentives including gifts and recommend a friend offers, as well banning referral fees between lawyers and insurers. There will also be measures put in place to establish independent medical panels to improve injury assessments, to tackle fraudulent and bogus claims.

Apart from the above, there is other recent evidence to suggest that the **2006 Act** has not yet been successful, e.g. Lord Young's report, entitled 'Common Sense Common Safety' (2010) called for a greater reduction on restrictions preventing beneficial activities; the private members' bill, the **Compensation Act 2006 (Amendment) Bill 2010**, unsuccessfully attempted to deter the fear of litigation by asking the courts to apply a *presumption* that defendants undertaking a desirable activity have satisfied the relevant standard of care. The media regularly decry its existence and are likely to continue to do so whenever a large settlement becomes public, such as a £10.8 million 'payout' to a brain damaged child in May 2012, or cases where bogus whiplash claims are dismissed. However in any assessment of the Act the ease of access to justice that 'compensation culture' may encourage is not necessarily a bad thing, particularly for those without the resources to pursue costly litigation.

Aim Higher

The debate surrounding whether we are living in a compensation culture regularly occupies newspaper coverage so keep aware of topical developments. Of particular importance are new proposals within the current government's policy agenda to tackle increasing insurance premiums by restricting the profit incentives for personal injury lawyers.

3 Negligence – Breach, Causation and Remoteness of Damage

INTRODUCTION

Questions involving breach, causation and remoteness of damage are popular with examiners, either as questions in their own right or most commonly as part of negligence. Breach of duty involves the consideration of multiple factors that influence the 'reasonable' standard of care expected. Causation and remoteness are made more complex with the possibility of an intervening act (a *novus actus interveniens*) breaking the causal chain. This chapter provides coverage of these areas of law through two problem questions and one essay question.

Checklist
Students must be familiar with the following areas:
(a) breach:
■ standards and guidelines used to assess whether the defendant's actions are in breach of a duty of care;
■ *res ipsa loquitur*;
(b) causation:
■ the 'but for' test and the decisions in the mesothelioma cases;
(c) remoteness:
■ reasonable foreseeability and the eggshell skull rule;
■ *novus actus interveniens*.

QUESTION 10

One day, while walking home, William trips and falls, damaging his knee. Several days later, while driving to work, he sees Victor crossing the road and brakes to avoid running into him. Unfortunately, due to the pain in his knee, he cannot fully press his brake pedal and, as a result, he runs into Victor. The collision occurs at a fairly slow speed and a normal person would only have suffered bruising as a result, but Victor has brittle bones and suffers two broken legs and a number of broken ribs. He is taken to the local hospital where, due to an administrative mistake, his right arm is amputated.

▶ Advise Victor.

How to Read this Question

This is a reasonably straightforward question covering the areas of breach, causation, remoteness including reference to the eggshell/thin skull rule and intervening acts. The relevant persons involved here are Victor as the injured claimant, with potential liability towards William and/or the hospital as possible defendants. As the nature of the event is relatively simple, care must be taken to discuss the relevant legal principles in depth, and ensure due coverage is given to the liability of both William and the hospital. Also don't over-elaborate on elements that are easily satisfied, e.g. the existence of a duty of care does not need a lengthy application of *Caparo v Dickman* (1990).

How to Answer this Question

The following points need to be discussed:

- ❖ breach of duty;
- ❖ the rules of causation and the egg-shell skull rule;
- ❖ a break in the causal chain with a possible intervening act by the hospital in amputating the arm;
- ❖ *res ipsa loquitur* in relation to the liability of the hospital.

Applying the Law

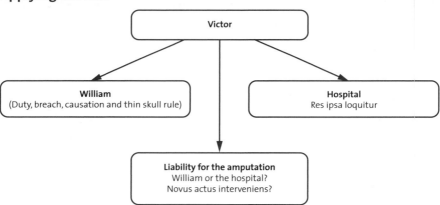

ANSWER

William

It is well-established law that a road user owes a duty of care to other road users, including pedestrians (*Donoghue v Stevenson* (1932); *Roberts v Ramsbottom* (1980)).[1] We must

---

1   In negligence answers, the depth of the analysis and application you give to establishing a duty of care is always dependent on the question. Spend too long on applying the *Caparo* criteria and you will run out of time and lose credit for not adequately discussing the more relevant issues that the question is demanding. Therefore be savvy in making appropriate choices. In cases where it is obvious a duty of care is held, there is no need for a lengthy discussion.

therefore consider whether he is in breach of this duty of care. The standard of care required is the objective one of a reasonable person's actions in William's position. In *Blyth v Birmingham Water Works* (1856), Alderson B stated that 'negligence is the omission to do something which a reasonable man … would do, or the doing of something which a prudent and reasonable man would not do'.

Applying this objective standard to car drivers, it is irrelevant that a particular driver is a learner (*Nettleship v Weston* (1971)). To hold otherwise, as Megaw LJ pointed out in *Nettleship*, would mean adopting a subjective variable standard which would create greater uncertainty and make it impossible to arrive at consistent decisions. Thus, William must be judged by the standard of the reasonable, competent driver, and he clearly does not meet this standard. The fact that this is due to a medical reason that is outside his control is irrelevant (*Roberts*), however doubt about this remains as seen in *Mansfield v Weetabix* (1998). The Court of Appeal held that where a medical reason that was not reasonably known to the defendant to have brought their performance below the objective standard of care, it could be a factor that is considered in deciding the defendant's negligence. By contrast William's knowledge of the knee injury and the foreseeably known consequences of the risk such injury may carry when driving may not be in his favour. Other factors such as the practicality of taking precautions to prevent the risk of harm, e.g. in this case to seek medical advice, remedy the pain or not to drive (*Latimer v AEC* (1953)), the relative seriousness of a failure to adequately brake to pedestrians and other road users (*Paris v Stepney* (1950)) and the reasonable size of the risk of injury from a failure to brake in an emergency (*Bolton v Stone* (1951)), would in all likelihood contribute to William breaching his duty of care.

Having decided that William is in breach of his duty, we must determine whether his breach caused Victor's injuries. Turning first to Victor's broken legs and ribs, applying the 'but for' test proposed by Lord Denning in *Cork v Kirby MacLean* (1952) and illustrated further in *Barnett v Chelsea and Kensington Hospital Management Committee* (1969), this damage would not have happened but for his breach of duty in failing to brake adequately. Hence William will be liable for Victor's broken limbs, provided that the damage is not too remote. The test for remoteness of damage is that the type of damage must have been reasonably foreseeable (*The Wagon Mound* (1961)). For harm to the person, as long as some personal injury is foreseeable, it does not matter that the exact consequences or its extent were unforeseeable (see, for example, *Bradford v Robinson Rentals* (1967); *Smith v Leech Brain* (1962)). Thus, William must take his victim as he finds him – that is, with brittle bones.

We must also consider whether William is responsible for Victor's amputated arm by applying the 'but for' test. But for William's negligence, Victor would not have been at the hospital later requiring an amputation. However the negligence of the hospital could constitute a *novus actus interveniens* breaking the causal chain. To break the chain it must be a new cause that disturbs the sequence of events and something unreasonable or extraneous or extrinsic (per Lord Wright in *The Oropesa* (1943)). Thus, the defendant will remain liable if the act of the third party is not truly independent of the defendant's negligence. It seems in William's case that the act of the hospital does satisfy this. In *Knightley v Johns* (1982) the court held that negligent conduct was more likely to break the chain of causation than non-negligent conduct and that, in *Knightley*, there were so many errors and departures from common-sense procedures that the chain of causation had been broken. In Victor's case, it seems that the hospital has been negligent through its administration, and there must have been some errors from similar standard procedures. Hence, the chain of causation has been broken and thus William remains liable for the broken legs and ribs. Liability for the amputation can only rest with the hospital if proven.

The Hospital

For Victor to pursue the hospital, it is assumed that a duty of care would be owed by medical staff to a patient. Proving a breach of duty, where the staff fell below the standard of a reasonably competent doctor in their position could be difficult. Traditionally courts have shown deference if bodies of medical opinion would agree with the course of care, and only intervened when there were conflicting views and the treatment could not be logically defended (*Bolam v Friern Hospital Management Committee* (1957); *Bolitho v City and Hackney Health Authority* (1997)). However Victor could use the maxim *res ipsa loquitur* – that is, the thing speaks for itself – to support his case. Where the maxim applies, the court may be prepared to find a breach of duty in the absence of specific evidence of the defendant's actions (see, for example, *Scott v London and St Katherine's Docks* (1865)).

For the maxim to be applicable, it must be shown:

(a) that the defendant is in control of the thing that caused injury to the claimant, present here with the hospital/doctor's control;

(b) that the accident would not have occurred in the ordinary course of events without negligence; amputation of the arm would not appear necessary from the injuries Victor arrived with;

(c) that there is no other explanation for the accident, no other apparent causes or explanations would explain the need for the amputation.

A recent example in a medical context can be seen in *Lillywhite v University College London Hospitals NHS Trust* (2005), in which it was observed that there would be strong evidence of negligence if an unexplained accident were to occur in relation to something under the defendant's control and if medical evidence were to show that this would not have occurred had proper care been taken. The application of the maxim will not shift the burden of proof, which will remain on Victor throughout (*Ng Chun Pui v Lee Chuen Tat* (1988)), but it will allow the court to draw an inference of negligence.

Thus, Victor is advised to sue William in respect of his broken legs and ribs, and the hospital in respect of the amputated arm.[2]

....

2 You should try to make time in an exam to sum up your answer at the end, as, apart from providing a conclusion, it gives you the opportunity to check that you have not made careless errors in relation to the names of the claimants/defendants. As here the conclusion does not have to be long but it neatly finishes off the analysis.

QUESTION 11

Last winter Stacey was driving in excess of the speed limit in a heavy snow storm when she skidded and crashed her car, injuring herself, killing Ahmet (the driver of a car coming in the opposite direction), and resulting in significant back and neck injuries to her passenger Leona.

Stacey was airlifted to hospital, where she was treated for facial injuries by Jackie, a junior doctor who was nearing the end of a double shift. Stacey's skin became infected, with the result that she had to have skin grafts. Jackie unfortunately prescribed the wrong anti-infection drug, and subsequent tests indicated that this error might have deprived Stacey of a 30 per cent chance of a complete recovery from her injuries without the need for skin grafts, although it is not clear at all whether she would have made a full recovery.

A few weeks after the accident Leona began to suffer from severe cramps in her back. It is known that the injury she suffered in the accident could cause this cramping, although it could also be caused by sciatica from which she had suffered in the past. Returning from a party, she climbed over a low wall to take a short-cut, which she had regularly done in the past. As she did so her back cramped and she fell to the ground, breaking her leg.

▶ **Advise the parties of their potential claims and liabilities in the tort of negligence.**

How to Read this Question

The question is a negligence scenario, which has layers of complexity in terms of the causation aspects. As the question suggests, all the parties need to be advised of claims and liabilities, so it is important to have a clear structure and for the reader to be able to clearly identify your reasoning and application. Notice the critical aspects of the question including the behaviour of Leona and the clear reference to Stacey's deprivation of a full recovery by 30 per cent. When you read such examination questions you should be thinking about highlighting such key points early on and/or making notes in your plan.

How to Answer this Question

The following points need to be discussed:

- ❖ (briefly) the establishment of a duty of care and breach of it;
- ❖ the issue of a loss of a chance;
- ❖ supervening causes;
- ❖ intervening acts.

Applying the Law

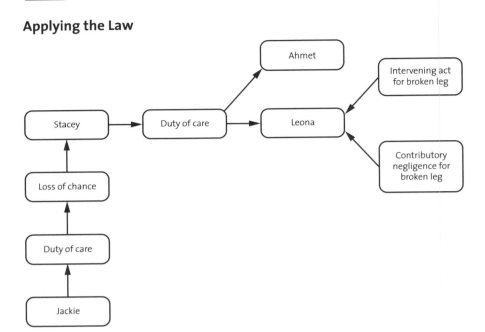

ANSWER

Ahmet and Leona[3]

Stacey would owe a duty of care to both Ahmet and Leona on the basis of the neighbour principle outlined by Lord Atkin in *Donoghue v Stevenson* (1932), as they are persons who Stacey could reasonably and foreseeably be likely to affect as a result of any negligence. A full *Caparo* assessment is not necessary but in any case proximity and the lack of policy factors make it fair, just and reasonable to impose a duty of care. Whether she breached that duty depends on whether her conduct fell below the standard expected of a reasonable person (*Blyth v Birmingham Waterworks* (1856); *Glasgow Corporation v Muir* (1943)). She would be assessed by the standard of the reasonable driver (*Nettleship v Weston* (1971)), and driving at excessive speed in poor weather conditions would fall short of reasonable care. Ahmet would not have died and Leona would not have suffered injury to her neck and back 'but for' Stacey's breach of duty (*Barnett v Chelsea and Kensington Hospital Management Committee* (1969)). Both would thus easily satisfy the requirement of proving factual causation. The test for legal causation is reasonable foreseeability of the type of damage suffered (*The Wagon Mound (No 1)* (1961)), and here it is clear that physical injury would be a reasonably foreseeable harm. The manner of the harm or the extent of harm need not be foreseen (*Hughes v Lord Advocate* (1963); *Bradford v Robinson Rentals* (1967)). Stacey is primae facie liable in negligence for the initial damage suffered.

....

3   The use of sub-headings such as these is absolutely fine and will convey the structural clarity and organisation of the answer. Feel free to use them explicitly as it will allow you to fully ensure that appropriate coverage to the various causes of actions is given.

Leona's Broken Leg

For Leona's claim for her broken leg, the issue is one of causation and the extent to which Stacey can be held to be liable for her further injury. Leona has a claim in negligence against Stacey for her damaged back, however it may be that the further injury suffered as a result of the cramping was an aggravation of that negligence, enabling a claim for the leg. First it would need to be shown on a balance of probabilities that it was the accident injuries that caused the cramping and not a recurrence of the sciatica. She would then need to prove that the damage she had suffered was not too remote a consequence of Stacey's breach of duty.

Stacey could point to a *novus actus interveniens*. The effect of such an act is to break the chain of causation from the defendant's breach of duty to the harm suffered by the claimant. An intervening act may arise through an act of the claimant themselves (*McKew v Holland, Weiland v Cyril Lord Carpets* (1968)). Here it is Leona's action in climbing the low wall given her back injury and whether it would be considered to be reasonable or not. If not then as in *McKew*, where an injured defendant was held to have acted unreasonably, putting himself in a dangerous situation by descending stairs knowing his leg was prone to 'give way', Leona's actions would be said to have broken the chain. The issue has been revisited by the Court of Appeal in *Spencer v Wincanton Holdings Ltd* (2009). The court took a more liberal approach in holding that the chain of causation remained unbroken when the claimant failed to wear his prosthetic leg and use crutches, eventually causing him to slip. The claimant's behaviour had not fallen within the type of recklessness in *McKew* and the behaviour was not wholly unreasonable. A related question would be whether the person's behaviour was reasonably foreseeable. In that context the decision in *Corr v IBC* (2008) is illustrative in that a reasonably foreseeable consequence must be judged at the time of the breach. Thus, if Stacey could have foreseen personal injury then any subsequent injury would be foreseeable. On the critical issue of reasonableness given her prior experience of climbing the wall and, in the context of returning from a party it may be held not unreasonable.

Stacey could claim contributory negligence under the **Law Reform (Contributory Negligence) Act 1945**. Such a finding only limits the portion of her liability (*Sayers v Harlow UDC* (1958)). Leona as a result of the wall climbing, could be subject to a reduction in any award if it is determined that Stacey is liable and she can argue that Leona failed to take reasonable care.[4]

Jackie

Jackie would owe a duty of care to Stacey for her injuries, as above. She would be judged by the skill level of the reasonable person in her position (*Bolam v Friern Hospital Management Committee* (1957)); the fact that she was a junior doctor would have no bearing (*Wilsher v Essex AHA* (1988)) on establishing whether she fell below the standard of care expected of her. By prescribing the wrong drug she is clearly in breach of her duty of care. The crucial issue here, though, is the extent to which she has *caused* Stacey foreseeable damage or any damage at all.

---

4   It is always worth considering whether there is an element of contributory negligence, particularly, as here, when you are told of the claimant's conduct which is connected to the cause of the harm.

The burden of proving the causal link between Jackie's misprescribing and Stacey's failure to recover is initially one of fact and it falls on Stacey to prove causation on a balance of probabilities. The facts indicate that this may be difficult for her. In recent years there has been consideration of the concept that a defendant's negligence deprived the claimant of the opportunity of avoiding a certain result – so-called 'loss of a chance'. The issue was considered in *Hotson v East Berkshire AHA* (1987), where the loss of a 25 per cent chance of a complete recovery was held not to give rise to a cause of action. Here the original misdiagnosis was held, on a balance of probabilities, not to have caused the subsequent disability in that it was likely to have happened even without the negligence of the defendant. The issue was revisited in *Gregg v Scott* (2005) where Baroness Hale commented that the difficulties of trying to establish liability for loss of a chance, meant that it would not be desirable to do so. This was especially given that an action would lie for damage that was *actually* caused by a doctor's negligence. It would appear unlikely that Stacey would succeed, but if so it would be Jackie's employer who would be liable, through the principle of vicarious liability as her actions were in the course of employment (*Lister v Helsey Hall* (2001)).

In conclusion, Stacey would be held liable for Ahmet's death, and most likely for the injuries suffered by Leona to her back and neck. Liability in relation to Leona's subsequent injury is less straightforward, although, applying *Spencer*, it may be that the court would have recourse to contributory negligence. It would seem unlikely that Jackie could be held to be liable to Stacey for her less than complete recovery.

Aim Higher

Focus on the real issues in the question and provide reasoned application of the cases and principles to the facts. This is how you are able to demonstrate to the examiner you are fully engaged with the subject matter, and where possible do provide a conclusion. Similarly in any negligence discussion it is always wise to consider any possible defences, perhaps particularly contributory negligence (especially where you have possible unreasonable conduct from the claimant as in this set of facts) (see the next chapter). For reasons of logical structure you should do this after you have discussed the liability of the party.

QUESTION 12

'Two causes may both be necessary preconditions of a particular result … yet the one may, if the facts justify that conclusion, be treated as the real, substantial, direct or effective cause and the other dismissed … and ignored for the purposes of legal liability …'

Per Lord Asquith in *Stapley v Gipsum Mines* (1953)

▶ Does this statement accurately reflect the law and, if so, does it allow a judge to choose any previous act as the real cause of the claimant's damage?

How to Read this Question

This question calls for a discussion of both the 'but for' test of causation and where there may be a break in the causal chain such as with a *novus actus interveniens*. A firm grasp of the case law will be necessary to convey your understanding of the relevant principles in determining the judge's conclusion of which particular cause is most relevant for the purpose of legal liability. Note the wording of the question which is indicating a relevant theme of the discussion: the extent of judicial freedom.

How to Answer this Question

The following aspects of causation need to be discussed:

- ❖ the 'but for' test;
- ❖ multiple and successive causes;
- ❖ *novus actus interveniens*;
- ❖ problems in proving causation (the mesothelioma cases).

Answer Structure

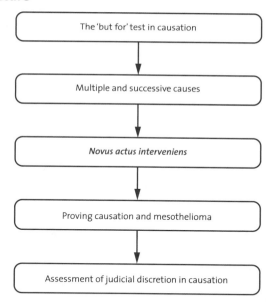

Up for Debate

Causation is a complex area of the law of tort, particular where there are multiple causes and where the courts have adapted the 'but for' test to accommodate both policy and fairness, such as with the mesothelioma cases. There is plenty of secondary literature and academic commentary that runs across all aspects of causation. An excellent and readable review of a selection of the cases is found in J Smith LJ, 'Causation: the search for principle' (2009) 2 Journal of Personal Injury Law 101. Similarly the scope, application and effectiveness of the modified but for test are discussed in articles such as S Bailey, 'Causation in negligence: what is a material contribution?' (2010) 30 Legal Studies 167, and J Stapleton, 'Unnecessary causes' (2013) 129 Law Quarterly Review 39.

ANSWER

The foremost causation test was best explained by Lord Denning in *Cork v Kirby MacLean* (1952), in which he said that 'if the damage would not have happened but for a particular fault, then that fault is the cause of the damage'.[5] A good example of this but for test is provided by *Barnett v Chelsea and Kensington Hospital Management Committee* (1969) where a doctor refused to examine a patient, who subsequently died from arsenic poisoning. It was held that the doctor was negligent in not examining the man, but that his negligence had not caused the man's death, as but for his negligence, he still would have died because he could not have been cured.

Though based on common sense, an area in which the 'but for' test can give rise to problems is where there is more than one cause of the claimant's injury: for example, where two persons both cause harm to the claimant, so that he still would have suffered harm but for the negligence of either of the defendants. This situation was considered by the Court of Appeal in *Holtby v Brigham and Cowan (Hull) Ltd* (2000). Here, the claimant suffered injury as a result of exposure to a noxious substance by two or more persons, but claimed against only one. The Court of Appeal held that the defendant was liable, but only to the extent that he had caused the claimant's injury. Though problematic the courts tend to approach causation as a matter of common sense, rather than from any theoretical point of view, including practical judgments on the facts such as the time between the first and the second cause, and whether the first cause was still indirect and operative (see *Wright (A Child) v Cambridge Medical Group* (2011)). As Lord Wright stated in *Yorkshire Dale Steamship v Minister of War Transport* (1942), 'Causation is to be understood as the man in the street, and not as either the scientist or the metaphysician would understand it.'

However an example where there is a risk of undue judicial discretion is where an act has occurred after the original negligent act of the defendant – a *novus actus interveniens*

---

5 A short quotation from a named judge enhances the quality of the answer.

situation. The judge must then decide which of the two acts is the real, substantial, direct or effective cause. The *novus actus* may be an act of the claimant, a third party or of nature. Taking these in turn, the latter act of the claimant that causes additional harm may be held to have broken the chain of causation between the original negligent act of the defendant and the additional harm suffered by the claimant. However, a judge does not have a completely free choice in deciding this; case law has determined that only where the latter act of the claimant is unreasonable will the causal chain be broken. Unreasonable is a subjective term and is difficult to interpret so the courts have taken a facts based approach. An example is *McKew v Holland and Hannen and Cubitts* (1969), in which the claimant, as a result of the defendants' negligence, suffered an injury that caused him to lose control of his leg. Despite this injury, the claimant still went down a steep flight of stairs that had no handrail, and subsequently fell when his leg gave way. The House held that this act was so unreasonable that the original negligence of the defendants was no longer the real and effective cause of the injury. In contrast in *Wieland v Cyril Lord Carpets* (1969), the claimant, as a result of the defendants' negligence, was unable to use her bifocal spectacles in the normal manner. As a result of this, she fell down a flight of stairs. It was held that the defendants were liable for this additional harm to the claimant because she had not acted unreasonably in continuing to wear them. Thus as can be seen the decision as to the reasonableness or otherwise of a claimant's (or other party's) conduct will often give the judge a certain amount of discretion.

Where the latter act is that of a third party, this latter act will be treated as the real cause of the claimant's additional damage where it is 'something unwarrantable … which can be described as either unreasonable or extraneous or extrinsic' (Lord Wright in *The Oropesa* (1943)). Thus, the latter act of the third party will not be treated as the true cause of the additional damage unless it is independent of the defendant's original negligence. If the act of the third party is itself negligent, the courts are usually willing to hold that this act is the true cause of the claimant's additional damage (*Knightley v Johns* (1982)). Again, judicial discretion here is rife.

A restriction on a judge's freedom to choose which previous act was the real cause of the claimant's injury is the need for the claimant to prove causation. This is where causation can intertwine with policy considerations where judges are concerned with providing corrective justice to the injured parties. Similarly concerns over the availability of proof and how certain medical science can be, has been a feature in modifying causation rules, particularly in the case of recovery for mesothelioma from asbestos exposure (see for example the statutory input from **s3(1)** of the **Compensation Act 2006**). A claimant who has difficulties in this area will usually rely on the decision of the House of Lords in *McGhee v National Coal Board* (1973) where the claimant recovered as he could show that the actions of the defendant materially increased the risk of damage. The House of Lords took a restrictive approach to *McGhee* in the later cases including in *Wilsher v Essex Area Health Authority* (1988). Indeed, in *Wilsher*, Lord Bridge stated that *McGhee* 'laid down no new principle of law whatsoever'. The area though has been significantly revisited by the Supreme Court in *Sienkewicz v Greif (UK) Ltd* (2011) and though it did not overrule the test, it maintained that the effect of **s3(1)** was that liability in tort must still be made out. The court added that the common law could still develop in this area, allowing even for the McGhee test to be abandoned if medical science made advances regarding the certainty of the diagnosis and its timing.

Lord Asquith's statement suggests that determining the relevant cause is straight-forward; however there is unpredictability as judges have developed their own tests, based on the peculiarities of the case, proof and policy. In this sense the ultimate decision rests with the judge, allowing them to interpret words such as reasonable, real and effective with a large degree of freedom.

Aim Higher

In essay questions the examiner is looking for evidence of critical analysis and arguments directed to the question or statement given. Your analysis can be drawn from the case law but also further reading, and even by advancing your own position on the state of the law. Certainly by reading secondary literature and citing academics in your answers, the level and sophistication of the criticisms you can demonstrate will only impress.

Common Pitfalls

Often in a question on negligence, certain aspects are assumed (or 'a given') such as the fact that Stacey owed a duty of care. When you know that the scenario is concerned with far more critical issues, do not waste your time addressing those points – keep such discussion concise so that you do not run out of time.

4

General Defences

INTRODUCTION

The general defences to tort are often tested by examiners. This may take the form of a specific essay question but is more often a part of another negligence discussion. Therefore ensure it forms a feature of your answer on any discussion of negligence liability, where it applies. Note that out of all defences, contributory negligence is regularly tested in questions, and can often be discussed where the claimant's own behaviour has in some way contributed to their harm. *Volenti* and illegality are similarly popular, with necessity and statutory authority being quite niche in terms of application and coverage (note they are not covered in the following questions). This short chapter has first a problem question and then a broad essay question.

Checklist
Candidates must be aware of the following defences:
(a) contributory negligence;
(b) *volenti non fit injura (volens)*;
(c) illegality;
(d) necessity;
(e) statutory authority.

QUESTION 13

Norman and Mark went out for a social evening using Mark's car. They called at a public house, where they both consumed a large amount of drink. Mark then drove Norman home and, due to his intoxicated state, crashed the car into a lamp post. Norman, who was not wearing a seat belt, was thrown through the car windscreen and was severely injured. Rita, who witnessed the accident, went to help Norman and cut her hands badly in so doing.

▶ Advise Norman and Rita of any rights that they might have against Mark. Would your advice differ if, rather than going out together, Norman had met Mark in the public house when Norman had had little to drink, but Mark was already intoxicated, and Norman had then accepted a lift from Mark?

How to Read this Question

This question involves multiple parties. It is important to remember that you need to establish liability first before you can discuss any defences, and therefore structure is critical. Hopefully the failure in wearing a seatbelt should have triggered your recall of contributory negligence from your learning. Note in this question there is a conditional circumstance attached so ensure this is dealt with in your answer as this will lose you credit needlessly. It is often best to compartmentalise this section and leave it to the end.

How to Answer this Question

The following points need to be discussed:

The liability of Mark to Norman:
- ❖ the defences available to Mark;
- ❖ *volenti* – consideration of statute law and previous common law *ex turpi causa*;
- ❖ contributory negligence in accepting the lift;
- ❖ contributory negligence in not wearing a seat belt.

The liability of Mark to Rita:
- ❖ the defences available to Mark;
- ❖ *volenti*;
- ❖ contributory negligence.

Applying the Law

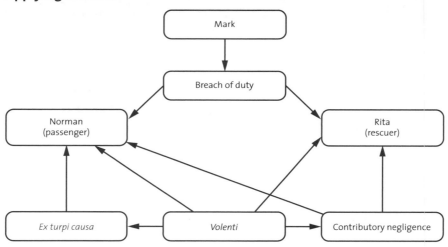

ANSWER

Norman must first show that Mark owes him a duty of care. In those situations in which a duty of care has previously been found to exist, there is no need to apply the modern formulation in *Caparo Industries plc v Dickman* (1990). In fact, a duty of care has been found to exist in a number of cases involving drivers and their passengers – for example, *Nettleship v Weston* (1971) – but, even without knowledge of such cases, we could deduce the existence of a duty of care as it is reasonably foreseeable that by driving carelessly, a passenger may suffer injury.[1]

Next, Norman must show that Mark was in breach of this duty – that a reasonably competent driver, in Mark's position would not have acted in this way (*Blyth v Birmingham Waterworks* (1856); *Nettleship*). It seems clear that a reasonably competent driver would not drink-drive given the risk of crashing as was the case here. Mark is in obvious breach of his duty not least as the behaviour is criminal.[2]

Norman will also have to show that this breach caused his injuries and the 'but for' test in *Cork v Kirby MacLean* (1952) proves the required causal connection, as but for the drink-driving and crash, he would not have caused Norman's injuries. Finally, Norman will have to prove that the damage that he has suffered was not too remote – that is, it must be reasonably foreseeable (*The Wagon Mound (No 1)* (1961)). This should not give rise to any problem, as all that Norman will have to show is that some personal injury was foreseeable, which is clearly the case with a passenger in Norman's position. He will not have to show that the extent was foreseeable, or the exact manner in which the injury was caused (*Smith v Leech Brain* (1962); *Hughes v Lord Advocate* (1963)).

The first possible defence however *volenti non fit injuria* – that Norman voluntarily submitted or consented to the risk of injury. The law is now firmly established under **s 149(3)** of the **Road Traffic Act 1988** which rules out *volenti* in road traffic situations.

(For completeness of coverage the answer considers the possibility of a *volens* defence. In the exam this would not be strictly compulsory though demonstrating a flavour of the common law principles would impress upon the examiner the breadth of knowledge and impress.)

Under the old common law, to establish that Norman was *volens*, Mark will have to show that Norman was able to choose freely whether to run the risk or not and that there were no constraints acting on his freedom of choice, such as fear of loss of his employment (*Bowater v Rowley Regis Corp* (1944)). In the instant case, no such restraints were acting on Norman. The next point is whether there was any agreement between Mark and Norman, whereby Norman agreed to accept the risk of injury. There is no evidence on the facts that we are given to suggest such an agreement, so we need to consider whether there was an implied agreement. In cases involving persons who have accepted lifts from persons whom they know to be intoxicated, the courts are usually unwilling to find that the person accepting the lift has impliedly agreed to waive his right to sue the intoxicated driver (*Dann v Hamilton* (1939)). In *Nettleship*, Lord

---

1 Again approach the duty of care situation pragmatically, and only develop the discussion at length if it is strictly necessary.

2 Do not forget the logical structure of a claim in negligence. Once duty of care has been established, the question then turns on whether a breach of that duty can be established. Once that is done then causation must be considered.

Denning stated that nothing short of an express or implied agreement would suffice to found a defence of *volenti*. However, this view has not been universally accepted. In *Dann*, the court held that *volenti* could apply to those situations in which the claimant comes to a situation in which a danger has been created by the defendant's negligence (although, on the facts of *Dann*, it was held that *volenti* had not been made out). Also in *Pitts v Hunt* (1990) and *Morris v Murray* (1990), it was held that the defence could apply in appropriate circumstances to passengers who accepted lifts from drivers who were obviously highly intoxicated. This though remains an academic discussion as the defence is ruled out by statute.

He may also attempt to raise the defence of *ex turpi causa non oritur actio* in that both he and Norman were jointly participating in an illegal activity – namely, driving a motor vehicle whilst under the influence of excess alcohol, contrary to **s4** of the **Road Traffic Act 1988**. This defence was upheld in *National Coal Board v England* (1954) and *Ashton v Turner* (1981), but there must be a causal connection between the criminal act and the damage that the claimant has suffered (*Delaney v Pickett* (2011); *Gray v Thames Trains* (2009)). Indeed the wider flexibility of *ex turpi causa* is reflected in Lord Hoffmann's reasoning in *Gray* who argued the defence is more policy than principle. This is best reflected in Beldam LJ's approach in *Pitts* who stated that it would be an 'affront to the public conscience' to allow the claimant to succeed. However in *Tinsley v Milligan* (1993), the House of Lords preferred a test of whether the claim is based directly on the illegal conduct, and this test has been used by the Court of Appeal in *Vellino v Chief Constable of Greater Manchester* (2002). The law on illegality has recently been revisited by the Court of Appeal in *Joyce v O'Brien and Tradex Co Ltd* (2013) who stated that the defence and the causation threshold would be satisfied where the character of a joint criminal enterprise was such that it was foreseeable that a party could be subject to an increased risk of harm as a consequence of the crime. Active encouragement was not necessary. On the facts here, which are analogous but distinguishable from *Pitts* there is no evidence of encouragement; however it could be made out that it would be foreseeable by Norman given the co-drinking, and then subsequent drive that increased risk of harm was self-evident, thus leading to a conclusion that the activity caused the damage. Thus the defence could apply.

Mark as a final option may be able to raise the defence of contributory negligence to reduce the damages that he will have to pay Norman (**s1(1)** of the **Law Reform (Contributory Negligence) Act 1945**). By **s1(1)**, where a person suffers damage as the result partly of his own fault and partly of the fault of any other person, his damages will be reduced by such an extent as the court thinks just and equitable, having regard to the first person's share in the responsibility for the damage. Mark will have to show that Norman was careless for his own safety by not showing reasonable prudence (*Davies v Swan Motor Co* (1949); *Jones v Livox Quarries Ltd* (1952)). Norman has been careless in accepting a lift from a driver whom he knows to be intoxicated (*Dann*; *Pitts* at first instance; *Owens v Brimmel* (1977)). Thus, any damages that Norman receives will be reduced due to this particular act of contributory negligence. In addition, as Norman was not wearing a seat belt at the time of the crash, the extent of his injuries would have been reduced as he would not have been thrown through the windscreen. Norman's act has thus contributed to the extent of the damage he has suffered and so his damages could be further reduced by up to 25 per cent (*Froom v Butcher* (1975)).[3]

Turning now to Rita, she is a rescuer[4] and can sue Mark (*Haynes v Harwood* (1935)). Mark will almost certainly be unsuccessful in attempting to raise the defence of *volenti* against Rita (*Haynes v Harwood* (1935); *Chadwick v British Transport Commission* (1967)). The only situation in which a rescuer will be held to be *volens* is where a rescue is attempted in circumstances in which there is no real danger (*Cutler v United Dairies* (1933)), which is not the case here. Mark may try to run the defence of contributory negligence against Rita in an attempt to reduce any damages payable to her, but the courts are reluctant to find rescuers guilty of contributory negligence. This has been done where the circumstances warrant it (*Harrison v British Railways Board* (1981)) but, in judging whether or not the rescuer has been careless for her own safety, the courts consider how the claimant may have been placed in an emergency. The court will be sympathetic to a claimant who makes a wrong decision in the agony of the moment (*Jones v Boyce* (1816) and more recently see *Tolley v Carr* (2010)). Thus, on the facts that we are given, it seems unlikely that a finding of contributory negligence would be made against Rita, who could recover in full against Mark.

If Norman had met Mark in the public house when Norman had very little to drink, but Mark was already intoxicated, then prima facie it would be easier for the court to find that Norman was *volens* to the risks of being a passenger in Mark's car. In *Dann*, it was said that if the drunkenness of the driver was extreme, the *volenti* defence might apply. However, even if this were to apply to Mark, **s149(3)** would still render the defence invalid. On the basis of illegality, it is less clear but it may appear more likely for the defence not to apply. The claimants' role in the enterprise of drink-driving is far lessened such that it would now be less likely to pass the causation threshold, and therefore less foreseeable that such a risk of harm may occur as a result of the pursuit of the activities (*Pitts*; *Joyce*).

QUESTION 14

Discuss the operation and effectiveness of the so-called 'general defences' in tort.

How to Read this Question

The question demands that the candidate explains and offers critical insight in relation to the operation of the general defences. As well as requiring explanation of how the defences are applied, it also necessitates consideration of their limitations and

---

3 Emphasise that contributory negligence, unlike the other general defences is only a *partial* defence which in effect is used to change the apportionment of his liability, as reflected through a reduction in the amount of damages that can be recovered.

4 Look out for those who could be classified as 'rescuers', who may be in a special position, as the courts give them additional protection, and they are less keen in finding that they consented to the risk or contributed to the harm suffered.

uncertainty around their margins. It is a very broad question so you can choose varied examples from the range of defences that you are aware of, though you must make editorial choices in timed conditions as you cannot possibly cover everything.

How to Answer this Question

A competent answer could contain broad coverage of the range of defences. This can include;

- ❖ contributory negligence;
- ❖ *volenti non fit injuria*;
- ❖ illegality;
- ❖ statutory authority, necessity (*where time and space permits*).

Answer Structure

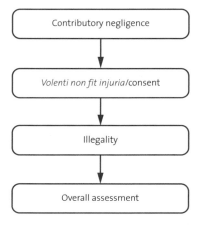

```
┌─────────────────────────────────┐
│      Contributory negligence     │
└─────────────────────────────────┘
                 │
                 ▼
┌─────────────────────────────────┐
│  Volenti non fit injuria/consent │
└─────────────────────────────────┘
                 │
                 ▼
┌─────────────────────────────────┐
│            Illegality            │
└─────────────────────────────────┘
                 │
                 ▼
┌─────────────────────────────────┐
│        Overall assessment        │
└─────────────────────────────────┘
```

Up for Debate

The general defences are a critical aspect of the law of tort, providing the only resort left to a defendant who is primae facie liable. Many of the general defences have many conceptual criticisms. For a more nuanced and conduct based repositioning of *volenti non fit injuria* read C Tan, 'Volenti non fit injuria: an alternative framework' (1995) 3 Tort Law Review 208; for a case comment on the problematic *Smith v Finch* (2009) see M Porter, 'Blame the victim' (2009) 159 New Law Journal 337–8, and browse through the Law Commission report 'The illegality defence: a consultative report' (Consultation Paper no 189, TSO 2009) or see P Davies, 'The illegality defence: two steps forward, one step back? (2009) Conv 182–208.

ANSWER

The first defence to consider is the statutory partial defence of contributory negligence. Under this defence, damages are reduced by the amount the claimant is judged to be responsible for their own harm. The **Law Reform (Contributory Negligence) Act 1945**, s1(1) of the Act, states that dependent on fault the quantum of damages that they receive 'shall be reduced to such an extent as the court thinks just and equitable'. The previous common law position was that it was an 'all or nothing' defence.

In order for the defence to operate, it must be demonstrated that the claimant failed to take care of their own safety and that failure was at least a partial cause of the damage that was suffered. So it is necessary to prove that the claimant was at fault, that the claimant had fallen below the required standard of care and then to determine the contribution of both of the parties to the damage suffered. Sometimes it will be obvious that the claimant has contributed to their own injury, for example by being a partial cause of the accident (see, for example, *Baker v Willoughby* (1970)) or in other cases purely a significant impact on the damage caused: for example failing to wear a seat belt (*Froom v Butcher* (1975)).

The standard of care applied is the usual negligence objective standard of the reasonable person in that situation though with special consideration to children and their relative appreciation of the risks and whether it would be obvious to them (*Gough v Thorne* (1966) contrasted with *Morales v Eccelstone* (1991)).

On occasions, a claimant will simply have made an error of judgement and, depending on the situation – say, for example, an emergency – they may not be held to have fallen below the standard of care. See *Tolley v Carr* (2010) where it was held that someone going to the aid of a crash victim on a motorway was not liable for contributory negligence. In other situations, the court has developed useful guidelines, such as where a person fails to wear a crash helmet or seat belt (see *Froom v Butcher* (1975) and *Smith v Finch* (2009)).

The next situation to consider is that in which the defendant has consented to run the risk of being injured, expressed in the Latin maxim *volenti non fit injuria* and this is a complete defence. It is necessary for the defendant to prove two key criteria: first, that the claimant had knowledge of the risk involved in terms of the nature of it and also its extent and, second, that the claimant *willingly* agreed to run that risk. The courts apply an objective test, which considers the claimant's behaviour in relation to determining the first limb, but mere knowledge of the risk does not mean that a claimant consented to it (*Smith v Baker* (1891)). In *Smith*, an important point was made by the House of Lords, which was considering the extent to which a person consents to being placed in a position of danger at work. When the choice is, effectively, 'do the job and run the risk, or have no job', the employee cannot be said to have consented freely to run that risk (see also *ICI v Shatwell* (1965) for a different result).

In certain situations, it is unlikely that *volenti* would apply, despite the risk that the claimant has undertaken. Rescuers, for example, are generally not subject to the defence (*Chadwick v BTC* (1967)) and persons who take their own lives while held in custody (*Kirkham v Chief Constable of Greater Manchester* (1990) – a mentally ill patient could not be *volenti*; and *Reeves v Chief of Police for the Metropolis* (1999) – the police could not claim *volenti* for an act that they were duty-bound to prevent). The fact, however, that a person is intoxicated, as in the case of *Morris v Murray* (1990), does not necessarily mean that *volenti* will not apply. Sporting injuries have provided another specialist application of the defence, although there is a distinction made between a participant who agrees to run the risk of injury through the normal playing of the sport/game within the rules (*Simms v Leigh Rugby Football Club* (1969); *Condon v Basi* (1985)).

Finally, it is worth noting that statute has placed a limitation on the *volenti* defence. **Section 149** of the **Road Traffic Act 1988** does not permit the defence of *volenti* in a situation in which a passenger sues a driver. This is related to the fact that compulsory third-party insurance is required for all road vehicles and was instrumental in *Pitts v Hunt* (1990).

The general defence of illegality, *ex turpi causa non oritur* action means that a person cannot base their legal claim upon an illegal act. The basis of the defence is that it would generally be considered as offensive to permit a claim for a person who was committing a crime. A classic application can be seen in the case of *Ashton v Turner* (1981), where it was established that there should be a causal link between the criminal and the tortious act (*National Coal Board v England* (1954)). The test to determine whether the defence applies seems to relate directly to the criminal conduct of the person involved (see *Cross v Kirkby* (2000) and *Vellino v Chief Constable of Greater Manchester Police* (2001)), however there is little doubt that there is lack of clarity and predictability about the principle perhaps highlighted by the varying rationales in the judgments in the *Pitts* decision. The recent case of *Joyce v O'Brien and Tradex Co Ltd* (2013) confirmed the public policy basis of the doctrine and its inherent flexibility, such as leaving it open to determine which type of criminal offence should ordinarily attract the defence. Indeed the House of Lords in *Gray v Thames Trains Ltd* (2009) discussed the two versions of illegality, with Lord Hoffmann also determining it was more in the character of a 'policy' than a principle. This policy was on the basis of deterrence, the public notion of who should deserve a share of resources and the overall consistency with the criminal law. Such a broad policy though exposes its practical limitations and illegality has received regular calls for its abolishment.

Thus there are significant considerations to take into account when attempting to plead the general defences. Issues of policy, statutory input and judicial discretion are factors that may affect the success and effectiveness of the defences. It is clear that not all of the defences are as 'general' in their application as they might seem at first glance; and the relationship between *volenti* and contributory negligence is interesting in so far as they are often pleaded together.

Aim Higher

Always ensure you give a reasoned and concise application of the defence, and know defences are always worth considering on a read through of the question. The defences are also problematic, so completing the extra reading will help develop your critical instincts, especially in areas such as the operation of illegality which is open to debate. For example understanding the distinctions drawn in the *Gray v Thames* case will enhance the analytical level of your work, or consider the debate surrounding the *Smith v Finch* decision in relation to not wearing cycle helmets. Similarly cases concerning contributory negligence and the apportionment of liability are very common, so using your research skills read some more recent cases such as the Court of Appeal rulings in *Paramasivan v Wicks* (2013) or *Smith v Chief Constable of Nottinghamshire Police* (2012).

Common Pitfalls

Frequent problems seen from candidates include not remembering that *contributory negligence* is only a partial defence, under *volens* forgetting that a person consents to run the risk of *an* injury, rather than, necessarily, the one that they actually suffer, and generally forgetting that the burden is on the defendant to prove that a defence applies, after liability has been established. Similarly candidates must draw a clear distinction between acts that contribute to the extent of damage, and acts that may contribute to the accident which causes the damage.

5 Employers' Liability

INTRODUCTION

Questions on employers' liability are regular features in examinations. As the topic is only a specialised branch of the law of negligence, it does not introduce any new legal concepts, but generally demands the broad understanding of negligence principles such as duty, causation and remoteness. The topic is often closely associated with vicarious liability so please refer to the next chapter for examples of questions that involve elements of employers' liability. Similarly your course may also include some historical coverage of breach of statutory duty though the rules on this have been changed due to the effect of the **Enterprise and Regulatory Reform Act 2013 (s 69)**. This chapter does not substantially cover statutory duty, but contains two problem questions that highlight the close relationship between vicarious liability and employer's liability.

Checklist

Students must be familiar with all of the above topics and especially:

(a) the provision of competent fellow employees;
(b) the provision of safe plant and equipment;
(c) the provision of a safe place of work;
(d) the provision of a safe system of work.

QUESTION 15

Ken is employed by Lomad plc as an electrician. One day, he is asked to repair a ceiling fan located in Lomad's workplace, and is told to dismantle the fan and take it to the electrical workshop for repair. In order to save time, Ken attempts to repair the fan whilst standing on a stepladder. As he is doing so, he drops his pliers, which land on Martin's head. Because Martin is of a rather nervous disposition, he is off work for two months following this accident, rather than the two days that would be normal for such an injury. Following this incident, Ken decides to comply with his instructions and dismantles the fan but, while he is doing this, his screwdriver snaps and a piece of metal enters his eye.

▶ Advise Martin and Ken of the claims available to them.

How to Read this Question

This is a straightforward question on employers' liability, involving two claimants against the defendant employer. There are issues of both primary liability by the employer Lomad plc to both Martin and Ken, and a possible vicarious claim by Martin for the negligent actions of Ken. In your own answer feel free to adopt your own sub-headings which will help organise your knowledge. Notice key aspects of the facts here such as Martin's prior nervous disposition, and when discussing vicarious liability be careful in noticing the effect of employer instructions on the subsequent tortious conduct.

How to Answer this Question

The following points need to be discussed:

- ❖ the duty to provide a safe place of work;
- ❖ vicarious liability for Ken's action;
- ❖ the eggshell skull rule;
- ❖ the duty to provide safe equipment and the **Employers' Liability (Defective Equipment) Act 1969**.

Applying the Law

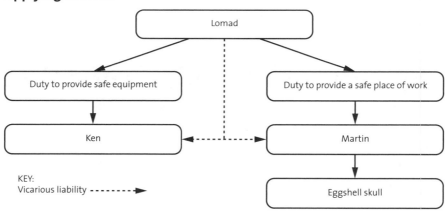

ANSWER

Martin can claim against Lomad in respect of their primary duty owed to him. Lomad has a duty to provide Martin with a safe place of work. This is not an absolute duty, but merely places on the employer the duty to take reasonable steps to provide a safe place of work: *Latimer v AEC* (1953). The question therefore is whether Lomad has taken such reasonable steps. It has instructed Ken to take the fan to the electrical workshop to repair it, but the duty to provide a safe place of work is non-delegable and so the employer may entrust the performance of this work to an employee, but cannot rely on this delegation to exclude their potential liability (*McDermid v Nash Dredging and Reclamation* (1987)). Following *McDermid*, we can see that Lomad is in breach of its duty to provide a safe place of work, and as causation poses no major concerns Lomad would be potentially liable.

Considering Lomad's secondary vicarious liability, for any tort committed by Ken in the course of his employment then there must be an employer–employee relationship between Lomad and Ken.[1] On the facts this can be assumed (*Mersey Docks and Harbour Board Ltd v Coggins and Griffith (Liverpool) Ltd* (1946)). Ken must also have committed a tort when Martin suffered his injuries. In order to establish liability Martin must owe a duty of care under normal *Donoghue v Stevenson* (1932) principles and this is satisfied in that he can reasonably foresee that any lack of care on his part may cause injury to Martin. Ken will be in breach of this duty if a reasonable person placed in his position would not have acted in this way (*Blyth v Birmingham Waterworks* (1856)). As a reasonable person would not have carelessly dropped the pliers, it is likely there would be a breach. However the courts will weigh up certain factors to justify their conclusion. Factors such as the potential seriousness of the harm given the height of a ceiling fan (*Paris v Stepney* (1950)), how it is reasonably likely that such a careless mistake undertaken by a layperson may occur (*Bolton v Stone* (1951)) and the convenience in complying with the instructions (*Latimer v AEC* (1953)) all add weight to the conclusion of breach. This breach must cause Martin's injury and the 'but for' test in *Cork v Kirby MacLean* (1952) proves the required causal connection. Additionally, the harm suffered by Martin must not be too remote, in that it must be reasonably foreseeable (*The Wagon Mound (No 1)* (1961)). All that Ken needs foresee is some personal injury; he need foresee neither the extent (*Smith v Leech Brain* (1962)), nor the exact manner in which the damage occurs (*Hughes v Lord Advocate* (1963)). These criteria can be satisfied as physical injury to others in the course of him using tools to fix a ceiling fan can be reasonably foreseen. Thus Ken has been negligent in the course of his conduct.

Finally we are told that Ken is an electrician and, in repairing the fan, he is prima facie acting within the course of his employment. However, there is an express prohibition that he should not repair the fan. The authorities show that acting in contravention of a prohibition will not automatically take the act outside the course of the employment: for example, *Rose v Plenty* (1976) and *Limpus v London General Omnibus* (1862). What a prohibition can do is to limit those acts that lie within the course of the employment, but it cannot restrict the mode of carrying out an act that does lie within the course of the employment (see, for example, *Limpus*). Thus, the question that must be decided is whether Ken, in repairing the fan *in situ*, has done an unauthorised act or whether he was merely carrying out an authorised act in an unauthorised manner, based on the Salmond test. The court would have to decide whether the authorised act was repairing the fan (that is, the wide approach to course of employment, as in *Rose v Plenty* and *Limpus*) or whether it was to repair the fan in the electrical workshop (the narrow construction, as in *Conway v Wimpey* (1951)). It is likely that a court would take the former approach and thus Lomad would be liable for Ken's negligence.

However, in recent years, the courts have taken a narrow view of course of employment where deliberate acts are concerned (see *Heasmans v Clarity Cleaning Ltd* (1987); *Irving v*

---

1 Take care to distinguish employers' *primary* liability (their own negligence) from *vicarious* liability (liability for their employees' negligence).

Post Office (1987)). In *General Engineering Services v Kingston and St Andrews Corp* (1989), firemen who drove very slowly to the scene of a fire were held not to be within the course of their employment with one of the grounds being slow driving was not in furtherance of their employer's business. Such factors as well as the inherent risks involved in the employment are still relevant even after the ruling in *Lister v Hesley Hall* (2001) that focused on whether there was a sufficiently close connection as to make it fair and just to impose vicarious liability. This was confirmed in *Mohamud v WM Morrison Supermarkets* (2014). Here we are told that the reason for Ken's action was to save time – which is in furtherance of the employers' business and therefore distinguishable from that in *General Engineering Services.*[2]

Lomad would be liable for the full extent of harm as the thin-skull rule would result in losses for the two month duration (from being off work due to his nervous disposition), being recoverable. The disposition would not have to be foreseen (*Dulieu v White* (1901)).

Turning now to Ken's damage, Lomad, as his employer, is under a duty to provide Ken with safe equipment (*Smith v Baker* (1891)). It is no defence for Lomad to show that it purchased the screwdriver from a reputable supplier because, by **s 1(1)** of the **Employers' Liability (Defective Equipment) Act 1969** (which survives the effect of **s 69** of **Enterprise and Regulatory Reform Act 2013**), where the defect is attributable to the fault of a third party, it is deemed to be attributable to negligence on the part of the employer. If the screwdriver was relatively new and it can be shown that nothing has happened since it left the manufacturers to cause the defect, the defect can be attributed to the manufacturer (*Mason v Williams and Williams Ltd* (1955)). However, if the screwdriver had been in use for some time, it may be difficult to show that the defect was due to fault on the part of the manufacturer (see *Evans v Triplex Glass* (1936)). The duty to provide safe equipment is merely one to take reasonable care (see *Toronto Power v Paskwan* (1915)) and Lomad will not be liable if it had not been negligent (*Davie v New Merton Board Mills* (1959)).

QUESTION 16

Iambic plc owns some premises and decides to have the rather old-fashioned central heating system replaced with a modern, efficient system. It engages Lead Ltd to carry out this work and Lead Ltd sends two plumbers to Iambic's premises. While the plumbers are working, one of them carelessly leaves a blowlamp running and the partition to an office catches fire. Jenny, who is working in the office, is burnt. Peter, who is an employee of Iambic plc, carelessly leaves a screwdriver on the floor of another office, and Katherine trips over it and twists her leg. In the ensuing commotion caused by these two accidents, an unknown thief enters the premises and steals a sheepskin coat belonging to Richard, another employee of Iambic plc. Richard kept his coat in a cupboard that was not provided with a lock.

▶ **Advise Jenny, Katherine and Richard.**

2 For more on vicarious liability, see the next chapter.

How to Read this Question

This is a perhaps more complex employer's liability question with three claimants, and as is frequently the case there is a requirement for a discussion on vicarious liability too. Notice that there is an independent contractor involved here which will form a key part of the discussion, and therefore you should be aware of the general rule on such situations as well as the limits placed on the duty of care. Ensuring a good structure with a clear separation of the claimants would be the best strategy to address the question.

How to Answer this Question

The following points need to be discussed:

❖   the liability of Iambic plc for the negligence of Lead Ltd;
❖   the liability of Iambic plc for the negligence of its employees;
❖   the liability of Iambic plc for the negligence of Peter;
❖   employers' liability – the limits on the duty of care.

Applying the Law

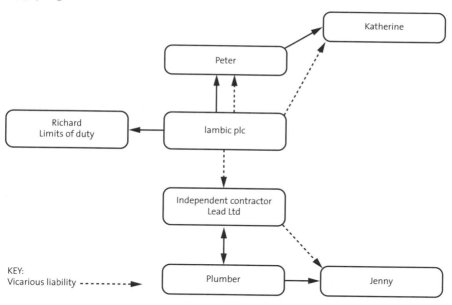

ANSWER

Jenny[3]

It is clear that the plumber himself owes Jenny a duty of care under normal *Donoghue v Stevenson* (1932) principles, in that he can reasonably foresee that any lack of care on his part may cause injury to Jenny. The plumber will be in breach of this duty if a reasonable

---

3   Dealing with the claimants individually avoids a confused answer. The time spent planning and structuring the answer to a problem question before starting to write it is never wasted.

plumber placed in his position would not have acted in this way (*Blyth v Birmingham Waterworks* (1856)) and it is submitted that a reasonable plumber would not have carelessly left a blowlamp running. This breach must have caused Jenny's injury and the 'but for' test in *Cork v Kirby MacLean* (1952) proves the required causal connection. Additionally, the injury suffered by Jenny must not be too remote, in that it must be reasonably foreseeable (*The Wagon Mound (No 1)* (1961)). All that the plumber need foresee is some personal injury; he need foresee neither the extent (*Smith v Leech Brain* (1962)), nor the exact manner which the harm occurs (in this case via the office catching fire whilst Jenny is still inside) (*Hughes v Lord Advocate* (1963)). This has been satisfied so the plumber can be said to have been negligent towards Jenny.

As the plumber is an employee of Lead Ltd, Lead Ltd will be vicariously liable for any tort committed by an employee-plumber in the course of his employment. The employer–employee relationship is self-evident, and with the tort having been committed by the plumber as discussed above, the final question is whether the tort was in the course of employment. As we are told that 'while the plumbers are working, one of them carelessly …' it would seem that the plumber has been careless within the course of his employment. The fact that the carelessness is gross and its consequences are obvious will not take the action outside the course of employment (*Century Insurance v Northern Ireland Road Transport Board* (1942)). Hence, Jenny could sue Lead Ltd in respect of her injury.

Jenny's potential claim against her own employer Iambic plc may be hampered by the fact that Lead Ltd appears to be an independent contractor. The normal rule is that an employer is not liable for the torts committed by an independent contractor during the course of the contractor's duties, as negligence is fault based (*Morgan v Girls Friendly Society* (1936); *D and F Estates v Church Commissioners* (1989)). However there are five points that need to be satisfied to overcome this rule and these were outlined in *Woodland v Essex Country Council* (2013); however these are unlikely to apply in such a context and not least be overcome due to lack of vulnerability or a special antecedent relationship between Jenny and Iambic plc. Nonetheless there is a non-delegable duty imposed by common law which may arise where an independent contractor is employed to carry out work that is extra-hazardous (*Alcock v Wraith* (1991)). In *Alcock*, the Court of Appeal held that a crucial question was: 'Did the work involve some special risk, or was it from its very nature likely to cause damage?' It is suggested that plumbing does not satisfy these criteria; the use of a blowlamp may carry some special risk, but Iambic plc could claim that the plumber's negligence was not connected to the performance of his work and that, as an employer, it is not liable (*Padbury v Holliday and Greenwood* (1912)).

Katherine

Following the analysis we used with the plumber, Peter has been negligent as regards his conduct to Katherine, as the ingredients of duty, breach and damage are all present. We are told that Peter is an employee of Iambic plc and, assuming that when he left the screwdriver on the floor he was acting within the course of his employment which given his physical presence is likely, Iambic plc could be vicariously liable for his negligence. In addition to this secondary liability, Iambic plc, as Katherine's employer, has a primary duty to provide Katherine with a safe place of work. This is not an absolute duty, but merely requires Iambic plc to take reasonable steps to provide a safe place of work (*Latimer v AEC* (1953)). We need to decide therefore whether Iambic plc has taken such steps. Iambic plc has presumably instructed Peter not to leave any obstructions on the floor, but the duty to provide a safe place of work is non-delegable. In other words, an employer may entrust the performance of this duty to an employee, but he cannot thereby discharge his duty. Following *McDermid v Nash Dredging and Reclamation* we can see that Iambic is likely to be in breach of its duty to provide a safe place and system of work.

Thus, Katherine is advised to sue Iambic plc for breach of its primary duty to provide a safe place of work and for being vicariously liable for Peter's negligence.

Richard

Concerning Richard, the courts have held consistently that the duty that an employer owes is a duty to safeguard the employee's physical safety (and this includes his mental state: (*Walker v Northumberland County Council* (1994); *Daw v Intel Corporation (UK) Ltd* (2007)), but does not extend to protecting the economic welfare of the employee (*Crossley v Faithful & Gould Holdings Ltd* (2004)). This whole area was considered extensively in *Reid v Rush and Tomkins* (1990), in which this distinction was upheld. In *Deyoung v Stenburn* (1946), in a similar fact situation, it was held by the Court of Appeal that no duty arose to protect the employee's clothing from theft (see also *Edwards v West Hertfordshire General Hospital Management Committee* (1957)), hence Richard cannot sue Iambic plc for the loss of his coat. On the facts given, it seems most unlikely that he could sue either the plumber or Lead Ltd (as being vicariously liable) or Peter or Iambic plc (as being vicariously liable) for the loss of his coat, as such loss would be of a type that would not be reasonably foreseeable and no duty of care would arise in respect of it. This situation differs from that in *Stansbie v Troman* (1948), in which a contractor left a house unoccupied and the front door unlocked. The contractor was found liable for the subsequent theft of some property from the house, because, in that situation, it could be foreseen that a thief might enter and steal property from the house.[4] Thus Richards's options for recovery for his coat are limited.

Aim Higher

One of the more interesting aspects of late has been the growth in cases relating to employee 'stress'. Appreciating how the basic requirements fit this new challenge will help you understand the tests more fully. Ensure more generally that you have a good grasp of the relationship between negligence, employer's liability, vicarious liability and the case law that underpins the heads of liability.

---

4 Information you are considering in the question.

Common Pitfalls

You must understand the multiple forms of liability that an employer might be exposed to on just one set of facts, as employer's liability can appear complicated. This is a topic where you must read the question carefully. Failing to take account of the basic range of employer's duties by just superficially referring to issues (for example equipment) is a common mistake. A good answer will set out the basic landscape, and then may focus on the most salient aspects.

6

Vicarious Liability

INTRODUCTION

Vicarious liability is a topic that is regularly tested by examiners, either as a question in its own right or as part of a question on negligence or in particular employers' liability. Please see the preceding chapter for many of the employer contexts in which a vicarious claim can be made out, and as a rule of thumb where an employee has committed a tort, a discussion of vicarious liability is always worth inclusion and consideration. However note that it is not an independent tort in its own right but is concerned with who can be held liable for the purpose of granting a remedy. This is precisely because employers are deep-pocketed defendants who are likely to offset their loss through indemnity insurance, so claimants would be in a better position suing an employer rather than an employee who may not be in a position to compensate. Much of the difficulty in vicarious liability questions are over whether an employer–employee relationship is present and most of all whether the employee was acting in the course of employment. It is important to remember that for vicarious liability to exist you must establish tortious conduct between the employee and the claimant. The first three questions in this chapter are problem scenario questions, with the final question an essay question on the general state of vicarious liability.

Checklist
Students must be familiar with the following areas:
(a) the definition of 'employer' and 'employee';
(b) the course of employment and the development of the close connection test laid down in *Lister v Hesley Hall Ltd* (2001);
(c) frolics and detours;
(d) the courts' differing attitudes to careless and deliberate acts;
(e) the effect of the *CCWS* judgment.

QUESTION 17

Factor X (FX), an events management company, was contracted to provide corporate hospitality by Womberfield Stadium for clients attending a sporting event. In order to exclude the general public from the exclusive corporate hospitality area, FX engaged its usual contactors, Crew Service (CS), to provide security for the day in question. The security staff's instructions from FX were detailed and included a specific instruction not to admit people without a ticket, along with an instruction that should there be any problem with a non-ticket holder trying to enter, the member of staff should radio a member of FX staff and wait for them to attend to resolve the situation.

The centrepiece to the hospitality buffet was an elaborate chocolate fountain. Paula, an FX employee, assembled the fountain incorrectly and did not test it as she had been instructed to do. As a result of the incorrect assembly, the fountain later toppled over, scalding several guests and knocking one unconscious. During the commotion, Scally tried to sneak into the event but was caught by Louie, one of the security staff. Louie violently twisted Scally's arm and threw him to the ground, breaking Scally's wrist and cutting his head.

▶ Advise FX.

How to Read this Question

This question involves consideration of the principles of vicarious liability in situations in which an employee has been negligent and also those in which the employee has committed a wilful act. It also involves the question of who may be held to be an employer in cases in which there is more than one possibility combined with varying relationships. The situation of independent contractors under vicarious liability is commonly examined and thus it is important to clarify the position of the various defendants, so look for tell-tale signs and clues. Remember in order for vicarious liability to be applicable there must be tortious conduct (in this case by Paula), so it will require some discussion.

How to Answer this Question

The following points require discussion:

❖ the negligence liability of Paula to the guests;
❖ the vicarious liability of FX for the acts of Paula;
❖ the battery liability of Louie to Scally;
❖ the vicarious liability of FX or CS for the (deliberate) acts of Louie.

Applying the Law

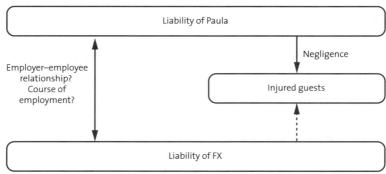

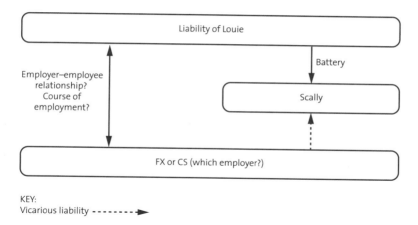

KEY:
Vicarious liability - - - - - - - - ▶

ANSWER

There should be no problem in demonstrating that Paula owed a duty of care to the guests. To determine the existence of a duty of care under *Caparo Industries plc v Dickman* (1990) would require a consideration of the reasonable foreseeability of harm, the proximity of the relationship between the claimant and defendant, and whether it is fair, just and reasonable to impose the duty on the defendant. In the circumstances, it is highly probable that Paula owes a duty of care, as it is foreseeable that improper assembly and a lack of testing of the fountain could lead to damage (*Kent v Griffiths* (2001)); proximity is present given the physical closeness and it is fair, just and reasonable to impose such a duty, given the absence of policy reasons to deny a duty.

Whether Paula was in breach of that duty depends upon an assessment of the reasonableness of her conduct: (*Blyth v Birmingham Waterworks* (1856)). It is unlikely that she has performed to the required standard and is therefore in breach of her duty, and factors such as the seriousness of the harm (potential scalding) (*Paris v Stepney* (1951)), the relative probability of an accident occurring (*Bolton v Stone* (1951)) and the practicality of the precaution in testing it (*Latimer v AEC* (1953)) point to a clear breach.

Next, the guests would have to demonstrate causation through the 'but for' test (*Barnett v Chelsea and Kensington Hospital Management Committee* (1969)); here but for Paula's failure to test and correctly assemble the fountain, the guests would not have been injured. It must also be determined whether the damage suffered was too remote a consequence of the breach (*The Wagon Mound (No 1)* (1961)) – in other words, was the damage of a type or kind that was reasonably foreseeable? In this case, all that would need to be shown would be that personal injury was reasonably foreseeable which on the facts it was. Paula is therefore very likely to be held to have been negligent.

. . . .

1   Establishing Paula's liability in negligence is a crucial stage in a vicarious liability answer, and though the order in which you organise this aspect of your discussion is a choice of your own, remember that it is a precondition for vicarious liability to exist, so make sure it is clear in your discussion.

Can FX be vicariously liable for Paula's actions? Paula must be an employee of FX. We are told that she is. Next it must be shown that Paula is acting in the course of her employment. The traditional test previously used was known as the Salmond test. The question was to determine whether his/her act was something that was a wrongful or unauthorised manner of doing an authorised act, or whether it was so far removed from what was authorised as to be independent from it (*Century Insurance v Northern Ireland Road Transport Board* (1942)); however the courts latterly in *Lister v Helsey Hall* (2001) have preferred a broader approach of looking at whether such a connection was sufficiently close. Here Paula was clearly in the course of her employment while setting up the chocolate fountain; irrespective that it was done carelessly, or in an unauthorised manner. Accordingly, the advice to the injured guests would be to sue FX for the damage that they have suffered.

As far as Louie is concerned, it is likely that he has committed battery, an element of the tort of trespass to the person. Battery is defined as a direct, intentional application of force by the defendant in the absence of the claimant's consent. The force must be direct (*Reynolds v Clarke* (1725)) and intentional (*Letang v Cooper* (1965)), so in the circumstances, Scally would have little trouble in proving these elements. Additionally, any form of touching or application of force is capable of being a battery (*Cole v Turner* (1704)): clearly, an arm twist and being thrown to the ground would suffice. There would also be little chance of Louie claiming self-defence, as the force used must be reasonable (*Turner v MGM* (1950); *Cross v Kirkby* (2000)); Louie has committed the tort of battery; therefore Scally could potentially sue Louie's employer for the tortious act.

Louie is employed by CS; however, it would appear from the facts that he has been 'lent' to FX by virtue of the fact that FX has hired-in security from CS. In *Mersey Docks and Harbour Board v Coggins and Griffiths* (1947), the House of Lords held however that the contract was not always decisive but that there was a presumption that the permanent employer would be liable unless it could overcome the burden of proving otherwise (which it could not). In *Viasystems Ltd v Thermal Transfer Ltd* (2005), the Court of Appeal considered that the question of whether an employee was 'deemed to be the temporary employee of the hirer of his services', turned on control. It was also held that more than one employer could be vicariously liable, depending on the facts and the integration of the employee into the business of both employers. Applying *Viasystems* and *Hawley v Luminar Leisure* (2006), FX may well be vicariously liable as it issued instructions and could be said to have control over the performance of the task; failing that, there is the possibility that both employers might share liability to Scally.

The final determination is whether an employer can be held vicariously liable for deliberate employee torts.[3] The appropriate test now is whether the nature of the employment was of sufficiently close connection to the wrongdoing as to be fair, just and reasonable to hold the employer liable (*Lister*). It is clear the scope of the employment itself and its relationship to

---

2 Understanding the effect of recent case law and the various tests that determines the employer–employee relationship is a mark of a good candidate. Here, conveying that there may be joint liability also shows a firm grasp of the case law and the effect of the *Viasystems* precedent.

3 Not only does this express Louie's liability for a tort, it also makes clear that as this is an intentional tort, there are differing implications for the purpose of vicarious liability, rather than where an employee has been merely negligent.

the tortious conduct is critical in this assessment (*Warren v Henley's Ltd* (1948); *Limpus v London General Omnibus* (1862); *Beard v London General Omnibus* (1900)). Multiple questions are often asked in this assessment such as the furtherance of employers' aims, the risks created of the wrong-doing by placing the employee in such a position, the granting of authority and the extent of any employer prohibitions. However the employer simply creating the opportunity for the interaction between their employee and the victim will not be suffi-cient as in *Mohamud v WM Morrison Supermarkets* (2014). In that case there was also training and warnings not to engage in confrontations and thus the employer was not liable. By con-trast *Mattis v Pollock* (2003), involved an assault by a doorman at a nightclub, and the employer was vicariously liable partly based on their encouragement for the aggression and how it naturally served the interests of the nightclub. The behaviour of the employer will be relevant (perhaps overlapping with their own non-delegable duty of care to staff), which on the present facts was the express instruction to await for assistance from an FX member of staff in the case of a non-ticket holder. This shows both responsibility and perhaps an attempt to limit the sphere of the employment but the prohibition still relates to his general conduct (*Ilkiw v Samuels* (1963)). Depending on the determination of who the relevant employer is, there is some degree of doubt whether this would be in the course of employment.

QUESTION 18

Gamma plc employs David as a driver and Elaine as a salesperson. One day, Elaine has to call on a customer but, as her car is being serviced, she asks David if he can drive her to the customer's premises. David agrees, but when they are in the car, he tells Elaine that he must first call at his private house to collect a suit to take to the dry cleaners. Whilst on the way to the house, David sees a patch of oil that has been spilt on the road and says to Elaine: 'See that oil – I'll show you how to control a skid.' David then drives onto the patch of oil, but fails to control the subsequent skid and hits a wall, injuring Elaine and dam-aging beyond repair a valuable painting that Elaine is carrying in her briefcase.

▶ **Advise Elaine.**

How to Read this Question

This is an uncomplicated question on vicarious liability that involves the issue of frolics and detours and the recent attitude of the courts when considering 'course of employ-ment' in situations involving deliberate acts by the employee. As is typical of exam ques-tions, be sure to identify all the relevant issues and it would be worth considering the scope of any defence or any peculiar features that would justify a discussion, for example reference to her *valuable* painting. Also notice the two aspects of the discussion, the ori-ginal detour and then later on the action of skidding over the oil. Distinguishing them would be wise.

How to Answer this Question

The following points need to be discussed:

❖ the liability of David to Elaine;

❖ the vicarious liability of Gamma plc;

❖ consideration of course of employment as regards deliberate acts of the employee.

Applying the Law

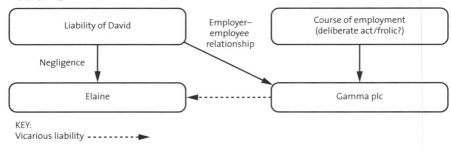

KEY:
Vicarious liability ---------➤

ANSWER

Elaine must first show that David owes her a duty of care. In those situations in which a duty of care has previously been found to exist, there is no need to apply the incremental test preferred by the House of Lords in *Caparo Industries plc v Dickman* (1990). In fact, a duty of care has been found to exist in a number of cases involving drivers and their passengers: for example, *Nettleship v Weston* (1971).

Next, Elaine must show that David was in breach of his duty – that is, that a reasonable person or rather a reasonably competent driver in David's position would not have acted in this way (*Blyth v Birmingham Waterworks* (1856); *Nettleship v Weston* (1971)). It seems clear that a reasonable driver would not drive deliberately on to a patch of oil; it is a highly risky activity (*Bolton v Stone* (1950)), and the potential harm is of serious physical injury (*Paris v Stepney* (1951)). Such factors point to a clear breach. In terms of causation but for David's breach of driving recklessly on to the oil, Elaine's injuries would not have occurred (*Cork v Kirby MacLean* (1952)). Finally, Elaine will have to prove that the harm suffered was not too remote – that the type of harm was reasonably foreseeable (*The Wagon Mound (No 1)* (1961)), the extent of the injury or the exact manner in which the injury was caused need not be foreseen (*Smith v Leech Brain* (1962); *Hughes v Lord Advocate* (1963)). Elaine could easily establish that David would have foreseen the risk of a loss of control leading to injury, and therefore David could be held liable. With respect to the property damage, David may not have foreseen that Elaine would be carrying such valuable property, but he could have foreseen that Elaine would be carrying some property on her person and authority suggests this will be sufficient for full recovery (*Vacwell Engineering v BDH Chemicals* (1971)).

Next we must consider whether Gamma plc is liable for David's actions when he decided to detour, and whether this amounts to acting in the course of his employment given it could be classed as a 'frolic of his own'. In *Storey v Ashton* (1869), employers were held not liable when the employee, after completing his work, embarked on a detour. It was held that this detour constituted a new and independent journey that had nothing to do with his employment and was, therefore, outside the course of his employment. This problem was considered by the House of Lords in *Williams v Hemphill Ltd* (1966). Lord Pearce stated that it was a question of fact in each case whether the deviation was so unconnected with the employer's business that the employee was on a 'frolic of his own'. Having considered *Joel v Morrison* (1834) and *Storey*, Lord Pearce stated that to constitute a frolic of his own, the employee's journey had to be entirely unconnected with the employer's business, as opposed to a mere detour for the employee's selfish purposes. However, on the facts of *Williams*, Lord Pearce held that the presence of passengers whom the employee had to take to their destination made it impossible to say that the detour was entirely for the employee's purposes. Applying this criterion to our case, the presence of Elaine will make it impossible to say that the detour was undertaken entirely for David's selfish purposes and thus David is likely to remain in the course of his employment.

What of the situation when he drives on to the patch of oil? The court has taken a much more restrictive approach to course of employment where 'deliberate' wrongful acts have occurred, as can be seen by decisions of the Court of Appeal in *Heasmans v Clarity Cleaning Co Ltd* (1987) and *Irving v Post Office* (1987). In *Heasmans*, an employer was held not to be vicariously liable for the actions of an employee who was employed to clean telephones, but who made unauthorised telephone calls costing some £1,400. See also *General Engineering Services v Kingston and St Andrews Corp* (1989). The fact is that, in driving on to the oil, David was not acting for the benefit of his employer does not automatically take the act outside the course of his employment. The question will also be whether the act was purely for gratification and self-interest purposes (see *Hilton v Thomas Burton Rhodes* (1961) and *N v Chief Constable of Merseyside Police* (2006)).

In *Lister v Hesley Hall Ltd* (2001), the House of Lords, in reviewing the law on course of employment, thought it necessary to concentrate on the relative closeness of the connection between the tort and the nature of the employment, taking a broad approach to nature of employment. The close connection approach though difficult to interpret and leaving a large measure of discretion was also used by the House of Lords in *Dubai Aluminium Co v Salaam* (2003) and the Court of Appeal in *Mattis v Pollock* (2004). The law was recently revisited by the Supreme Court in *The Catholic Child Welfare Society & Ors v Various claimants* (2012). Though confined to the peculiars of the case and the incidence of sexual abuse Lord Phillips emphasised the point of an employer increasing the risk of harm to the potential victim, through a causative link in placing the tortfeasor in a position to further the interests of their 'employer'. Such considerations would help determine whether there was a sufficiently close connection. Similar reasoning appears in *Maga v Trustees of the Birmingham Archdiocese of the Roman Catholic Church* (2010). A court would have to decide whether the connection to David's work was sufficient using this test but there appears to be a link between the driving and the risks inherently attached, as it was for work purposes and the interests of the business.

QUESTION 19

Delta plc owns a small office. Delta asks Frank, an electrician, to undertake various works at the company premises and tells Frank that his work will take about one week.

---

4   The preceding discussion is showing both awareness and analysis of the relevant case law and of course citing a judge and a rationale of the judgment would add analytical quality to the answer.

While Frank is working in Delta's offices, he carelessly rewires a switch and Gloria, an employee of Delta, is injured when she uses the switch. Henry, who is visiting Delta in an attempt to sell some office equipment, is also injured when he trips over a length of electrical cable that Frank has left in a corridor.

▶ Advise Gloria and Henry.

How to Read this Question

This question involves a consideration of the liability of an employer for the acts of an independent contractor. It would be best in terms of structure to consider grouping Gloria and Henry together for the original tortious conduct by Frank to avoid any duplication in your discussion.

How to Answer this Question

The following points need to be discussed:

❖ the liability of Frank;
❖ the liability of Delta or Frank (an employee or an independent contractor);
❖ any non-delegable duties of Delta for the torts of Frank (an independent contractor).

Applying the Law

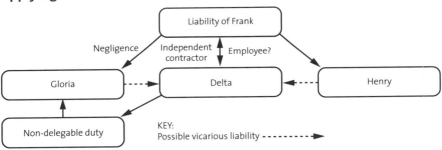

ANSWER

We must decide whether Gloria and Henry could sue Frank for the tortious conduct under traditional negligence and, if so, whether Delta plc is vicariously liable for Frank's actions. Both must first show that Frank owes them a duty of care. In those situations in which a duty of care has previously been found to exist, there is no need to apply the incremental test preferred by the House of Lords in *Caparo Industries plc v Dickman* (1990). In fact, a duty of care has been found to exist in a similar situation in *Green v Fibreglass Ltd* (1958). However, even without knowledge of this case, we could deduce the existence of a duty of care. It is reasonably foreseeable that, by carelessly rewiring the switch, a person who uses it may suffer injury, with both physical and temporal proximity being satisfied along with the fair, just and reasonable criterion as there are no policy reasons to deny a duty.

Next, it needs to be shown that Frank was in breach of this duty – that a reasonable person, or rather a reasonably competent electrician, in Frank's position, would not have acted in this way (*Blyth v Birmingham Waterworks* (1856); *Bolam v Friern Hospital Management*

Committee (1957)). It seems clear that a reasonable electrician would not rewire a switch carelessly, or leave a loose electrical cable exposed in a corridor. The likelihood of injury (*Bolton v Stone* (1951)), the seriousness of electrical shock and tripping over a cable (*Paris v Stepney* (1951)), coupled with the simple practicalities in avoiding such risks and taking care, e.g. removing the cable from the corridor (*Latimer v AEC* (1953)), all point to a clear breach. Both Gloria and Henry will also have to show that this breach caused her injuries and the 'but for' test in *Cork v Kirby MacLean* (1952) proves the required causal connection. Finally, both will have to prove that the damage that was suffered to both was not too remote – that is, that it was reasonably foreseeable (*The Wagon Mound (No 1)* (1961)). This should give rise to no problem, as all that Gloria and Henry will have to show is that some personal injury was foreseeable; the extent need not be foreseeable, or the exact manner in which the injury was caused (*Smith v Leech Brain* (1962); *Hughes v Lord Advocate* (1963)). In our case physical injury was at least foreseeable and therefore both could overcome this threshold.

Given then that Frank is negligent; can Delta plc be held vicariously liable? It needs to be decided whether Frank is an employee of Delta plc, or whether he is an independent contractor. It is extremely difficult to formulate a universal test for an employee. The original test, laid down in *Yewens v Noakes* (1880), was the 'control' test: the employer had the right of control as to the way in which the employee carried out his work. This test has obvious problems when the person concerned has a particular skill. In *Stevenson, Jordan and Harrison Ltd v MacDonald* (1952), Denning LJ proposed the 'business integration' test: does the person do his work as an 'integral part of the business' (when he will be an employee), or is he merely 'accessory' to it (when he will be an independent contractor)? In *Ready Mixed Concrete v Minister of Pensions* (1968), MacKenna J laid down several conditions for a contract of employment, one of which was that the worker agrees to be directed as to the mode of carrying out the work. However, this condition seems to be lacking in Frank's case, leaving him as an independent contractor. Similarly the modern approach taken in *Market Investigations v Minister of Social Security* (1969) was to take a fuller and multiple assessment of the facts of the case. Looking at the facts of Frank and Delta plc, it would seem that Delta plc has the right to tell Frank what work is to be done, but not how to do it, so that Frank is an independent contractor.

However if this is overcome it seems reasonably clear that Frank was acting within the course of his employment. Provided that the relevant act (that is, the rewiring of the switch) was an authorised act, the fact that Frank has carried it out in a wrongful and unauthorised manner will not take the act outside the course of his employment (*Century Insurance v Northern Ireland Road Transport Board* (1942)).

As regards Gloria, Delta plc is under a non-delegable duty to take reasonable care for the safety of its employees (*Wilsons and Clyde Coal v English* (1938)). By the phrase 'non-delegable', the employer cannot delegate responsibility for performance. Thus, although the standard rule is that an employer is not liable for the actions of an independent contractor (*Morgan v Girls Friendly Society* (1936); *D and F Estates v Church Commissioners* (1989)), Delta plc will be liable to Gloria for failing to take reasonable care for her safety.

....

5   You need to distinguish clearly between the employer's vicarious liability (through Frank's negligence) and Delta's direct liability to Gloria as an employee.

Concerning Henry, as he is not an employee of Delta plc, he may only rely on suing Frank in negligence as established earlier.

However, there are some situations in which an employer is liable for the torts of an independent contractor (see the fact-specific criteria in *Woodland v Essex County Council* (2013) for example). One of the situations that may be relevant as regards common law non-delegable duties is where the independent contractor is employed to carry out work that is extra-hazardous (*Honeywill and Stein Ltd v Larkin Bros* (1934); *Alcock v Wraith* (1991)). In *Alcock*, the Court of Appeal held that a crucial question was: 'Did the work involve some special risk or was it from its very nature likely to cause damage?' The work here was not extra-hazardous and so Delta plc will not be liable (*Salsbury v Woodland* (1969)).

If it were decided that Frank's work was extra-hazardous, Delta plc might be able to claim that Frank's negligence was merely collateral to the performance of his work and that it was not liable (*Padbury v Holliday and Greenwood* (1912)).

QUESTION 20

Recent developments in the law of vicarious liability 'represent sound and logical incremental developments of the law' (Lord Phillips in *Catholic Child Welfare Society v Various Claimants and the Institute of the Brothers of the Christian Schools* (2012)).

▶ Discuss the accuracy of the above statement.

How to Read this Question

This question requires you to consider the developments in the law of vicarious liability and examine whether they are sound and logical. Vicarious liability as you will know is heavily fuelled by case law that has attempted to grapple with the tests of when an employer–employee relationship will be said to exist, but more critically whether an employee has acted within the course of their employment when the tortious conduct was carried out. Once you have defined the nature of vicarious liability you should highlight these debates with a close reading of the main cases.

How to Answer this Question

The following points need to be discussed:

- ❖ defining vicarious liability;
- ❖ the development of the tests establishing an employer–employee relationship;
- ❖ the course of employment – Salmond;
- ❖ the course of employment and intentional wrong doing – Lister;
- ❖ difficulties in interpreting the Lister close connection test;
- ❖ the effect of *CCWS* and policy;
- ❖ overall assessment.

Answer Structure

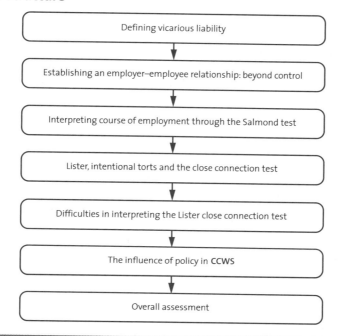

```
┌─────────────────────────────────────────────────────┐
│            Defining vicarious liability              │
└─────────────────────────────────────────────────────┘
                          ↓
┌─────────────────────────────────────────────────────┐
│  Establishing an employer–employee relationship: beyond control  │
└─────────────────────────────────────────────────────┘
                          ↓
┌─────────────────────────────────────────────────────┐
│  Interpreting course of employment through the Salmond test  │
└─────────────────────────────────────────────────────┘
                          ↓
┌─────────────────────────────────────────────────────┐
│  Lister, intentional torts and the close connection test  │
└─────────────────────────────────────────────────────┘
                          ↓
┌─────────────────────────────────────────────────────┐
│  Difficulties in interpreting the Lister close connection test  │
└─────────────────────────────────────────────────────┘
                          ↓
┌─────────────────────────────────────────────────────┐
│          The influence of policy in **CCWS**          │
└─────────────────────────────────────────────────────┘
                          ↓
┌─────────────────────────────────────────────────────┐
│                 Overall assessment                   │
└─────────────────────────────────────────────────────┘
```

Up for Debate

Vicarious liability poses some fascinating conceptual, doctrinal and policy based questions. It is important to note that it is not an independent tort in itself but a mode of liability which leaves the employer liable for the tortious conduct of an employee. It is often justified due to the presence of insurance and that it would deter future harm by putting greater responsibility on the employer to improve standards, supervision or the training of employees. For a thorough critical overview, considering both the relationship with other aspects of employer's liability such as the non-delegable duty of care, and the policy underpinnings of vicarious liability see C McIvor, 'The use and abuse of the doctrine of vicarious liability' (2006) 35 Common Law World Review 268. Other sources of difficulty originate from the difficulties posed in establishing an employer–employee relationship, see for example E McKendrick, 'Vicarious liability and independent contractors: a re-examination' (1990) 53 MLR 770, and for an overview of the conceptual problems with the stretching of this requirement see P Morgan, 'Recasting vicarious liability' (2012) 71(3) Cambridge Law Journal 615. Similarly the other significant challenge has been in the interpretation of course of employment, and on this see P Giliker, 'Rough justice in an unjust world' (2002) 65 Modern Law Review 269 and 'Lister revisited: vicarious liability, distributive justice and course of employment' (2010) 126 Law Quarterly Review 521. Finally an interesting and recent judicial perspective on vicarious liability can be found in an article by the recently retired Lord Hope, 'Tailoring the law on vicarious liability' (2013) 129 Law Quarterly Review 514.

ANSWER

It is important to emphasise that vicarious liability is not a tort in its own right but a means of holding an employer (in most cases) liable to pay compensation where there has been a tort committed by one of its employees, and it has occurred in the course of their employment. Though these criteria appear principled enough, the test to determine an employer–employee relationship and latterly whether conduct occurred within the course of their employment has proved considerably problematic.

Nonetheless where the law might have developed sensibly and logically, at least initially, is in the determination of an employer–employee relationship. The old historical emphasis placed on control which was relevant in an industrial era, rather than the modern workplace has slowly diminished. Justice Cooke in *Market Investigation v Minister of Social Security* (1969) stated that control was only one factor to consider and the degree of risk and responsibility the individual assumes would be relevant in the determination of the relationship.

Similarly other tests such as whether the worker was sufficiently integrated into the business (*Stevenson, Jordan and Harrison v McDonald* (1952)), has encouraged greater emphasis to be placed on all the relevant circumstances including, e.g. whether uniform is worn or whether losses are borne by the individual employee (contrast *Hawley v Luminar* (2006) with *Ready Mixed Concrete v Minister of Pensions* (1968)). Indeed in response to modern working practices, determining the relationship in the case of temporary employment, where an individual is hired out, has seen many cases where the terms of the contract are taken as not decisive (*Mersey Docks v Coggins* (1947)). For the purpose of vicarious liability there may even be dual liability between two relevant employers as found in *Viasystems v Thermal Transfer* (2006) and confirmed latterly in the *CCWS* case. In *CCWS* Lord Phillips endorsed the approach taken in *Viasystems* by Rix LJ when the question to be asked was whether the employee is so much part of the work, business or organisation of both employers that it is just to make both employers answer for the negligence.

Thus emphasis placed on what is 'just' has underpinned the development of the law and this was borne out in the *CCWS* case, where even though no formal employer–employee relationship existed, the relationship between the teaching brothers and the institute was akin to employment, and factors such as the hierarchical structure of the institute, and that the brothers furthered its mission and objectives, ultimately proved persuasive.

Evidently this expansion of the previously narrow control test, to something more varied nuanced and flexible, underlines the law's development in line with modern practices of the workplace. Yet it also risks sacrificing consistency and certainty in how judges should approach the application of legal doctrines and tests, leading to the over-extension of this element of vicarious liability.

Similar determinations have been reflected in the development of the test of whether the conduct was in the course of employment. The emphasis previously placed on the circular aspects of the Salmond test, of whether it was a wrongful and unauthorised mode of doing an act authorised by a defendant often created arbitrary distinctions. This included a fine division drawn in cases where an employer provided express prohibitions. The law maintained vicarious liability if the prohibition was merely as to the conduct whilst carrying out their employment duties (*Rose v Plenty* (1976); *Limpus v London General Omnibus* (1862)). However vicarious liability was denied when the prohibition related to the scope of the employment (*Beard v London General Omnibus* (1900)) or when the employee's conduct more generally was such that it amounted to a 'frolic of his own' (*Storey v Ashton* (1869); *Hilton v Thomas Burton* (1961)).

However the flaws in the Salmond test are best exposed in the case of intentional tortious wrong-doing and the way in which it might encourage a narrow view of the specific tortious conduct having to be authorised by the employer. This would make it impossible to satisfy the test. In overruling a previous case of *Trotman v North Yorkshire County Council* (1999), the court in *Lister v Hesley Hall* (2001) found that the broader question to ask is whether the torts are so closely connected with his employment that it would be fair and just to hold the employers liable. Thus in the word of Lord Steyn where Salmond encouraged overly conceptualistic reasoning, the motivation in the case was rather to deliver principled and practical justice, and thus take a far wider approach to the duties of employment, and the close connection that needed to be found.

However the interpretation of close connection naturally has led to a lack of clarity as there is no guidance on the type or degree of connection required, as outlined by Lord Nicholls in *Dubai Aluminium v Salaam* (2002) where *Lister* was applied. It therefore appears that courts will make evaluative judgments about who should bear the losses including rather problematically assessing the employer's behaviour, e.g. whether the employer's own conduct encouraged or at least created an enhanced risk of the tort as in *Mattis v Pollock*. Similarly a practical focus on the location and time where the acts took place or whether the employment was a mere pretext to an independent activity will also be significant (contrast *Weddell v Barchester Healthcare* (2012) and *Wallbank v Wallbank Fox Designs* (2012)). As the courts are essentially judging the nature and gravity of the acts there is scope for a large degree of inconsistency as seen in *Weir v Chief Constable of Merseyside Police* (2003) and *N v Chief Constable of Merseyside Police* (2006).

The logical development of the case law has been shaped by strong policy considerations that justify vicarious liability. This was confirmed by Lord Phillips in *CCWS* who was influenced by Canadian authorities such as *Bazley v Curry* (1999), asserting that 'Vicarious liability is imposed where a defendant, whose relationship with the abuser put it in a position to use the abuser to carry on its business or to further its own interests, has done so in a manner which has created or significantly enhanced the risk that the victims would suffer.... The essential closeness of connection between the relationship between the defendant and the tortfeasor and the acts ... involves a strong causative link.'

In light of the recent Jimmy Saville sex abuse scandal, vicarious liability has captured a lot of public attention. As Lord Phillips in *CCWS* outlined, citing reasoning by Lord Millett in

Lister, the courts have taken a claimant-centred approach at least in contexts such as schools, prisons and old people's homes where there is an inherent risk in such assaults, given the proximity and the positions of trust that are occupied by employees. In so doing vicarious liability as a species of liability has logically developed away from the confines of control in the cases of identifying employers and the strictures of the Salmond test, to a broad case by case approach. It appears there has been a strong shift to the broad aims of corrective justice and in the process a strong deterrent message is sent to employers to ensure they adopt appropriate practices and standards, so that innocent parties are not harmed.

Aim Higher

Make sure you can differentiate between independent contractor and employee, or 'hired out' employee. As cases such as *Viasystems* and *Hawley* have examined these relationships quite closely, it is worth getting familiar with the tests, including the up to date analysis provided by Lord Phillips in *The Catholic Child Welfare Society & Ors v Various claimants* (2012). Indeed consider how vicarious liability has developed since the case, as inclusion of recent case law as in the Court of Appeal decisions in *Cox v Ministry of Justice* (2014) and *Mohamud v WM Morrison Supermarkets* (2014). Similarly in order to grapple with many of the conceptual problems besetting vicarious liability the Claire McIvor article is well worth reading, and will enhance your critical instincts.

Common Pitfalls

You are most likely to encounter vicarious liability as a problem question, sometimes mixed up with other areas of negligence. Do not forget to determine whether the 'other' negligence will satisfy the tests for liability before addressing vicarious liability. In other words ensure you have discussed the tortious conduct of the employee before discussing vicarious liability. The depth that you can naturally give to such a discussion on the tortious conduct depends largely on what the facts of the question demands in terms of coverage. If there are other critical issues to discuss, you have to be wary of time demands. The other major pitfall is to muddle an employer's liability to their employee and their vicarious liability for an employee's negligence. Ensure the discussion is kept distinct in your answer (even though judges themselves have often obscured the difference!).

7 Occupiers' Liability

INTRODUCTION

Occupiers' liability is a specialised branch of the tort of negligence and is tested in most examinations year after year. The area is governed by statute – namely, the **Occupiers' Liability Act 1957** and the **Occupiers' Liability Act 1984**. Thus, in addition to the common law concepts of duty, breach, causation and remoteness, attention must be paid to the statutes and the particular sections that elaborate on the common law principles. Be aware that in moving around a premises, a person may well change in status from a visitor to a non-visitor – and therefore being at first subject to the **1957 Act** to being subject to the **1984 Act**. By doing so, it will be much more difficult for that person to demonstrate that they are owed a duty of care, and this difference should be brought out in answers. This chapter has three problem questions and one essay question. Many students find occupiers' liability challenging insofar as questions can involve many issues, so it is important to be wise with timing, focus on the critical issues and have a sound grasp of the statutes to assist with your structure.

Checklist

Students must be familiar with the following areas:

(a) the definitions of occupiers, visitors and non-visitors;
(b) the duty regarding children and skilled persons, independent contractors as well as the legal effect of warnings;
(c) the exclusion of duty;
(d) the circumstances under which a duty to a non-visitor arises and the nature of this duty as distinct from a duty to visitors.

Aim Higher

Strong candidates show a grasp of all the relevant features that comprise occupiers' liability including 'premises' and 'occupier' but without dwelling on these where they are not relevant. You must concisely apply the relevant provisions of the statute. Also, most tort students will have a statute book that is accessible to them in the exam, so it will serve little purpose to copy out entire and lengthy sections as this will not receive much credit and it will also waste time. Better candidates will paraphrase the key section or even better to simply refer to sections and apply them on the facts without over describing the section. In addition *Tomlinson v Congleton* (2004) is well worth reading to fully appreciate some of the broader policy underpinnings of this area of tort law.

Common Pitfalls

Weak candidates fail to remember that, ultimately, occupiers' liability is a specialist application of the tort of negligence and, therefore, operates within the same confines of duty (albeit statutory), breach and damage, which means that common-law principles can still apply once a duty is established. However remember you must focus on the most relevant parts of the discussion in the time allocated. Also, there is a tendency not to differentiate clearly enough between the two Acts with particular confusion in regards to the precise nature of the duty under both Acts. Similarly it is important to know the effect of warnings, and properly distinguish whether a warning is there to discharge the duty or to exclude liability. Warnings are reflected in sections in both of the **Occupiers Liability Acts** and close reference to the case law would be wise.

QUESTION 21

Harry inherits a large and dilapidated house from his mother. He moves in and decides to have substantial renovations carried out by Askew Alterations Ltd, a local company that specialises in renovating old property. Whilst these alterations are in progress, Harry decides to hold a party to welcome his new neighbours.

Barney and his five-year-old daughter Clara attend. Clara becomes bored and wanders into a room marked 'Danger – do not enter', where she is injured. Barney, while looking for Clara in that room, turns on a light switch that has not been completely finished and suffers an electrical shock.

Danny, who is aware that Harry's mother kept a good wine cellar, goes down to the cellar intending to help himself to some wine, but slips on a cork on the steps and breaks both his legs.

▶ Advise Barney, Clara and Danny.

How to Read this Question

This is a broad-ranging occupiers' liability question, in that it involves independent contractors, children as well as visitors becoming non-visitors. Therefore a firm grasp of both the relevant occupiers' liability statutes will be required. As there are three claimants, adopting a structure that separates the relevant discussion would be good for clarity purposes, and so the use of sub-headings may be helpful in the answer. Notice some of the key features on the facts, we have a warning sign here, and a parent in Barney who has allowed his daughter to wander in a property currently being renovated. It is always important to highlight such key issues in your answer plan so that these points are not omitted in your discussion.

How to Answer this Question

The following points need to be discussed:

❖ the application of the **Occupiers' Liability Act 1957** including;

❖ Harry's duty to visitors including Barney, Clara and Danny;
❖ the effect of the warning notice;
❖ Harry's duty to Danny under the **Occupiers' Liability Act 1984**.

Applying the Law

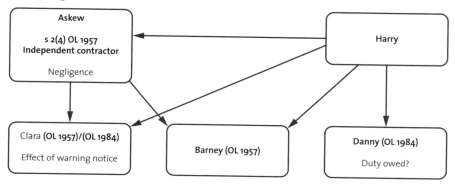

ANSWER

Harry is the occupier of his house, as he has 'sufficient control over the premises (**s 1(2)** of the **Occupiers' Liability Act 1957**, *Wheat v Lacon* (1966)). However given the extent of control for such substantial renovations Askew could be an effective occupier but, for the purpose of this discussion, Harry will be deemed to be the sole occupier. Barney, Clara and Danny are initially Harry's visitors as they are invited (*Wheat*, **s 1(1) OLA 1957**), and it is self-evident that Harry's house would satisfy the condition of being a premises (**s 1(3)**).

Harry owes visitors the common duty of care (**s 2(1)** of the **Occupiers' Liability Act 1957**) to take such care as in all of the circumstances to see that the visitor will be reasonably safe in using the premises for the purposes for which he is invited. It is the visitor who must be reasonably safe and not the premises (see *Ferguson v Welsh* (1987)). Thus, the fact that repairs are being carried out to Harry's house, does not in itself constitute a breach of duty.

Barney

Prima facie, it is a breach of duty to allow persons to come into contact with unsafe light switches, but Harry has attempted to discharge his duty via the notice. The notice seems to be insufficient as a warning, as it does not describe the nature of the danger in any way and so, by **s 2(4)(a)**, would not be enough to make the visitor reasonably safe.

However, Harry could rely on **s 2(4)(b)**. This section states the occupier will not be liable for the work of an independent contractor where the occupier had acted reasonably in entrusting the work to an independent contractor and had taken such reasonable steps to satisfy himself that the contractor was competent and that the work had been properly done.

The renovation is covered by s2(4)(b), as it is reasonable to entrust it to independent contractors, and as we are told that Askew Alterations specialises in renovating old property, it would seem that it is competent. The question, therefore, is what (if any) steps Harry ought reasonably to have taken to satisfy himself that the work had been properly done. Despite the words 'had been properly done', it was held by the House of Lords in *Ferguson v Welsh* (1987) that it could apply where the work was still being done and had not been completed. The rule is that the more technical the work, the less reasonable it is to require the occupier to check it (*Haseldine v Daw* (1941); *Woodward v Mayor of Hastings* (1945)). In Harry's circumstances, it would seem that as the work is technical, there is no requirement to check that the work had been properly done and Harry has discharged his duty by employing reasonable independent contractors, if this is indeed the case.

Hence, Barney may not be able to sue Harry, if s2(4)(b) applies, but he could sue Askew Alterations in negligence. Askew Alterations owes Barney a duty of care under normal *Donoghue* principles.

Clara

By s2(3)(a) of the **1957 Act**, Harry must be prepared for children to be less careful than adults. In *Latham v Johnson and Nephew Ltd* (1913), Lord Hamilton stated that there may be a duty not to lead children into temptation. Having said this, if the danger is obvious, even to a child, the occupier will not be liable (*Liddle v Yorkshire (North Riding) County Council* (1934)). Indeed the broad nature of the duty is that all visitors are to be kept reasonably safe and that there was no duty to safeguard children from harm from all possible circumstances (*West Sussex County Council v Lewis Pierce* (2013)).

With very young children, of course, almost anything can be a danger, but here an occupier will be able to rely on the decision of Devlin J in *Phipps v Rochester Corp* (1955). It was held that reasonable parents would not allow small children to go unaccompanied to places that may be unsafe. It should have been clear to Barney that Harry's house was in the process of redecoration and hence contain danger that might not be obvious to a small child. Following *Phipps*, Barney has not acted reasonably and that Harry was justified in relying on Barney to look after Clara. Harry could also argue that the sign 'Danger – do not enter' is a warning that discharges his duty under s2(4)(a), but to achieve this, the warning must in all of the circumstances be enough to enable the visitor to be reasonably safe. The sign does not seem to be a warning at all, in that it does not describe the danger. It would not be enough in all of the circumstances to discharge the duty owed to a small child, though there may be some scope to turn the child into a non-visitor and so the application of the **1984 Act** may be relevant (see Danny). It would also be relevant to consider whether injury was sustained due to the state of the premises or as a result of any activity she undertook there which is unclear on the facts: see *Revill v Newberry* (1996) and recently *Siddorn v Patel* (2007). In the latter case, it was held that the statute would not apply and ordinary negligence principles would apply and so Clara could alternatively sue Harry or Askew in negligence.

Danny

Although Danny was initially a visitor, on entering the cellar, he became a non-visitor.[1] An occupier may place a spatial limitation on the visitor's permission to enter (*The Carlgarth* (1927)) and, by implication, Danny must have known that he did not have Harry's permission to enter his wine cellar and, consequently, Danny became a trespasser when he entered the cellar.

Any duty now owed to Danny is governed by the **Occupiers' Liability Act 1984**. By s1(3) of the **1984 Act**, an occupier will only owe a duty to a non-visitor if all three of the conditions in the section are satisfied: it seems unlikely that requirement (a) that of having knowledge of the danger or having reasonable grounds of a cork on the floor would necessarily be known (*Keown v Coventry Healthcare NHS Trust* (2006); *Ratcliff v McConnell* (1999); *Rhind v Astbury Water Park Ltd* (2004)). Requirement (b) is arguably not satisfied, as Harry had no reason to suspect that his guests would go down to the cellar. Hence, no duty is likely in respect of Danny's accident in the cellar: see, also, *Tomlinson v Congleton Borough Council* (2003).

QUESTION 22 `--------------------------------------------`

Eric owns a waxworks museum in the seaside town of Westsea. He decides to have a new air conditioning system installed in the museum by Coolit plc, but Coolit can only carry out this work at the height of the tourist season. Rather than delay the job until winter, or shut down while the work is being done and lose income, Eric decides to allow the public into the museum while the new air conditioning system is being installed. He places notices around the museum stating 'Danger – Work in Progress'. While the employees of Coolit are working in one part of the museum, some scaffolding that they have erected in another part of the museum collapses. The scaffolding injures Florence, who paid to enter the museum, and George, who entered without paying through the open back doorway that Coolit's employees were using to bring in equipment.

▶ **Advise Florence, who has suffered a fractured skull and had her spectacles broken, and George, who has suffered a broken shoulder and has had his new suit ruined.**

How to Read this Question

This is a similar problem question to the previous one. A clear and distinct structure, with concise application will be required, and again you need to be aware of the independent contractor rules, i.e. Westsea hires Coolit plc to carry out the installation work, but more critically there is scope of both being classed as occupiers. There is similarly a warning sign here, and also note the differing harms suffered and the relevant rules for recovery for the differing types of damage.

`..........................................................................................`

1   Note that the **Occupiers' Liability Act 1984** refers to non-visitors and not trespassers. Note the key distinction between the **1957 Act** and the **1984 Act** is the difficulty in satisfying **s1(3)** of the **1984 Act**, by which a duty is owed to a non-visitor, in contrast to the **1957 Act** where all visitors are owed the 'common duty of care' to ensure they are kept reasonably safe.

How to Answer this Question

The following points need to be discussed:

❖ the status of Eric and Coolit both being occupiers;
❖ Eric's duty to Florence and the application of **s 2(4)(b)** of the **Occupiers' Liability Act 1957**;
❖ the liability of an occupier to a non- visitor like George under the **Occupiers' Liability Act 1984**;
❖ the type of harm that is recoverable.

Applying the Law

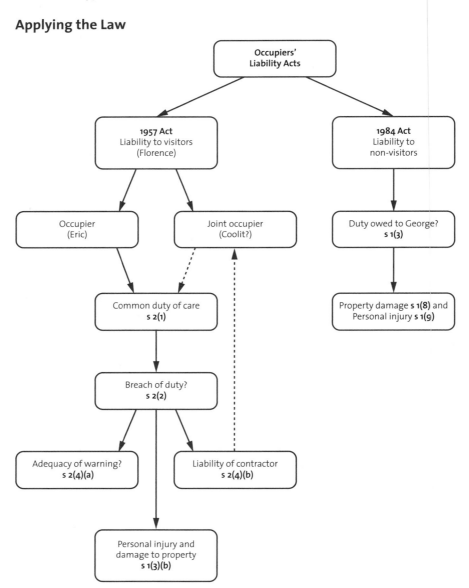

ANSWER

Eric is the occupier of the museum as he has sufficient control over the premises (*Wheat v Lacon* (1966)). In addition, Coolit may also be an occupier of the museum, for there is no need for control to be exclusive (*Wheat*). The museum satisfies being a premises under **s1(3)** of the **Occupiers' Liability Act 1957**. The question is whether Coolit, as an independent contractor, has sufficient control, as in *AMF International v Magnet Bowling* (1968). This is, of course, a question of fact and, as presumably the installation of an air conditioning system in a waxworks museum would involve extensive work, Coolit may well be held to be an occupier and so also be liable together with Eric.[2]

Florence

Florence is Eric's visitor. Eric owes Florence the common duty of care by **s2(1)** of the **Occupiers' Liability Act 1957**. By **s2(2)**, the duty is to take such care as in all of the circumstances of the case to see that the visitor will be reasonably safe in using the premises for the purposes for which he is invited. It should be noted that it is the visitor who must be reasonably safe and not the premises, so the fact that renovations are taking place does not, by itself, constitute a breach of duty (see, for example, *Ferguson v Welsh* (1987)). The question as to whether the occupier is in breach of his duty is always a question of fact depending on the exact circumstances of the case.

Eric will, however, seek to rely on the defence contained in **s2(4)(b)**[3] of the **1957 Act** – this section states the occupier will not be liable for the work of an independent contractor where the occupier had acted reasonably in entrusting the work to an independent contractor and had taken such reasonable steps to satisfy himself that the contractor was competent and that the work had been properly done.

There is nothing in the facts of the problem to suggest that Coolit is anything but competent. The question, therefore, is what (if any) steps Eric ought reasonably to have taken to satisfy himself that the work had been properly done. Despite the words 'had been properly done' in the subsection, it was held in *Ferguson v Welsh* (1987) that the obligation could arise where the work was still being done and had not been completed. The rule is that the more technical the work, the less reasonable it is to require the occupier to check the work (cf. *Haseldine v Daw* (1941) and *Woodward v The Mayor of Hastings* (1945)).

The work of installing an air conditioning system is certainly technical, but we are told that the damage was caused by scaffolding collapsing. If this danger was obvious to a reasonable observer, Eric should have been aware of the danger and cannot bring himself within **s2(4)(b)**. However, if the careless work of Coolit was not apparent upon such examination, Eric will not be in breach.

---

2 Determining who the occupier is, is the first step in a case of occupiers' liability, and though there are many instances where this will be self-evident, for completeness it is always worth establishing at the outset. In cases such as these where there is scope for more than one occupier, then a discussion is more essential.

3 When citing statutes, ensure that the section, subsection and (if appropriate) the paragraph are accurate.

Next, we need to consider whether the notices stating 'Danger – Work in Progress' discharge any duty owed by the occupier. By s 2(4)(a) of the 1957 Act, where damage is caused to a visitor by a danger of which he has been warned by the occupier, the warning is not to be treated without more as absolving the occupier from liability, unless in all of the circumstances it was enough to enable the visitor to be reasonably safe.[4] 'Work in Progress', here does not indicate the nature of the danger and it is a question of fact whether this is adequate in allowing a visitor to be reasonably safe. In *Rae v Mars UK* (1989), it was held that where an unusual danger exists, the visitor should not only be warned, but a barrier or additional notice should also be placed to show the immediacy of the danger. On the facts of the present case, this had not been done. As the scaffolding fell on Florence, it seems that, in addition to the notice, the area should have been roped off to keep visitors away from any possible danger.

Hence, the advice to Florence is that Eric may be able to avail himself of this statutory defence, so she would be better advised to sue Coolit under the **Occupiers' Liability Act 1957** as occupiers and/or in negligence. Florence can recover for both the injury to her person and the damage to her property: **s 1(3)(b)** of the **1957 Act**.

George

George is clearly not a lawful visitor of Eric or Coolit. The duty owed to George is covered by **s 1(3) Occupiers' Liability Act 1984**. In George's case, requirement (a) is satisfied as Eric was aware of the danger (as can be shown by his placing of the warning notices): *Woollins v British Celanese* (1966); *Rhind v Astbury Water Park Ltd* (2004); *Keown v Coventry Healthcare NHS Trust* (2006).

However requirement (b) is not satisfied, as Eric has no reason to anticipate George's presence is or could be in the vicinity of danger. In both *Donoghue v Folkestone Properties Ltd* (2003), and *Tomlinson v Congleton Borough Council* (2003), the position of trespassers was considered and it was held in both cases that there was no duty owed in respect of obvious dangers and that no duty was owed where persons freely and voluntarily undertook an activity that involved some risk (see the High Court decision in *Andrew Risk v Bruford College* (2013) as a recent application). In George's case, it could be argued that the danger from the activity involving scaffolding is obvious and that using the back door to enter the premises involved an element of risk in that any warnings would not be apparent to George. Either way the question to then be determined is whether it was reasonable to take precautions to protect against the risk. This is a similar judgment to what is found in **s 1(4)** and it is argued here that it would be reasonable to protect against unsafe scaffolding for the potential seriousness that such harm could do.

Even if the duty does arise, it can be discharged by a reasonable warning: **s 1(5)** (but see the discussion above). By **s 1(9)**, injury only includes personal injury, and damage to property is expressly excluded (**s 1(8)**). Thus, in the unlikely event of George being able to establish liability under the **1984 Act**, the damage to his suit would be irrecoverable.

---

4   An accurate and a precise reading of the words of the statute will allow you to fully apply the specifics to the facts of the scenario.

QUESTION 23

Gordon is the landlord of the Tamar public house and family restaurant, owned by Pilgrims Brewery. Recently some refurbishment was undertaken, and Gordon engaged Cowboys Limited (CL) to carry out the work. He had never used them before, but they were recommended to him by a customer as being cheap and cheerful. Work was completed in the dining area first and the premises were reopened. Bharat, a customer, tripped over a poorly secured floorboard, on his way to the salad bar, breaking his arm and smashing his glasses. In the commotion that followed, Bharat's young son managed to slip away and walked out of the door. He was attracted to the children's play area, which was adjacent to a landscaped water feature. He slipped on the edge, fell in the water and drowned.

CL were also contracted to upgrade the wiring and fusebox. Gordon had warned CL that the wiring was in poor condition. Sparkie, an employee of CL, was put in charge of the work in the cellar. She cut the wrong wire, received an electric shock and suffered severe burns to her hands.

Meanwhile, Wesley, a regular customer, wanted to have a look at the progress of the work in what was formerly the lounge bar. He squeezed through some plastic fencing that was used as a barrier to keep people out of the area, ignoring a sign stating: 'Danger – Keep Out – No Persons Beyond This Point Without Permission of the Contractors. No Liability for Injury is Accepted, Howsoever Caused.' The area was not properly lit and he tripped over some tools left on the floor. As a result he cut open his head and broke his watch.

▶ **Advise the parties as to their potential liabilities by reference to the duty owed by an occupier of premises.**

How to Read this Question

This is a wide-ranging and complex question on occupiers' liability which engages a number of issues. It is fairly typical in that it requires an evaluation of both **Occupiers' Liability Acts**, but there are many issues here as there are parents, children, contractors and warnings to consider. Again having an organised structure is crucial so you do not lose credit unnecessarily. Focus on the salient facts and these include the reasons why CL is hired, the attraction of the play area, that the warning also contains an exclusion provision and, finally, the types of harm incurred.

How to Answer this Question

The following points need to be discussed:

- ❖ the **OLA 1957** and the duty held to visitors including Bharat and his son as parent and child;
- ❖ the potential for the application of **s 2(4)(b)** in relation to Gordon and CL;
- ❖ the position of visitors in the exercise of their calling in relation to Sparkie;
- ❖ the duty held to adult trespassers (Wesley) and the impact of warnings.

Applying the Law

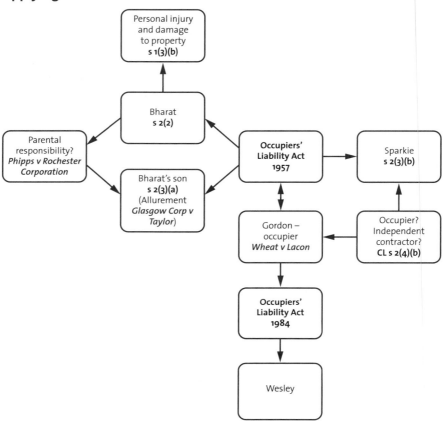

ANSWER

Gordon through Pilgrims Brewery could both be classed as the occupiers of the public house as both have sufficient control over the premises (*Wheat v Lacon* (1966)) and there does not need to be physical possession or occupation, nor for it to be exclusive (*Harris v Birkenhead Corporation* (1976)). The public house satisfies being a premises under **s 1(3)** of the **Occupiers' Liability Act 1957**. The question is whether CL, as an independent contractor, has sufficient control, as in *AMF International v Magnet Bowling* (1968) as they can also be classed as an occupier. This is, of course, a question of fact but the refurbishment is reasonably extensive and so CL may well be held to be an occupier.

The duty owed under the **1957 Act** is to visitors, generally understood to mean those with permission to be on the premises for the purpose that they are there. This would include licensees, invitees or persons entering under a legal right. The duty is elaborated in **s 2(2)** of the **1957 Act** and is expressed as a duty to take such care as in all the circumstances to see that the visitor will be reasonably safe in using the premises for the purposes for which he is invited.

Bharat and Bharat's Son

Bharat is a visitor on the premises occupied by Gordon and is owed a duty of care under the **1957 Act**. His injury stems from the state of the premises and thus it could be argued that Gordon has breached his duty of care, by failing to ensure Bharat's reasonable safety while on the premises, and is therefore liable (**s 2(2)**). The damage suffered is of a type or kind that is foreseeable (*Jolley v Sutton LBC* (2000)) and thus the requirements for liability would be made out. Liability extends to both personal injury and damage to property under **s 1(3)(b)** of the **1957 Act**, so Bharat could be compensated for his broken arm and his broken glasses.

So far as the death of Bharat's son is concerned, the **1957 Act** states in **s 2(3)(a)** that an occupier should expect that children will be less careful than adults. This, effectively, imposes a higher duty of care on the occupier; this does not mean that an occupier has an absolute duty in relation to children on their premises (see *West Sussex County Council v Lewis Pierce* (2013)); however parental responsibility is also taken into consideration given whether it would be likely that children would be left free to roam (*Phipps v Rochester Corporation* (1955); *Perry v Butlins* (1998); *Maloney v Lambeth LBC* (1966)). It is unclear whether Bharat was made aware of the water feature, although placing an obvious (to an adult) danger next to a play area, could operate as an allurement (*Glasgow Corporation v Taylor* (1922)) to a child. This would strengthen the position that it would fall below the standard of care required of an occupier given children are likely to roam in such a family environment. The only doubt would be the question of what more a reasonable parent in Bharat's situation could have done to exercise control over their child.[5]

Gordon and CL

Gordon may wish to try and pass the liability on to CL relying on **s 2(4)(b)** of the **1957 Act**. This section states the occupier will not be liable for the work of an independent contractor where the occupier had acted reasonably in entrusting the work to an independent contractor and had taken such reasonable steps to satisfy himself that the contractor was competent and that the work had been properly done. We are told that Gordon used them because they were 'cheap and cheerful', perhaps as opposed to professional and effective? In terms of taking steps to satisfy himself that the work has been properly done the rule is that the more technical the work, the less reasonable it is to require the occupier to check (cf. *Haseldine v Daw* (1941) and *Woodward v The Mayor of Hastings* (1945)). The issue will turn on whether the loose floorboard would have been obvious on a reasonable inspection. If it was not, then it is likely that Gordon, subject to the finding that CL was a competent contractor, could escape liability.

Sparkie

Gordon is likely to be able to avoid any liability in relation to Sparkie's injuries. This is because in **s 2(3)(b)** of the **1957 Act** it is provided that an occupier may expect that a skilled worker in the exercise of their calling will appreciate and guard against any special risks

---

5   Do not be afraid to leave the question of liability uncertain. It is perfectly acceptable to raise doubt largely on the basis of insufficient information given in the problem.

ordinarily incident to it, so far as the occupier leaves him free to do so (see also *Roles v Nathan* (1963) and the recent High Court decision in *Yates v National Trust* (2014)), where it was held that a tree surgeon would be expected to guard against risks when climbing a tree. Here, Sparkie, representing to be an electrician would be expected to take reasonable care of her own safety to the extent that it related to her job which is present due to her suffering electric shock.

Wesley

It is clear that Wesley is not a visitor when he enters the former lounge bar. He probably was Gordon's visitor in the Tamar public house, but exceeded the terms of his permission to be there (*The Calgarth* (1927)) by entering a prohibited area.[6] Given that there is a physical barrier and a warning sign expressly stating that permission to enter must be given by the contractor, there is, at least arguably, a presumption that, by virtue of *AMF v Bowling*, CL would be considered to be the occupier.

Whether Wesley is owed a duty of care depends on the test set out in **s1(3)** of the **1984 Act**. The fact that a warning notice was deployed by CL would be suggestive of the fact that they knew that a danger existed. However, it is unlikely that CL would be held to believe that Wesley would come into the vicinity of the area (*White v St. Albans City and District Council* (1990)) and whether this was an obvious risk to an adult trespasser in any case (*Tomlinson v Congleton BC* (2003)).

If a duty of care was held to exist then CL would probably escape liability by virtue of the fact that their warning was sufficient (**s1(5)** of the **1984 Act**). Adult trespassers who have been provided with a warning but trespass nonetheless are usually held to have consented to run the risk of injury (*Ratcliff v McConnell* (1999)). The attempt by CL to exclude liability would be irrelevant if no liability arose, and there is academic uncertainty about whether the **Unfair Contract Terms Act 1977 s2(1)** would apply. Either way Wesley would not be able to make a claim in respect of his damaged watch as property damage is not recoverable under the **1984 Act s1(8)**.

QUESTION 24

Discuss the extent to which the law on occupier's liability respects individual responsibility and freedom to participate in activities, even those carrying obvious risks.

How to Read this Question

This is a wide ranging question, and note the question does not specify an Act so you are entitled to use the breadth of your knowledge to highlight points and principles. It would be wise for reasons of coverage to highlight cases from both Acts. The use of the words

---

6 Look out for the possibility of a visitor in an occupiers' liability question becoming a non-visitor by 'straying' outside the area they were allowed to be in, as here with Wesley, and thus being subject to the **1984 Act**. This is very commonly examined.

individual responsibility and freedom highlight some of the philosophical concerns underpinning occupiers' liability, and there is no doubt the spirit of such concerns was seen in the case of *Tomlinson v Congleton* (2004). Note the question is asking you to discuss the extent, so attempt to emphasise the limits that the law has drawn in your discussion.

How to Answer this Question

The following points need to be discussed:

- ❖ the context of the two **OL Acts**;
- ❖ the difference between activity and state of the premises;
- ❖ the duty owed under the **1957 Act** and considerations of children and professionals;
- ❖ the duty owed under the **1984 Act**;
- ❖ the effect of warnings and exclusion clauses;
- ❖ the significance of *Tomlinson v Congleton* (2004);
- ❖ overall assessment.

Answer Structure

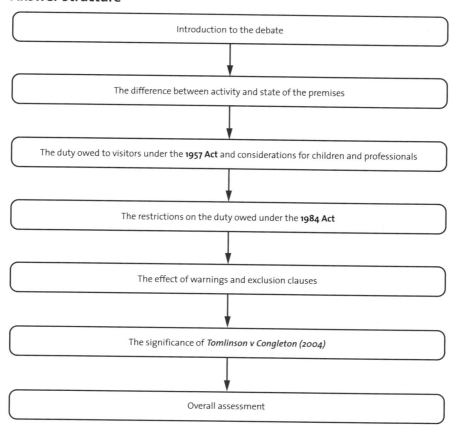

Introduction to the debate

↓

The difference between activity and state of the premises

↓

The duty owed to visitors under the **1957 Act** and considerations for children and professionals

↓

The restrictions on the duty owed under the **1984 Act**

↓

The effect of warnings and exclusion clauses

↓

The significance of *Tomlinson v Congleton (2004)*

↓

Overall assessment

Up for Debate

The law on occupiers' liability is governed by two separate statutes in the form of the **Occupiers Liability Acts 1957** and **1984** which cover both visitors and non-visitors respectively. The law in this area is a blend of policy and one of the leading cases is *Tomlinson v Congleton* (2004), with both Lord Hoffmann and Lord Hobhouse providing good judgments to read. It is a case which denied recovery out of respect for free will and the individual responsibility to partake in activities in spite of obvious risks. The motive behind this decision was largely to avoid any chilling effect on pursuing socially desirable activities. For a comment on this case see M Lunney, 'Occupiers and obvious risks' 11 Tort L Rev 140, and for a policy appraisal of the relevance of insurance in the reasoning of many judicial decisions see J Morgan, 'Tort, insurance and coherence' (2004) 67 Modern Law Review 384. For a comparative perspective, Richard Buckley provides insight into how the Canadian occupier regime contrasts with our own in 'Occupiers liability in England and Canada' (2006) 35 Common Law World Review 413.

ANSWER

The law on occupiers' liability (OL), as reflected in both the **1957** and **1984 Acts** outlines various concepts, definitions and principles in drawing three way a balance between the duties imposed on occupiers, the autonomy given to individuals by the limits of the law's intervention, and in the process allowing occupiers to be free from the threat of unjustified compensation claims.

It is important to highlight that OL only extends to 'dangers due to the state of the premises …' (**s 1(1) 1957 Act**), and it has been made clear on many occasions that the risk must be one that is concerned with the premises or the land, rather than a claimant's own risky activities which happens to be on the land (*Keown v Coventry Healthcare NHS Trust* (2006); *Donoghue v Folkestone Properties Ltd* (2003)). In this sense, occupiers' liability does not over-stretch to hold occupiers liable when the cause is not their premises.

Second, it is important to contrast duties that are owed under both the Acts, with occupiers owing visitors a duty to keep them reasonably safe in using the premises for the purpose for which they are invited under **s 2(2) 1957 Act**. To this extent it is only reasonably safe, as a matter of objective fact and not absolutely safe, so in *West Sussex Country Council v Pierce* (2013) it was held that a school was not liable for a sharp edge on a water fountain as there was no evidence that the water fountain was not reasonably safe. The school was no more obliged as an occupier to take such steps in respect of the water fountain than it would be in respect of any of the other numerous edges, corners or surfaces which children might come into contact with.

The Act however does demand more by way of the fact that children are less careful than adults, and thus whose unrestricted freedom and willingness to participate in activities must be mitigated by occupiers (**s 2(3)(a)**) as reflected in the common law; *Glasgow*

Corporation v Taylor. Similar restraint is reflected in the approach to allurements, as there is a duty not to lead children into temptation and it would affect the reasonable foresight of an occupier alerting them to the danger posed to children (*Latham v Johnson and NephewY*; *Jolley v Sutton LBC* (2000)). However there is some scope given for additional parental responsibility with regards to supervision and it is likely to be very fact-dependent (*Phipps v Rochester* contrasted with *Perry v Butlins* (1997)). By contrast however a lower standard is expected to those who are on the premises in the exercise of their calling (s 2(3)(b)) (*Roles v Nathan* (1963) and *Yates v National Trust* (2014)) which seems an appropriate common sense distinction.

By contrast the far more restricted duty under s 1(3) and s 1(4) of the **1984 Act** results in an occupier only owing a duty to ensure the non-visitor does not suffer injury by reason of the danger. The conditions are if he is aware of the danger or has reasonable grounds to believe it exists, believe the non-visitor may be in its vicinity and overall the risk is such that he may reasonably be expected to protect against it. Thus if the occupier is unaware of the danger he cannot be said to owe a duty as in *Rhind v Astbury Water Park* (2004), and this is only actual knowledge, or the facts from which the natural inference of risk of danger can be drawn (*Swain v Natui Ram Pun* (1996)). Similarly as *Donoghue* highlights only where the occupier has at least reasonable grounds to know of trespassers in the vicinity of the danger at the relevant time will the requirement be satisfied, thus further demonstrating that the law is not imposing disproportionate liability on occupiers.

The effect of warnings justifies inclusion in both statutes and what is required to discharge the duty within those warnings will depend on a range of criteria including its details, prominence and the relationship between the danger and the warning amongst others. However the scope of the requirements are different with **OL 1957** s 2(4)(a) asking whether the warning was adequate enough to enable the visitor to be reasonably safe and *Darby v National Trust* (2001) confirms the limits imposed on a occupier who would not be expected to warn against obvious risks. Likewise the wording is to keep reasonably safe, so a warning could merely redirect the entrant to somewhere safer (Lord Denning in *Roles v Nathan* (1963)). The effect of warnings is also supported by the *volenti* defence available under both Acts (s 2(5) **1957 Act** and s 1(6) **1984 Act**).

However the law has drawn limits, to the effect of exclusion notices, liability can be restricted or modified or excluded (s 2(1) **1957 Act**) but not to the extent that it would breach the **Unfair Contract Terms Act 1977**, i.e. personal injury or death due to negligence cannot be excluded. However the position of trespassers is unclear, and though a similar provision as in the **1957 Act** may apply, it would seemingly be an unfair loophole if the spirit of a duty of common humanity (as in *BRB v Herrington* (1972)) could simply be excluded. This would be drawing the limits of the law too early in allowing occupiers to wilfully disregard any risks once they have placed an exclusion notice.

The essence of the question posed is the extent to which the law should impose liability on an occupier for freely chosen activities that inherently carry a risk. In the seminal case of *Tomlinson v Congleton* (2004), it was held that the law would pose no obligation for an occupier to take steps to prohibit them. Lord Hoffmann famously stated: 'If people want to climb mountains, go hang gliding or swim or dive in ponds or lakes that is their affair.'

The case is critical as it is partly premised on drawing a line in the limits of blame culture. Lord Hobbhouse was concerned that imposing liability would restrict the liberty of the individual to engage in dangerous, but otherwise harmless, pastimes. Similarly he argued that it would not be acceptable for the coastline and other beauty spots to be lined with warning notices, and this sentiment was later captured in statute with s1 of the **Compensation Act 2006**.

The **Occupiers' Liability Acts** therefore attempt to strike a balance between paternalism and protection for those who are unduly put at risk by an occupier, to one of free will and responsibility not to burden occupiers with liability. The law is attempting to encourage individuals to act responsibly but otherwise be free to participate in activities without the law's intervention. In the case of children the law has shown a tendency to be paternal but, increasingly of late, the law has been more sympathetic to occupiers, interpreting reasonable in favour of occupiers who for lack of limitless funds cannot be expected to protect against all hazards.

Product Liability

INTRODUCTION

Product liability is a niche area of tort law, with particular attention paid to the effect of the **Consumer Protection Act 1987** and this is often the subject for many essay questions. However ensure you are aware of the relevant traditional common law principles too. There are two problem questions and one essay question in this chapter.

Checklist
Students must be familiar with the following areas:
(a) the common law position:
■ the dictum in *Donoghue v Stevenson* (1932);
■ intermediate examination;
■ the problems regarding defective product economic loss;
(b) the position under the **Consumer Protection Act 1987**:
■ defects;
■ persons liable;
■ defences;
■ loss caused;
■ the invalidity of exclusion clauses.

QUESTION 25

'Although many manufacturers feared the introduction of the **Consumer Protection Act 1987**, they are in a no worse position since the Act than before.'

▶ **Critically discuss the above statement.**

How to Read this Question

This question is typical of the essays that examiners may set. It requires a discussion of the main elements of **Part 1** of the Act and a comparison of the statutory and common law regimes regarding product liability. The effect of the Act on manufacturers must be analysed, with particular reference to recent cases. Note, however, that the question requires you to discuss critically; it will not be sufficient merely to list the statutory requirements.

How to Answer this Question

In particular, the following points must be discussed:

- ❖ the position under the **Consumer Protection Act 1987**;
- ❖ persons liable – **s 2**;
- ❖ the definition of defect and guidelines for assessing safety – **s 3**;
- ❖ the burden of proof;
- ❖ the defences, especially the state-of the-art defence – **s 4**;
- ❖ the position at common law;
- ❖ the requirement of causation and foreseeability;
- ❖ the limitations on property damage;
- ❖ whether manufacturers are in a worse position after the introduction of the Act.

Answer Structure

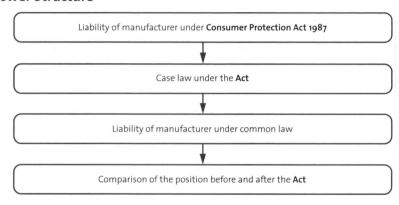

Liability of manufacturer under **Consumer Protection Act 1987**

Case law under the **Act**

Liability of manufacturer under common law

Comparison of the position before and after the **Act**

Up for Debate

Product liability is now largely governed by the **Consumer Protection Act 1987**, and thus much of the case law has considered whether the scope of its various sections applies to particular circumstances. It is a relatively niche area of law not as prominent in the law of tort and it has traditionally been difficult for claimants to recover under the statute. For an interesting and student-friendly introduction to many of the important principles in product liability see C Johnston, 'A personal (and selective) introduction to product liability law' (2012) 1 Journal of Personal Injury Law 1, and for a critical survey of some of the problems found in the case law see M Mildred, 'Pitfalls in product liability' (2007) 2 Journal of Personal Injury Law 141.

ANSWER

Part 1 of the **Consumer Protection Act 1987** was introduced into English law to implement the EC **Directive 85/734/EEC** relating to product liability. The main provision of the Act is to be found in **s 2(1)**, which states that where any damage is caused wholly or partly by a defect in a product, the persons detailed in **s 2(2)** shall be liable for the damage, regardless of any negligence on the producers' part. This change from 'fault' liability, as demonstrated by the leading negligence case of *Donoghue v Stevenson* (1932), to 'strict' liability was viewed with concern by manufacturers. They prophesised increased costs and a failure to introduce new products for fear of liability. However, in reality there has been very little litigation in this area and many commentators have argued that the legal position was barely altered by the Act.[1]

By **s 3**, a product contains a defect where 'the safety of the product is not such as persons generally are entitled to expect'. Thus, it can be argued that the **1987 Act** only requires the product to be reasonably safe; it does not impose a requirement of absolute safety. As almost any product is capable of being unsafe if misused (for example, a kitchen knife or an electric fire), the Act does not attempt to define safety, but instead provides a list of guidelines to be taken into account when considering what is meant by the term (**s 3(2)**).

For all of the defences contained within the Act, the burden lies on the defendant to prove the defence. This could be seen as reversing the burden of proof from the previous situation under the common law and shifting the pressure therefore to the manufacturer to prove the defence.

The state-of-the-art defence is permitted by **s 4(1)(e)** and is wider than that allowed in **Art 7(e)** of the original EC Directive and in *A v National Blood Authority* (2001) the court held that liability under the Directive is defect based and that any question of fault by the manufacturer is irrelevant. Thus, a product is defective if it does not provide the level of safety that a person is entitled to expect, whether or not that level of safety could have been achieved by the manufacturer. The **Art 7(e)** defence will not be relevant where there are known risks or risks that can reasonably be ascertained. *Abouzaid v Mothercare (UK) Ltd* (2001), demonstrates that a manufacturer is in a worse position under the Act than at common law.

One small relief for manufacturers is that *Richardson v LRC Products Ltd* (2001) confirmed that under **s 3**, all of the circumstances had to be taken into account, including any instructions or warnings, and the absence of any claim that the product was 100 per cent effective. Thus, if a manufacturer makes no claim that his product is 100 per cent effective, a failure does not necessarily prove the existence of a defect. However, in *Richardson*, it was reiterated that **s 4** only affords a defence where the defect is one of which up-to-date scientific knowledge is ignorant. In *Pollard v Tesco Stores Ltd* (2006), the Court of Appeal could be said to have been more sympathetic to manufacturers in that it held that despite the cap on the dishwasher powder not complying with BSI standards, it was not defective.

To see to what extent this has changed the law, it is necessary to consider the common law (*Donoghue v Stevenson* (1932)).

1   With an essay question it is important to address the key issue highlighted in the question, therefore mentioning why the change was 'feared' will give the answer some early focus and perspective in the introductory paragraphs.

The first problem that a consumer had was identifying the manufacturer, and even then the remedy may have been practically worthless where manufacturers were based entirely outside the jurisdiction. In such a case, under the **1987 Act**, the consumer could proceed against an importer into the EU (**s 2(2)(c)**), and one of the advantages of the Act from the consumer's point of view is the number of potential defendants that are available under **s 2(2)**.

The next hurdle that a consumer had to overcome was to show the absence of reasonable care. It could be difficult to show that the defect arose in manufacture, especially where the product had left the manufacturer's control some time previously as in *Evans v Triplex Safety Glass* (1936), and it is often very difficult for a claimant to fulfil the burden of proof, not least where there are several possible defendants in the chain of production.

This problem for the consumer remains under the Act, as **s 4(1)(d)** provides that it is a defence for the manufacturer to show that the defect did not exist in the product at the relevant time, a defence successfully claimed by the defendant in *Piper v JRI Manufacturing Ltd* (2006) in relation to a defective prosthetic hip. However, there is a shift in the burden of proof in that it is left for the defendant to establish this, rather than the claimant. Nevertheless, causation remains a problem for the consumer, both at common law and under the **1987 Act**, but unlike the common law, there is no requirement of foreseeability of damage under the Act.

Liability under the Act does not extend to damage caused to the product itself (**s 5(2)**), whereas at common law, recovery for defective product economic loss was allowed in *Junior Books v Veitchi* (1983). However, *Junior Books* has been subject to intense judicial criticism and has since been restricted so practically the common law and the **1987 Act** are identical.

Thus, it can be seen that it is incorrect to state that manufacturers are in no worse a position since the Act than before. Although there are relatively few decided cases under the Act, research by consumers' organisations has suggested that companies are now more willing to settle claims where damage is caused by a defective product than before the introduction of the Act. It is suggested that the shift in the balance between the parties is due to the changes introduced by the Act. Thus, manufacturers are worse off in that a consumer has few requirements to establish that the manufacturer was at 'fault' and only that the product was 'defective', foreseeability of damage not being an issue, and the defendant – the manufacturer – will suffer the burden of any defence. In particular, it seems clear that recent cases have curtailed the extent of the state-of-the-art defence in **s 4(1)(e)**, so that manufacturers who would escape liability under common law negligence are now liable under the **1987 Act**. However, apart from the lower limit of £275 for property damage, below which an action may not be brought, the manufacturer is in the same position as before as regards causation or defective product economic loss.[2]

---

2 Similarly the concluding paragraph should seek to bring together arguments made in the body of the answer and directly address the question set.

Aim Higher

The statutory scheme under the **Consumer Protection Act** is rooted in EU law. If you are attempting an essay-type question in this area it may be wise to reflect on that fact, and the differences in the level of protection between the **CPA** and the product liability directive.

Common Pitfalls

In problem questions relating to this area, a common error is to forget the 'pure economic loss' exclusion. Remember, the defendant will be liable for personal injury and consequential damage caused by the defective product, but not for the value of the product itself.

QUESTION 26

Trudi bought her children – Andy and Bea – new laptop computers from a local dealer, Chipit, for £260 each. The laptops, exclusive to Chipit, were manufactured by Bytesize and made from components supplied by Ram Ltd, a company based in India. Trudi bought the particular model as it was rated as having low energy consumption and was described as an ideal, portable study tool.

A week after the purchases, Andy's computer overheated, due to a faulty internal fan. The computer caught fire, but he was there on hand to extinguish the flames and no further damage occurred. Bea took her computer away to university and was not aware of what had happened to her brother's computer. Bea's computer was left on standby for an evening while she went out with friends. The computer caught fire and the resulting blaze extensively damaged Bea's room, as well as causing significant smoke damage to the rest of the house. Chavez, a housemate, suffered minor burns as he attempted to extinguish the fire.

It transpired that Bytesize was aware of a potential fault in the fans but had not passed the information on to Chipit.

▶ **Advise Andy, Bea and Chavez.**

How to Read this Question

The question requires a consideration of the provisions of the **Consumer Protection Act 1987** and the common law in relation to defective products. There are three claimants here so be sure to make references to them all, and note the supply chain here which would warrant a discussion of who is the relevant manufacturer of the product. Ensure you highlight key facts and assess their importance in your answer such as, the knowledge that Bytesize has of the fault, and the purpose of the product itself.

How to Answer this Question

The answer should contain:

- ❖ an explanation of the key terminology of the **Consumer Protection Act** – product, producer (**s 2**);
- ❖ an evaluation of the criteria necessary to show a defect (**s 3**);
- ❖ the nature of restrictions placed on property damage (**s 5**);
- ❖ common law under the rule in *Donoghue v Stevenson* (1932);
- ❖ the need to demonstrate foreseeability of damage;
- ❖ the nature of restrictions placed on property damage.

Applying the Law

Strict liability

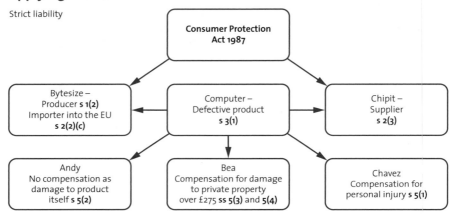

Fault liability

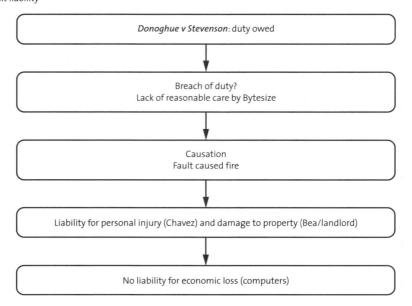

ANSWER

All of the parties should be advised that they might have a claim under the **Consumer Protection Act 1987**, which imposes a form of strict liability in relation to damage caused by defective products, as well as under the common law. Any person who suffers some form of personal injury or damage to their property caused by a defective product may use the Act: as with the common law (see *Stennet v Hancock* (1939)), the ability to sue extends to third parties who suffer damage as a result.[3]

Section 1(2) of the Act can impose liability on to a producer of a product which is defined as 'any goods or electricity' going on for our purposes ... 'A product which is comprised in other products, whether by virtue of being a component part ...'. That definition would thus include the fan, were it to be separated from the computer.

A producer, according to **s1(2)**, is widely defined and liability is imposed by **s2** in respect of any damage caused wholly or partly by a defect in a product. It is not only the actual manufacturer who attracts liability, but also those who represent that they are the manufacturer, such as own-branders (**s2(2)**). In that situation, Chipit could be held to be a manufacturer, but it would depend on the extent to which it identified Bytesize as the 'true' manufacturer of its exclusive product, e.g. marketing and labels. Chipit might be liable as the supplier as provided for by **s2(3)**; however as Chipit is readily identifiable as the manufacturer recourse through this route could be unnecessary in any case.

Bytesize is unquestionably a manufacturer within the meaning of the Act. Although Ram Ltd made the components, one of which was the ultimate cause of the defect, the Act provides in **s2(2)(c)** that an importer into the European Union of a product manufactured outside will be held to be a producer which is similarly satisfied by Bytesize.

According to **s3(1)**, a product is defective if it is not as safe as persons generally are entitled to expect. The section extends this notion of safety to 'products comprised in that product', such as in our case, the fan. It is for Andy and Bea to prove the link between the defect and the damage suffered according to the decision in *Foster v Biosil* (2001). In determining whether a product is in fact reasonably safe, the Act provides that all of the circumstances should be taken into account and includes a list of indicators in **s3(2)**. These relate to the marketing of the product, instructions and/or warnings (*Richardson v LRC Products* (2000)), what might reasonably be expected to be done with the product (*Bogle v McDonalds Restaurants Ltd* (2002)) and the time at which the product was supplied by the producer to another. Thus it does not mean that a product must be 100 per cent safe; merely that it should, according to all of the circumstances, be reasonably so. A low-energy computer is marketed to be used with it being left on standby to be expected. Both Andy and Bea were using the computers as they were intended and on that basis the computers were not as safe as a person would be reasonably entitled to expect (*A v National Blood Authority* (2001))

---

3 This identifies and clarifies that the answer will involve consideration of both the common law and statute, and conveys to the examiner that you are aware of the distinction between the two.

and were therefore defective. The strict liability nature of the Act means that Andy and Bea need only prove a causal link between the defect and the damage suffered, they are not obliged to show blameworthiness, so the fact that Bytesize was aware of the fault would be irrelevant in a case under the Act.

Section 5(1) sets out the type of damage giving rise to liability under the Act. Death, personal injury and property damage are all expressly permitted; thus, at first glance, Andy, Bea and Chavez would not have a problem in claiming against Bytesize for their losses and injury. As above, a third party can claim for damage caused by a defective product. So far as property damage is concerned, there is a monetary threshold of £275, so that if damage to property does not exceed that amount, there can be no claim (**s 5(4)**). So with the computers at £260, this will exclude recovery for Andy, as only the computer is damaged, though with Bea's situation there is extensive damage and so a claim would be likely to succeed if above that threshold amount. Another factor will limit Andy's ability to claim, however, and would also affect the amount of Bea's claim. The Act excludes damage to the defective product itself (**s 5(2)**), so neither of the computers by virtue of the fan, would be able to be claimed for.

At common law negligence the classic duty case in relation to defective products is *Donoghue v Stevenson* (1932) where Lord Atkin made specific reference to the fact that a manufacturer of products owes a duty to the ultimate consumer. All of the parties would be able to establish that Bytesize owed them a duty of care.

The mere fact of the defect would probably enable the breach element to be satisfied. A breach of duty requires a person to fall below the standard of the reasonable person (*Blyth v Birmingham Waterworks* (1856)) and, in this situation, Bytesize would have fallen below that threshold by permitting the defective computers to enter circulation, particularly given its suspicion of the potential fault and certainly being aware of the potential seriousness of such a defect. The breach would need to cause the final injury. The classic formulation is the application of the 'but for' test elaborated by Denning J in *Cork v Kirkby MacLean Ltd* (1952) and here but for the faulty component and assembly of which Bytesize were aware, the harm would not have occurred. The last hurdle is demonstrating that the damage was of a type or kind that was reasonably foreseeable, and thus not too remote a consequence of the breach (*The Wagon Mound (No 1)* (1961)). The damage that has been suffered due to a faulty fan, which caused overheating and a fire, would certainly be reasonably foreseeable. As a result, Bea would be able to claim for the damage to her property, and Chavez and the landlord would be able to claim for their injury and losses. As with the Act, however, common law will not provide a remedy for damage to the computers themselves. This would be regarded as pure economic loss for which no remedy in negligence exists.

Think Point

Had Bea spent money on downloading music or other media on to her computer, would she be able to claim damages in respect of the fact that these would have been lost?

QUESTION 27

Dee goes to a café bar, Minchelli, with her friend, Cheryl. Cheryl buys them both bottled lager brewed by Stevensons. Dee drinks the beer straight from the bottle, but when she later pours the dregs into a glass, she finds the remains of a decomposing spider. Dee is immediately sick over her friend's designer handbag, and subsequently suffers from gastroenteritis for several days, requiring time off work and causing her considerable discomfort.

▶ **Advise Dee and Cheryl.**

Would it make any difference to your answer if you knew:

(a) that Stevensons has gone out of business; or
(b) that the beer was imported by Stevensons from (i) Germany or (ii) America?[4]

How to Read this Question

This question is obviously closely based on the facts in *Donoghue*, but it will necessitate applying current law, i.e. the **Consumer Protection Act 1987**. It might give some opportunity for you to demonstrate comparatively how much better the position is now than previously, however it is important not to dwell on this excessively. Ensure you address the two aspects of the question adequately.

How to Answer this Question

Your answer should contain:

❖ comparison with *Donoghue v Stevenson*;
❖ the **Consumer Protection Act** including who was the producer;
❖ that the product was defective;
❖ that the defect caused their injuries;
❖ recovery for property and economic loss;
❖ identifying liability when products are imported.

Applying the Law

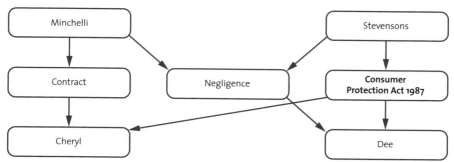

---

4 Where a question asks if something will make a difference to your answer, it usually will! When a question is broken down into different parts, as here, it is advisable to assess the relative worth, and the attention to be given to each part, if the marks have not been broken down by the examiner. Similarly ensure that you make it clear in your answer when you are addressing this part of the question.

ANSWER

The facts of this problem clearly bear a close similarity to the leading negligence case of *Donoghue v Stevenson* (1932). However, whereas Ms Donoghue had to rely on a majority decision in the House of Lords to establish her right to a remedy, Dee and Cheryl can rely on the **Consumer Protection Act 1987** (**CPA**),[5] which imposes strict liability on the producer of a defective product. Dee therefore only has to prove the identity of the producer, that the product was defective and the causal[6] link between the defect and her injury to obtain compensation.

In *Donoghue*, it was never finally established whether there was a snail in the ginger beer, as the question for the courts was solely whether a duty was owed by a manufacturer to the ultimate consumer, but we are told here that the spider exists.

The producer under the **CPA** is defined in **s 1(2)(c)** to include the processor, so this would encompass brewing. Stevensons is thus the producer, and by virtue of **s 2(1)** will be strictly liable for damage caused by their defective product. (Unlike Ms Donoghue, there is no requirement to prove a breach of duty, or fault, which would have involved showing how and why the snail got into the bottle and whether reasonable care would have prevented it from doing so.)

A defective product is one which by virtue of **s 3(1)** is not 'as safe as persons generally are entitled to expect',[7] bearing in mind such factors as how it is marketed and any warnings and instructions given with it. The courts have had relatively few chances to interpret the **CPA**, but see *Abouzaid v Mothercare* (2000) and more recently *Pollard v Tesco Stores Ltd & ors* (2006). Although the section does not impose absolute liability (see *Bogle v McDonalds* (2002), where it was held that very hot coffee was not 'defective'), it is unlikely that any court would say that a contaminated drink was 'reasonably safe', which is likely to be the minimum that persons generally are 'entitled to expect'.

The only remaining hurdles for Dee would seem to be to prove causation; that the harm falls within the definition of damage for the purposes of the **CPA**; and to rebut contributory negligence on her part, a defence specifically provided for in the Act (**s 6(4)**). To dispose of the latter point, it might be argued by Stevensons that to drink directly from the bottle added to her harm, but given modern habits this is unlikely to succeed.

The **CPA** does not deal with causation specifically, so applying general tort principles of the 'but for' test in *Barnett v Chelsea and Kensington Hospital* (1969), it can be said that the fact that she was immediately sick suggests that 'but for' the sight of the spider she would not have vomited or become subsequently ill. (As a practical point, Dee or Cheryl

---

5 Most examiners will be happy for you to abbreviate the names of statutes in exam conditions, but it is essential to give the full title initially, and show your chosen abbreviation.

6 Beware the simple spelling mistake often made, causal is not casual!

7 Including a short extract from a statute will increase the sharpness and accuracy of the response, as it will allow you to be more specific in the application of it to the problem.

could be advised to photograph the insect as evidence of both the existence of the defect and causation, as in many cases the absence of such evidence is a weakness of product liability cases.) Her vomiting and gastroenteritis, as personal injury, would fall within s 5(1).[8]

Stevensons could try to plead one of the statutory defences in s 4, but the most common, that the defect was undiscoverable scientifically (s 4(1)(e)) is unlikely to apply in this fact situation, and the fact that the bottle was sealed makes it unlikely that the defect occurred after it left Stevensons (s 4(1)(d)).

The introduction of strict liability under the **CPA** therefore makes it highly unlikely that Dee would have to rely on her common law rights under *Donoghue*.[9] However, as there are a few minor exclusions from the Act, such as liability for private property under £275 (s 5(4)), it may be that Cheryl may have to establish fault to recover for her designer handbag if it is valued at less than £275. If it is over this figure, she could claim as damage to property from Stevensons under s 5(1), or alternatively from Minchelli for breach of contract.

Neither the **CPA** nor the common law gives a right to recover the cost of the lager, i.e. damage to the defective product itself (s 5(2) and despite *Junior Books v Veitchi* (1983)),[10] and Cheryl would be left to pursue this case against Minchelli for breach of her contractual implied rights under the **Sale of Goods Act 1979**, s 14, as the lager is not of satisfactory quality.[11]

Thus although some commentators have argued that there has been little advantage to consumers from the introduction of the **CPA**, it is likely that Dee and Cheryl's cases in the twenty-first century would be settled quickly because of the move to strict liability, provided the difficult factual questions of causation could be established, and unlike Ms Donoghue would not require resort to the highest court for a remedy.

(a) If Stevensons had gone out of business, liability under the **CPA** will not transfer to anyone else in the supply chain. The retailer, Minchelli, will only be liable under the **CPA** if it had put its own brand name on it or in some other way held itself out as the producer (s 2(2)(b)) or was unable to provide the name of the producer or other party in the supply chain (s 2(3)). At common law a retailer who should have spotted the

---

8 Students sometimes judge that loss of earnings amounts to 'economic loss' purely because we are considering financial losses. However, this would be part of the personal injury assessment as such losses flow from, in this case, Dee being ill.

9 Here the fact that the common law right still exists is acknowledged, but little depth is given to it as in practice it will no longer be necessary to rely on it.

10 This alerts the examiner that you appreciate the debate surrounding this area, but are wise not going into further details as the question does not demand it in the time you are given.

11 Though not essential at all, and only if there is time, including reference to the contractual position would highlight the close relationship between contract and tort in product liability within the broader law of obligations generally.

defect or been suspicious of the manufacturer may be in breach of duty (*Fisher v Harrods* (1966)), but if as here the lager was in a sealed opaque bottle there would be no chance of intermediate inspection, and if Minchelli had had no problems with Stevensons' products in the past it is highly unlikely that there has been a lack of reasonable care.

(b) (i) If the lager was imported from Germany, Dee would have to sue the German manufacturer (**s 2(2)(c)**). As the **CPA** was based on an EU Directive, the law in the UK and Germany should be harmonised, but doing so would not be straight-forward because of jurisdictional differences etc.

(ii) If the lager was imported from America, outside the EU, then Stevensons will be held liable, in effect standing in for the producer, **CPA s 2(2)(c)**. As this is strict liability, it does not matter how much, or little care Stevensons has taken when selecting the manufacturer.

9

INTRODUCTION

Questions on nuisance are popular with examiners and students alike. There are some grey areas in the tort with much of its complexity due to the fact that there are few hard-and-fast rules as to what constitutes an unreasonable interference. Recently, a number of nuisance cases have involved arguments relating to the **Human Rights Act 1998** and you should be aware of the importance of these developments. Also note there is a natural relationship between the law of nuisance and the rule in *Rylands v Fletcher* which is the topic of the next chapter. Be aware of the importance of remedies in a nuisance discussion and this area has been revisited by the Supreme Court in the recent case of *Coventry v Lawrence* (2014). There are three problem questions and one essay question in this chapter.

<table>
<tr><th colspan="2">Checklist</th></tr>
<tr><td colspan="2">Students must be familiar with the following areas:</td></tr>
<tr><td>(a)</td><td>the types of activity capable of constituting a nuisance;</td></tr>
<tr><td>(b)</td><td>the factors indicating whether an interference is unreasonable and the relative importance of these factors inter se;</td></tr>
<tr><td>(c)</td><td>the possible defendants in a nuisance action;</td></tr>
<tr><td>(d)</td><td>the defences and especially the invalid defences;</td></tr>
<tr><td>(e)</td><td>the undecided point regarding recoverability of damage for personal injury and economic loss;</td></tr>
<tr><td>(f)</td><td>public nuisance;</td></tr>
<tr><td>(g)</td><td>the relevance of the Human Rights Act 1998, especially Art 8 of the European Convention on Human Rights (ECHR);</td></tr>
<tr><td>(h)</td><td>in addition, nuisance questions may contain elements of negligence and the rule in Rylands v Fletcher (1868).</td></tr>
</table>

QUESTION 28

Sarah owns a house in a small village that she leases to May. May owns four dogs, which she keeps in kennels in the garden. The dogs spend large amounts of the day and night barking, and this annoys her neighbours, Terence and Ursula. Victor, another neighbour, finds the noise during the day particularly annoying, as he works nights and has to sleep during the day. All of the neighbours complain to May, who refuses to do anything. Consequently,

Ursula lights a large bonfire in her garden in the hope that the smoke will stop the barking. Terence, whose hobby is woodworking, takes the television suppressor off his electric drill and uses it in the evenings to interfere deliberately with the reception on May's television.

▶ Discuss the liability of the parties.

How to Read this Question

This nuisance question has several features, and note that Sarah appears as the landlady in the first sentence and then she is not mentioned again. However, this does not mean she is not worthy of inclusion in your answer. Also note particular factual features including the duration of the barking, whether Victor is susceptible to the nuisance and the role of malice. Once key aspects are highlighted it is important that in such questions you clearly distinguish the relevant specific nuisance and the potential parties liable for them.

How to Answer this Question

The following points need to be discussed:

❖ the liability of landlord and tenant in nuisance;

❖ whether Ursula and Terence can sue;

❖ whether the barking of the dogs is a nuisance;

❖ whether Victor is a sensitive claimant;

❖ May's liability in public nuisance;

❖ the remedies available against May;

❖ the liability of Ursula in nuisance for the bonfire;

❖ the liability of Terence in nuisance for the interference with the television reception;

❖ the liability of the local authority under the **Human Rights Act 1998**.

Applying the Law

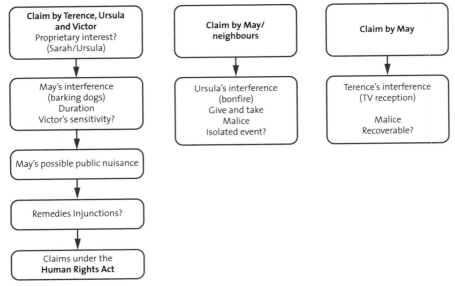

ANSWER

A nuisance is an unreasonable interference with a person's use or enjoyment of land or some right over or in connection with it. It is well established that noise can constitute a nuisance (*Halsey v Esso Petroleum* (1961); *Tetley v Chitty* (1986)), but not all interference gives rise to liability. As May is responsible for the dogs, she will be the potential defendant. Sarah will not be liable as the nuisance did not exist before she leased the premises; the premises have not been leased for a purpose that constitutes a nuisance (as in *Tetley*).

We must ascertain who can sue in respect of the barking and it has been held that only persons with an interest in land can sue (*Malone v Laskey* (1907)). On this basis, if Terence and Ursula are owners or tenants of the property, they can sue but if, for example, Terence is the sole owner, Ursula would not have the requisite interest in land required to found an action in private nuisance. Although in *Khorasandjian v Bush* (1993) and *Hunter v Canary Wharf Ltd* (1996), the Court of Appeal found that it was no longer necessary to have the classic interest in land required by *Malone*, when *Hunter* was decided in the House of Lords, the House confirmed that *Malone* was still good law.

There must be give and take between neighbours, and the interference must be substantial and not fanciful (*Walter v Selfe* (1851)). The shorter the duration of the interference, the less likely it is to be unreasonable (*Harrison v Southwark and Vauxhall Water Co* (1891)). As we are told that the dogs spend large amounts of the day and night barking, this noise would probably amount to a nuisance.

Victor can sue if he has the traditional interest in land, but, as a night worker, he may be a sensitive claimant. In *Robinson v Kilvert* (1889), it was held that a claimant cannot recover where the damage is solely due to the sensitive nature of the claimant's property. However, in *McKinnon Industries v Walker* (1951), it was held that once a nuisance has been established on the grounds of interference with ordinary use, a claimant can recover for the full interference however sensitive. Hence, if Victor can establish that the barking constitutes an unreasonable interference with his use or enjoyment of property, he will be able to fully recover, which is likely here. Any harm caused must also be foreseeable (*Cambridge Water Co v Eastern Counties Leather plc* (1994)), but this requirement gives rise to no problems for the claimants.

The remedies[1] available against May would be damages to compensate for the nuisance and an injunction to prevent further nuisance. The court does have power, under s 50 of the **Senior Courts Act 1981**, to award damages in lieu of an injunction. This power has traditionally been used very sparingly as outlined in *Shelfer v City of London Electric Lighting Co* (1895) which emphasised criteria such as the loss must be quantifiable, that it was relatively small and an injunction would be oppressive. However in *Coventry v Lawrence* (2014) Lord Neuberger advanced his own more flexible approach, emphasising that it was

---

1 Remember to consider remedies, especially when it can demonstrate the importance of injunctions in relation to nuisance and the effective protection they give to claimants.

a matter of discretion, and that a mechanistic application of the *Shelfer* criteria so that damages were only awarded exceptionally may risk unfairness. However on these facts, there seems no good reason not to award a partial injunction against May for example providing conditions on the freedom or keeping of the dogs. May could also be liable in public nuisance which requires there to be 'an act or omission which materially affects the reasonable comfort and convenience of life of a class of Her Majesty's subjects' (*Attorney General v PYA Quarries* (1957), Romer LJ) and in order to sue the claimant must be affected more than others in the class. Here, it could be said that Terence and Ursula are more acutely affected given their proximity.

Ursula has lit a large bonfire in her garden and this may not constitute a nuisance – the interference must be substantial and not merely fanciful (*Walter v Selfe* (1851)). In Ursula's case, the court would consider the duration of the interference, as the shorter the duration of the interference, the less likely it is to be unreasonable (*Harrison v Southwark and Vauxhall Water Co* (1891)). In particular, it seems that an isolated event is unlikely to constitute a nuisance (*Bolton v Stone* (1951)). However, although Ursula might claim that the bonfire is an isolated event, it does constitute a temporary state of affairs and is capable, in law, of being a nuisance: see, for example, *Crown River Cruises v Kimbolton Fireworks* (1996). As regards any interference with health and comfort, the court will take into account the character of the neighbourhood (*Bamford v Turnley* (1860)), as 'what would be a nuisance in Belgravia Square would not necessarily be so in Bermondsey' (*Sturges v Bridgman* (1879)).[2] As Ursula lives in a rural area, the occasional lighting of a bonfire might not constitute a nuisance, as there must be an element of give and take between neighbours. However, if Ursula by her lack of care allowed an annoyance from the bonfire to become excessive, she would become liable in nuisance (*Andreae v Selfridge* (1938)). The for problem Ursula, is that her possible malice may turn an otherwise non-actionable activity into a nuisance (*Christie v Davey* (1893) and *Hollywood Silver Fox Farm v Emmett* (1936)) as she cannot claim to be making a reasonable use of her land if she intends to cause damage.

Terence is deliberately interfering with May's television reception. Terence is clearly motivated by malice, as above so prima facie he would seem to have committed a nuisance. However, May has a problem, in that, in *Bridlington Relay v Yorkshire Electricity Board* (1965), it was held that the ability to receive interference-free television signals was not so important as to be protected in nuisance, something later confirmed in *Hunter*. Thus, May may have no remedy in respect of Terence's actions, though it is a principle that may be revisited.

Finally, we should consider any remedies that might be available to Terence, Ursula and Victor under the **Human Rights Act 1998**. Under **Art 8** of the **European Convention on Human Rights (ECHR)**, Terence, Ursula and Victor have the right to respect for private and

---

2   This short phrase is easily remembered (just remember which way round the two very different places in London appear!). The importance of locality is almost always worthy of inclusion in most private nuisance questions.

family life. In *Baggs v UK* (1987) and *Hatton v UK* (2003), it was taken for granted by the European Court of Human Rights that noise came within **Art 8**.[3] Under **s 6(1)** of the **1998 Act**, it is unlawful for a public authority to act in contravention of a **Convention** right. Also, and by **s 6(6)**, 'act' includes a failure to act (see *López Ostra v Spain* (1995)), consequently, it could be argued that by failing to institute proceedings for statutory nuisance, the local authority has failed to protect their rights although there is no indication that the local authority is or should be aware of the situation.

Aim Higher

Reading the case of *Coventry and others v Lawrence and Others* (2014) will provide a very in depth and effective oversight of the remedies of damages and injunctions, but also other areas of private nuisance such as the role of planning permission, the principle of coming to the nuisance as well as how to interpret the locality. Take a look at Lord Sumption's short judgment, in which in the clearest of terms he declares the position in *Shelfer* as out of date and proactively asserts the greater role of damages in the law of nuisance.

QUESTION 29

Beta Products plc owns a factory set in the centre of a manufacturing town and employs a considerable number of people. One day, the factory emits a quantity of acid fumes that damage the paintwork of the neighbouring houses and some residents' cars. In addition, Beta has recently installed some machinery that is considerably more noisy than the machinery it replaced and which annoys its immediate neighbours.

▶ Discuss any potential liability of Beta both at common law and under the **Human Rights Act 1998**.

How to Read this Question

At first sight, this question seems only to cover a few issues of nuisance. However it raises a number of common law concerns, as well as actions within the rapidly developing jurisprudence of the **Human Rights Act** actions. This question also demonstrates an overlap between nuisance, the rule in *Rylands v Fletcher* (as evidenced by the word 'emits') and the law of negligence, so be sure to give appropriate coverage of the issues.

How to Answer this Question

The following points need to be discussed:

❖ whether the neighbours are capable of suing in private nuisance;
❖ Beta's conduct in terms of utility, its isolation and the relevance of location to interference with health and comfort and physical damage;

3 When you have not been asked in the question to advise anyone in particular, it is valuable to consider all possible claimants/defendants. This last part of the answer demonstrates an awareness of the effect of the **Human Rights Act 1998** in this area, which has become increasingly prominent in recent years.

- ❖ the possibility of an action in public nuisance;
- ❖ additional actions in *Rylands v Fletcher* (1868) and negligence;
- ❖ the situation under the **Human Rights Act 1998**.

Applying the Law

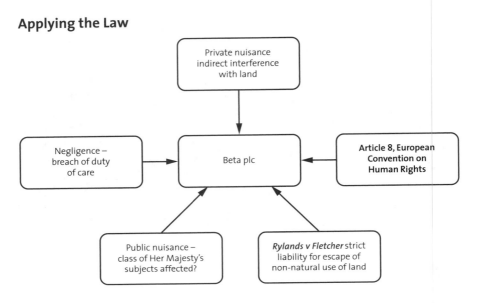

ANSWER

Traditionally, an interest in the land in question is a prerequisite for an action in nuisance (*Malone v Laskey* (1907) and *Hunter v Canary Wharf Ltd* (1997)), and thus residents with such an interest, e.g. freeholder or leaseholder can bring a claim.

A nuisance is an unreasonable interference with a person's use or enjoyment of land, or of some right over or in connection with it. However, not all interference necessarily gives rise to liability and there must be give and take between neighbours. Also, the interference must be substantial and not fanciful (*Walter v Selfe* (1851)). The courts have developed a number of guidelines that are used to determine whether any particular interference is unreasonable.

The court will consider whether Beta's emissions are an isolated event. In *Bolton v Stone* (1951), it was stated that a nuisance could not arise from an isolated happening, but had to arise from a state of affairs, however temporary. It could be argued that the escape of acid was due to a build-up of this material and thus the emission can constitute an actionable nuisance (*Midwood v Manchester Corp* (1905)). Though the premises are in the centre of a manufacturing town, the character of the neighbourhood is not to be taken into account where physical damage to property has been caused (*St Helen's Smelting Co v Tipping* (1865)), i.e. the damaged paintwork on the cars. We are told that Beta employs a considerable number of people, but the utility of the defendant's conduct is not critical in the assessment (*Adams v Ursell* (1913)) but public interest could be relevant at the remedies stage (*Coventry v Lawrence* (2014)). Thus, the fact that Beta provides employment is not a conclusive factor and therefore the emission looks likely to be an actionable nuisance.

It is well established that noise can constitute a nuisance (*Halsey v Esso Petroleum* (1961); *Tetley v Chitty* (1986)). It is clearly not an isolated event of limited duration, nor is there any evidence of sensitivity on the part of the neighbours. However, as the noise is an interference with health and comfort, the character of the neighbourhood must be taken into account (*Bamford v Turnley* (1860)). As Thesiger LJ stated in *Sturges v Bridgman* (1879), 'what would be a nuisance in Belgravia Square would not necessarily be so in Bermondsey'. As we are told that Beta's factory is in the centre of a manufacturing town, the neighbours would have to accept a certain amount of noise as part of everyday living.

As outlined in *Cambridge Water Co v Eastern Counties Leather plc* (1994), and confirmed in *Northumbrian Water v Sir Robert McAlpine Ltd* (2014), there must however be an element of foreseeability that such damage would incur either physical harm (to the cars) or amenity (the noise), and though knowledge and awareness would be important in the assessment, in relation to the increased level of noise this can be made out. With regard to the emissions, and given it passes the threshold of being a temporary state of affairs, an action under the rule in *Rylands v Fletcher* (1868) may be more applicable.

A problem to overcome is whether Beta has made a non-natural use of its land. After *Halsey*, it was held in *British Celanese v Hunt* (1969) that factories in industrial parks were a natural use of land. In *Transco v Stockport Metropolitan Borough Council* (2004), the House of Lords held that the requirement that the thing is likely to do mischief if it escapes should not be easily satisfied. It must be shown that the defendant has done something that he recognised or ought to have recognised as giving rise to an exceptionally high risk of danger or mischief if it escapes. The acid fumes and noise could come into this category. In addition, their Lordships considered the non-natural use requirement and held that the defendant's use of the land must be extraordinary and unusual. The House doubted whether the test of reasonable use was helpful, thus the fact that Beta's factory is situated in a manufacturing town, which might be relevant to reasonable use, still does not stop the use from being extraordinary and unusual. Hence it seems likely that Beta could be liable in a *Rylands* action.

Beta might also be liable in public nuisance (*Halsey v Esso Petroleum* (1961)). First, the persons affected by the nuisance must consist of the public or a section of the public (*AG v PYA Quarries* (1957)). Second, the claimant must have suffered damage over and above that suffered by the public at large. Thus, the car owners whose car paintwork is damaged could sue in public nuisance and they would not need any interest in land depending on whether there is damage over and above that suffered by the public at large.[4]

....

4   Here, brief application of relevant cases on public nuisance to Beta's use of the land is required, especially in relation to personal injury.

The claimants could sue Beta in negligence. Beta must owe them a duty of care (applying *Caparo Industries plc v Dickman* (1990)), and that it was breached by failing to act as a reasonable factory owner would (*Blyth v Birmingham Waterworks* (1856)). This may pose difficulty depending on proof of whether Beta fell below its standard trade procedure. Finally causation needs to be satisfied including whether the type of damage was not too remote and reasonably foreseeable. This can certainly be made out at least for the louder machinery (*The Wagon Mound (No 1)* (1961)).

Finally, a cause of action might arise under the **Human Rights Act 1998** with **Art 8** of the **European Convention on Human Rights** (**ECHR**) establishing the right to respect for private and family life.[5]

An action under the **Human Rights Act 1998** would raise no problems as regards interest in land (*McKenna v British Aluminium Ltd* (2002)). Indeed, it is clear from *Marcic v Thames Water Utilities Ltd* (2001), that the detailed law of nuisance is irrelevant with respect to a breach of **Art 8** (see also *Dennis v MOD* (2003)). However the practical effect will be that by course the **HRA** will not confer any additional independent remedies to those arguing their **Art 8** right was breached but with no interest in the land. Only the final award of damages to the proprietary interest holder under common law nuisance may reflect whether it amounts to just satisfaction under the **HRA** (*Dobson v Thames Water Utilities* (2011)).

Finally under **s 6(1)** of the Act, it is unlawful for a public authority to act in contravention of a **Convention** right. Also, and by **s 6(6)**, 'act' includes a failure to act (see *López Ostra v Spain* (1995)), and there may be limited scope to argue that the authorities failed to prevent Beta from being built or to intervene to ensure compliance with safety standards. **Article 8** has also been held to apply to toxic emissions from a factory (*Guerra v Italy* (1998)). However, following *Hatton v UK* (2003) and *Marcic v Thames Water Utilities Ltd* (2004), if the local authority had canvassed opinions of persons affected by the activities of Beta and considered these opinions before allowing the activities, it is possible that an action would fail.

QUESTION 30

Ricardo has recently bought an old manor house in the heart of the countryside which he intends to open to the public when it has been restored. The necessary building work caused considerable noise, dust and fumes to spread over the neighbouring district. The villagers nearby suffered disruption to their sleep on several occasions and they were unable to go into their gardens during the summer months because of the smells. They also found that their cars and paintwork were covered with grime. Additionally, the parish council had received a number of letters expressing fears that the visitors to the manor

---

5   It is essential to consider any **Human Rights Act** implications in relation to claims which might previously have been restricted to nuisance and negligence.

would disrupt the villagers' tranquillity in future, particularly in blocking the narrow streets with their cars. The council passed on these concerns, and the fact that the villagers were very angry, to Ricardo, but he failed to respond. He is in financial difficulties, and spends long periods away from the site.

During the building work, Dan, a specialist pipe-layer, is employed to replace the old drains. While digging a trench, he pierces an electricity cable and receives a severe electric shock. Dan has to have his arm amputated and he can no longer work.

That night, Marco, one of the villagers, organises a protest against the building work outside the boundary wall. During the course of the protest, he climbs over the wall, intending to place one of his protest banners directly under Ricardo's window. On the way back from doing this, he falls down the unfinished trench which had been left uncovered after Dan was rushed to hospital. Marco is a keen footballer but he has now badly damaged his legs and is unlikely to play again.

(i) Discuss the rights of the villagers in tort in connection with the disturbances, both current and potential, and indicate what remedies might be available to them. To what extent does it make a difference to your answer to know whether planning permission had been granted for this project?

(ii) Explain to Ricardo whether Dan and Marco are likely to have a successful claim against him in tort, and what their remedy might be. He also wishes to know if he may take a civil claim against Marco.

How to Read this Question

This question requires consideration of three different topics which may not have been taught together. It is lengthy so be sure to organise the claimants and defendants clearly in your head. In this sense it is a rare question as you will have to draw material from various areas of the course and this includes nuisance, occupiers' liability and even briefly the law of trespass. As it is in two parts, an assessment will have to be made as to the relevant weight to be given to each part of the question in terms of how much time to spend on each though it might be appropriate to assume that they are of roughly equal weight.

How to Answer this Question

The following points need to be discussed:

❖ the villagers' right to sue in private nuisance;
❖ whether the interferences are unreasonable including the effect of planning permission;
❖ potential remedies in private nuisance;
❖ the villagers' right to sue in public nuisance;
❖ Ricardo's potential liability under the **Occupiers' Liability Acts**;
❖ liability of Marco in trespass.

Applying the Law

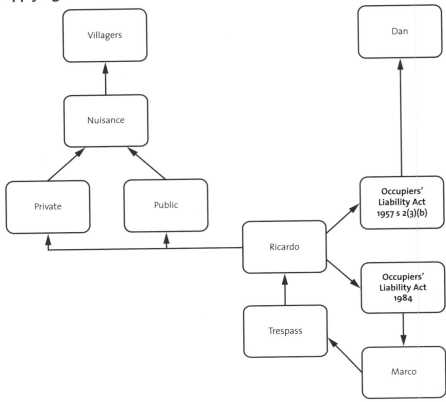

ANSWER

The villagers are concerned about the interference with their property and so would be able to consider taking action against Ricardo in either public or private nuisance. They might also consider an action based on the **European Convention on Human Rights (ECHR)**, incorporated into English law by the **Human Rights Act 1998**, because **Art 8** gives a right to respect for private life.

Private nuisance is 'an unlawful interference with persons' use or enjoyment of land or some right over or in connection with it'. The first important thing for the villagers is to establish whether they have the right to sue in private nuisance, because the House of Lords in *Hunter v Canary Wharf* (1997) confirmed the old principle of law in *Malone v Laskey* (1907) that only those with a proprietary interest in the land can claim. So only owners and tenants are likely to be able to sue.

Assuming that at least some of the villagers fulfil this criterion, it is clear that noise, fumes and smells have long been capable of constituting an unreasonable interference as in *Halsey v Esso Petroleum* (1961). In relation to the material property damage to their cars, there should be no difficulty in establishing this as in *St Helens Smelting Co v Tipping* (1865), but in relation to amenity damage the courts might require a balancing of factors between the claimants and the defendants because as was said by Thesiger LJ in *Sturges v Bridgman* (1879) 'what might be a nuisance in Belgravia Square would not necessarily be so in Bermondsey'. It would be taken into account that this was a rural area, which is described as previously 'tranquil', so it could be seen as unreasonable. However, the building work is likely to be temporary and the duration of the nuisance is an important factor. The courts have held though that even temporary disruption can be actionable (*De Keysers Royal Hotel v Spicer Bros* (1914)). Ricardo might try to argue that he is providing employment and that the public good of this outweighs the private harm, but the courts are unlikely to accept this as in *Dennis v Ministry of Defence* (2003). If he had obtained planning permission for this enterprise, that would not in itself be a defence to creating a nuisance (*Wheeler v Saunders* (1996)), unless it could be said to have changed the whole nature of the neighbourhood, which is unlikely here with the relatively small scale of the project (*Gillingham BC v Medway Docks* (1993)).[6] However given the case law has been mixed on this point Lord Neuberger in *Coventry v Lawrence* (2014) clarified and perhaps adopting a softer approach stated that whilst planning permission is normally of no assistance to the defendant, specific detailed permission would carry evidential value of the reasonableness of the activity that was permitted.

The villagers might wish to try to obtain an injunction to restrict the noise and dust etc. to particular times, and to prohibit the Manor from being opened to the public. The granting of an injunction is discretionary as it is an equitable right, and so the courts might decide to award damages instead (*Shelfer v City of London Electric Lighting Co* (1895); *Coventry* (2014)), although this is for the defendant to argue why an injunction should not be granted, not the claimants (*Regan v Paul Properties* (2006)). As we know Ricardo is already in financial difficulties, this might be enough to bring the project to an end anyway.[7]

The concerns about the blocking of the highway are likely to amount to public nuisance which requires there to be 'an act or omission which materially affects the reasonable comfort and convenience of life of a class of Her Majesty's subjects' (*Attorney General v PYA Quarries* (1957), Romer LJ) and in order to sue in tort the claimant must be affected more than others in the class. If the cars which were damaged were on public roads, as in *Halsey*, the owners could recover under public nuisance.

Dan could also possibly sue Ricardo under the **Occupiers' Liability Act (OLA) 1957**. As a visitor, he is owed the 'common duty of care' by virtue of **s 2(1)** by Ricardo, who would qualify as the occupier as he would seem to have sufficient 'control' over the property as

---

6 Drawing factual distinctions like this and judging how they relate to the given question is an example of good practice in your skills of application and problem-solving.

7 Again, try to use all the information given to make relevant points based on the legal situation. This will help you arrive at more convincing and reasoned conclusions.

we are told he is the owner (*Wheat v Lacon* (1966)). This is so unless his trips away are significant enough to mean that somebody else has control. The duty is to take 'reasonable care to ensure that visitors are reasonably safe' (**s2(2)**), and is by no means absolute liability as demonstrated in such cases as *Bowen v National Trust* (2011) where the defendant was not liable for a branch which fell on and injured children in a school party. Here, Ricardo could rely on **s2(3)(b)**, which states that 'those in the exercise of their calling' should in effect take care of themselves, and as long as Ricardo has not interfered with the way Dan works, it would seem that he has been injured in the course of his specialist work and therefore no liability attaches to Ricardo.

Marco is clearly a trespasser as he has no right to be on Ricardo's land. Thus if Ricardo owes him a duty at all it will fall to be determined under the **Occupiers' Liability Act 1984, s1(3)** which covers whether a duty of care is owed to 'non-visitors'. Marco would have to show that (a) Ricardo knew of the danger (here, the uncovered ditch); (b) knew or had reasonable grounds to suspect he was in the vicinity of the danger; and (c) it was reasonable in the circumstances for something to have been done to protect Marco from the danger.[8] Given that we are told that Ricardo is often away, and that the ditch had been left open very recently due to an emergency, it is highly unlikely that Ricardo will owe Marco a duty as the criteria cannot be made out. Alternatively it could be argued, that he knew he was running a risk by going at night on to property where building work was going on and so the defence of *volenti* would apply (**s1(6)** and see *Tomlinson v Congleton BC* (2003) and *Ratcliff v McConnell* (1999)).

Marco could be sued by Ricardo as he has committed the tort of trespass to land by coming directly on to land where he is not permitted to be. This ancient tort is actionable per se but Ricardo should be told however that he could only be granted nominal damages to mark the breach.

Neither Dan nor Marco appear to have a strong claim against Ricardo, but if they were to be successful they would be awarded damages, which would seek to put them in the position they would have been in had the tort never occurred, insofar as money can do that. Considering Ricardo's financial position, however, he may not be in a position to pay any claim unless he is adequately insured.

QUESTION 31

'The difficulties of proceeding with an action in private nuisance are grave, but the prospects of potential claimants have increased with the coming into force of the **Human Rights Act 1998**.'

▶ Discuss the above statement.

---

8   Here the opportunity is taken not just to recite or copy the statute, but to apply it directly to the facts. This is very good practice as it answers the question and conveys your knowledge and grasp of the law simultaneously.

How to Read this Question

This question is in effect in two parts. First, for you to consider the doctrinal difficulties in issuing a successful claim in private nuisance, which can include a range of the doctrinal and conceptual concerns that have arisen from the case law. The second half of the question is asking for your understanding of how the **Human Rights Act** may have provided better alternatives for claimants to pursue their claims.

How to Answer this Question

In particular, the following points need to be discussed:

❖ the restrictions on who can bring a claim in nuisance and for which type of interference;
❖ the guidelines in determining an unreasonable interference;
❖ possible defendants in nuisance claims;
❖ the development of nuisance through the **Human Rights Act 1998**.

Answer Structure

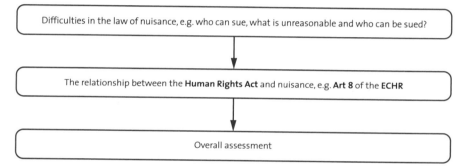

Difficulties in the law of nuisance, e.g. who can sue, what is unreasonable and who can be sued?

The relationship between the **Human Rights Act** and nuisance, e.g. **Art 8** of the **ECHR**

Overall assessment

Up for Debate

The influence and impact of the **Human Rights Act 1998** in private law is keenly felt in relation to the law of nuisance, and in particular the implications of **Art 8** of the **European Convention on Human Rights** as discussed in *McKenna v British Aluminium Ltd* (2002). For some of the case commentaries on the human rights effects on the law of nuisance see generally J Elvin, 'The law of nuisance and the human rights act 1998' (2003) 62(3) Journal of Personal Injury Law 648, and J O'Sullivan, 'Nuisance, human rights and sewage: closing the floodgates' (2004) 63(3) Cambridge Law Journal 552.

ANSWER

It was traditionally the case that only persons with an interest in the land affected can sue (*Malone v Laskey* (1907)) and, although this requirement was relaxed in *Khorasandjian v Bush* (1993), it was re-imposed by the House of Lords in *Hunter* (1997). Although this has narrowed the range of potential claimants, it has reintroduced some certainty as the exact link between the person affected and the land was somewhat uncertain following *Bush*. The decision in *Dobson v Thames Water Utilities* (2009) has further clarified this point, confirming the need for a link with the property, due to the fact that nuisance is a tort that protects interests in land, either the land itself, or the value of its amenity. It also seems, from the decision in *Bridlington Relay Ltd v Yorkshire Electricity Board* (1965), that interference with purely recreational facilities lay outside the tort of nuisance. In *Bridlington*, the court was concerned with the reception of interference-free television signals and in *Hunter* it held that an action did not lie for such interferences. Thus, an uncertainty has been removed, although the exact extent of 'purely recreational facilities' is not clear.

The courts consider a broad range of principles in determining what amounts to an unreasonable interference. First, is the duration of the interference. The shorter the duration of the interference, the less likely it is to be found unreasonable with one-off or isolated incidents not amounting to nuisance (*Harrison v Southwark and Vauxhall Water Co* (1891); *Bolton v Stone* (1951)). What is required is a state of affairs, however temporary (see *Midwood v Manchester Corp* (1905)).

The character of the neighbourhood is also a relevant factor where the interference is with health and comfort (*Bamford v Turnley* (1860)). This is also illustrated by the famous statement of Thesiger J in *Sturges v Bridgman* (1879), in which he said 'what would be a nuisance in Belgravia Square would not necessarily be so in Bermondsey'. Whether a particular interference with health and comfort is actionable will depend on the exact nature of the area and the interference in question, making the chances of success at trial difficult to predict with any confidence and thus creating different legal and social expectations based on subjective value judgments based on the locality of the area. Similarly Lord Neuberger admitted himself of his own circular reasoning in *Coventry v Lawrence* (2014) when addressing the issue of whether the defendant's use of land should be considered in addressing the character of the locality. His judgment that it should be considered but only to the extent that it is not creating a nuisance, results in a rather problematic process whereby the unreasonableness that makes it a nuisance has to be pre-judged, before even assessing locality.

Further confusion arises concerning the utility of the defendant's conduct, as the risk is that the more useful it is, the less likely it may be that interference with the claimant's land is unreasonable. However in *Coventry v Lawrence* (2014) the broad public interest was likely to be relevant in the determination to award damages ahead of an injunction. This would be especially true in, for example, temporary construction works or public infrastructure projects.

There are, however, additional areas that risk injustice within the law of nuisance. One problem concerns who can be sued in respect of any particular interference and there may be issues where the occupier of land from which the nuisance emanates did not create the thing that causes the nuisance. If the relevant nuisance was created by a trespasser, the occupier will only be liable if he continues or adopts it (*Sedleigh-Denfield v O'Callaghan* (1940)). If the occupier does neither of these things, it may be impossible to identify the trespasser, leaving the claimant unfortunately without a remedy. The common law rules have somewhat struggled to remain consistent, fair and predictable to support the needs of claimants.

However there is now the possibly far-reaching effect of the **Human Rights Act 1998** on the law of nuisance. **Article 8** of the **European Convention on Human Rights**, brought into the law by **s 1** of the **1998 Act**, establishes the right to respect for private and family life. **Article 1** of the **First Protocol** to the ECHR states that persons are entitled to the peaceful enjoyment of their possessions, and **Art 2** of the **Convention** establishes a right to life.

As **s 6(1)** of the **1998 Act** makes it unlawful for a public authority to act in a way incompatible with a **Convention** right and by **s 6(6)** an 'act' includes a failure to act, both the government and local authorities could be held liable for breaches of **Art 8**. **Article 8** has also been held to cover noise (*Baggs v UK* (1987); *Hatton v UK* (2003)) and toxic emissions (*Guerra v Italy* (1998)). Clearly, hazardous emissions could fall within **Art 1** and even **Art 2** if the emissions are sufficiently hazardous.

This new jurisprudence could have extensive effects on the law of nuisance. An action under the **Human Rights Act 1998** would raise no problems of interest in land, recovery of economic loss or application to personal injuries. Indeed, in *Marcic* (2001), in the High Court, the judge found for the claimant under **Art 8** while dismissing the claims based on nuisance and *Rylands* with it clear from the judgments in both the High Court and the Court of Appeal that much of the detailed law of nuisance is irrelevant in considering a breach of **Art 8**. In *Dobson v Thames Water Utilities No 2* (2011) the court though confirmed that the award of damages in nuisance to the property owners was relevant when considering any possible and limited award of damages for a non-property-owning claimant.

However it must be emphasised that the ECHR does not automatically bypass the normal rules of nuisance. A fair balance has to be struck between community and individual interests. In *Hatton*, it was held that in matters of general policy, on which opinions might differ widely, the role of the domestic policymaker should be given special weight.

Thus, taking an overall view of the law of nuisance there are a number of areas in which either the law is uncertain, or in which it would be difficult to predict with any confidence at all what decision a court would come to, faced with a particular set of facts, whether the common law of nuisance or the **ECHR** is invoked.[9]

QUESTION 32

Consider the extent to which the law of private nuisance provides coherent and consistent protection for those claiming an unreasonable interference with their enjoyment of the land.

9 Time should always be taken at the end of an essay to reach some conclusion on the question set.

How to Read this Question

This essay question is pervasive in allowing you to discuss a range of nuisance principles, cases and concepts from the view of those claiming interference. In this sense the implication in the question is the extent to which it is on the 'right side' of those claiming their land use is being affected. Ensure that there is due focus on whether it is indeed coherent and consistent. It would be best to begin with the definition of nuisance and then draw on specific features in an ordered and structured fashion. Also note that though there is some duplication in coverage with the previous question, the focus and theme of the question is different so you would be justified in developing points with greater depth.

How to Answer this Question

In particular, the following points need to be discussed:

- ❖ overall context and the balancing exercise;
- ❖ consistency of the factors, e.g. locality, duration and sensitivity of the claimant;
- ❖ limits on recreational rights, e.g. TV reception;
- ❖ restrictions on those who can sue and the **Human Rights Act**;
- ❖ the relationship between damages and injunctions.

Answer Structure

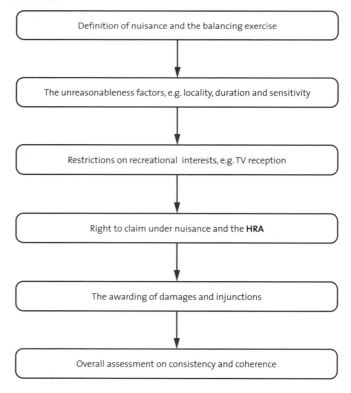

Definition of nuisance and the balancing exercise

↓

The unreasonableness factors, e.g. locality, duration and sensitivity

↓

Restrictions on recreational interests, e.g. TV reception

↓

Right to claim under nuisance and the **HRA**

↓

The awarding of damages and injunctions

↓

Overall assessment on consistency and coherence

Up for Debate

Nuisance is a popular topic with students as it often forms a coherent tort in its own right, and manages to be a tort which for neighbourly reasons we might all relate to. A very good starting point that explores the underlying foundations of nuisance and for example its relationship with negligence is M Lee, 'What is private nuisance?' (2003) 119 Law Quarterly Review 298. For an overview of two recent decisions see also Maria Lee's 'Nuisance and regulation in the Court of Appeal' (2013) 3 Journal of Personal Injury Law 277. Some of the earlier controversy which had human rights implications centres on the decision in *Hunter and Others v Canary Wharf Ltd* (1997) which maintained the restriction in standing as confirmed in *Malone v Laskey* (1907). For two critiques of the decision see P Cane, 'What a nuisance!' (1997) 113 Law Quarterly Review 515, and K Oliphant, 'Unblurring the boundaries of nuisance' (1998) 6 Tort Law Review 21.

ANSWER

Nuisance is defined as simply the unreasonable use by a man of his land to the detriment of his neighbour (*Lord Denning in Miller v Jackson* (1977)). One of the key issues with the tort is that it involves the striking of a balance between the rights of neighbours to be free to use their land without both unreasonable interference but also unreasonable restrictions and the challenge in determining this balance has been the allowance given to a measure of give and take and live and let live (*Bamford v Turnley* (1862); *Sedleigh-Denfield v O' Callaghan* (1940)). This instantly leaves a large degree of discretion to a judge to determine this balance, and thus those claiming an interference will have to be open that they cannot make undue and unfair expectations of others, thus it is unlikely that consistency in the application of the law will be a key feature, as there will be a greater emphasis placed on the fact sensitive nature of the individual cases.

This is best seen in some of the factors which are relevant to judging whether it is an unreasonable interference. The character of the neighbourhood is one such factor where the interference is with health and comfort (*Bamford v Turnley* (1860)). This is illustrated by the famous statement of Thesiger J in *Sturges v Bridgman* (1879), in which he said 'what would be a nuisance in Belgravia Square would not necessarily be so in Bermondsey'. Whether a particular interference with health and comfort is actionable will depend on thus the exact nature of the area and the interference in question, making the chances of success at trial difficult to predict with any confidence for claimants. Similarly it seems unfair to allow judges to decide subjective value judgments about the locality of the area and use it to deny recovery on the basis of what the claimant should expect. Similarly Lord Neuberger admitted himself of his own problematic and circular reasoning in *Coventry v Lawrence* (2014) when addressing the issue of whether the defendant's own use of land should be considered in addressing the character of the locality. His judgment that it should be considered but only to the extent that it is not creating a nuisance, results in a rather problematic process whereby unreasonableness has to be pre-judged. In other words in answering the question whether the defendant's conduct is a nuisance, one has to disregard the conduct of the defendant which amounts to a nuisance. This evidently has a lack of coherence in a logical application of the factor, and Lord Carnwarth who dissented on this point preferred an approach whereby the defendant's activity formed an established pattern of use.[10]

Many of the other factors that are considered leave little by way of established precedent. The broad flexibility of factors such as duration, its continuity and when such activity takes place leaves claimants restricted, at least prospectively, in assessing how much they can be expected to tolerate. This would no doubt lead to a lack of consistency (*De Keyser's Royal Hotel v Spicer Bros* (1914); *Andreae v Selfridge and Co. Ltd* (1938)). Similar concerns arise in the interpretation of sensitive use as a means to traditionally deny recovery to those who would not have suffered the nuisance otherwise; however an apparent move away to reasonable foreseeability might pose greater scope for successful claims, and a greater burden on possible defendants.

It is clear however that any interference has to be substantial and not a fanciful complaint (*Walter v Selfe* (1851)). In *Bridlington Relay Ltd v Yorkshire Electricity Board* (1965), it was confirmed that interference with purely recreational facilities (e.g. views) lies outside the tort of nuisance such as the reception of interference-free television signals, and the House of Lords in *Hunter* held that an action did not lie for such interferences. Lord Hoffmann, in that case, argued that were it to be held a nuisance, there would be the policy risk of hundreds of claimants arguing the building developers had created a nuisance, which would increase overall building costs significantly. Claimants it would appear need to make reservations before such building works; however how this might apply in domestic contexts is largely unclear. Similarly it is at least arguable, that *Bridlington* is a dated precedent. The ubiquity of TVs and people's reliance on such technologies including broadband internet, that suggests interference with such rights would surely not now be classed as merely fanciful. This imprecise nature of purely recreational facilities perhaps leaves claimants' prospects of claiming nuisance restricted.

Another restriction for claimants is the traditional requirement for a claimant in nuisance to have a proprietary interest in the land (*Malone v Laskey* (1907)). There is little doubt that the challenge and the broadening of rights for those claiming nuisance under *Khorasandijan v Bush* (1993) operated to support claimants with no such right having to be shown, the traditional position was restored in *Hunter*. Though as in the *Bush* case, other torts may be applicable that might protect personal distress and injury, nuisance as a cause of action is intended to protect the enjoyment of the land. This restriction is serving to confine the law of nuisance, leaving injured parties to only pursue a claim under the **Human Rights Act 1998**; however as confirmed in *Dobson v Thames Water Utilities No 2* (2011) the **HRA** by course does not entitle those without a proprietary interest to additional compensation, where those with such an interest are already compensated through a successful common law nuisance claim.

---

10 This section of the answer shows a high level of familiarity with an authoritative Supreme Court decision, and conveys analytical depth which can be highly creditworthy.

Finally it appears after the decision in *Coventry v Lawrence* (2014) that the use of damages as a remedy in nuisance might receive greater momentum, rather than the sparing nature in which it has currently been applied under *Shelfer v City of London* (1895). That the criteria is not to be applied rigidly, might free up the courts to award damages in lieu of an injunction. Whether this will be satisfactory to claimants is unlikely. The motivation behind actions in nuisance is to stop it. However, the positive approach taken to both planning permission and public benefit might serve to restrict the number of injunctions and enhance the discretion in the reward of damages.

In conclusion, the law of nuisance has inherent flexibility given it is tort that is premised on a balancing exercise, rather than say establishing a clear breach of duty as in negligence. As a result, finding consistency in application of principles, and coherence, in its development has been difficult. The relationship that nuisance has with both *Rylands v Fletcher*, negligence and human rights claims make it difficult for nuisance to be a clear, independent and transparent cause of action and therefore lacks the predictability that claimants, or even commentators would like. However with the interests of balancing the freedom of others, as well as the economic necessity of developing unused land, such inconsistency is likely to continue.

INTRODUCTION

Questions on *Rylands v Fletcher* (1868) as mentioned in the previous chapter are often intertwined with elements of negligence and nuisance. There are also some grey and undecided areas of the law, making it amenable to an essay question, and this chapter contains one, alongside two problem questions. Similar to nuisance where there is scope for a brief discussion of any claim under the **Human Rights Act 1998**, then you should make reference to it.

Checklist
Students must be familiar with the following areas:
(a) the elements of the rule itself, with special reference to: ■ the non-natural user requirement;   ■ the decision of the House of Lords in *Transco v Stockport MBC* (2004);   (b) defences, and especially the independent acts of third parties.

QUESTION 33

Delta Manufacturing plc owns and operates a factory situated on an industrial estate on the outskirts of a small town. One day, the environmental control system malfunctioned for some unknown reason and large quantities of toxic fumes were emitted. These fumes damaged paintwork on some houses in the town and some inhabitants also suffered an allergic reaction to the fumes. As a result of the adverse publicity, the town has seen a reduction in its normal tourist trade and the local shopkeepers are complaining of loss of business.

▶ Advise Delta Manufacturing plc of any liability that it might have incurred. Would your advice differ if Delta operated its factory under statutory authority?

How to Read this Question

It is important in answering this question to consider the possible causes of action in detail, paying particular attention to *Rylands v Fletcher* (1868) and nuisance, and the possibility of a negligence action. Therefore be sure to highlight the most relevant facts including this was an emission on apparently an isolated day for an unknown reason, and that it has caused various types of harm, physical, property and economic. As the question suggests the defence of statutory authority must also be considered for these actions.

How to Answer this Question

The following points need to be discussed:

- ❖ the ingredients of *Rylands v Fletcher* (1868), with special reference to non-natural use;
- ❖ the recoverability for property;
- ❖ the possibility of a claim in private or public nuisance;
- ❖ negligence and the problem of proof of breach of duty;
- ❖ statutory authority as a defence to the above actions;
- ❖ action under the **Human Rights Act 1998**.

Applying the Law

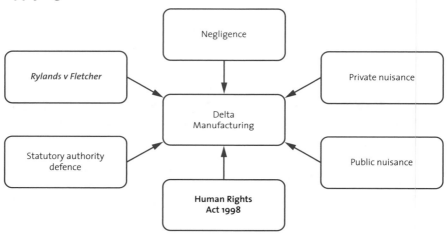

ANSWER

The rule in *Rylands v Fletcher* (1868), states that a 'person who, for his own purposes, brings onto his lands and collects and keeps there anything likely to do mischief if it escapes must keep it in at his peril, and if he does not do so, he is *prima facie* answerable for all the damage which is the natural consequence of its escape'. In addition, the defendant must have made a 'non-natural' use of his land and the harm caused must be foreseeable (*Cambridge Water Co v Eastern Counties Leather plc* (1994)).[1]

The fumes have been brought on to Delta's land for Delta's purposes. They have been brought on to Delta's land in the sense that they are not something that is there by nature, such as thistles (*Giles v Walker* (1890)) or rainwater (*Smith v Kenrick* (1849)). The toxic fumes are clearly likely to do mischief if they escape and there has been an escape from Delta's premises, as required by *Read v Lyons* (1947). As it is foreseeable that the fumes would cause harm, we must determine whether or not there has been a non-natural use of land, an

---

1 When dealing with *Rylands v Fletcher*, it is advisable to be able to quote the exact words used in the original judgment, as here. The elements of the tort can then be systematically addressed.

aspect that has given rise to much confusion. In *Rylands* itself, the word 'natural' was used to mean something on the land by nature, but later cases have construed the word as meaning 'ordinary' or usual. In *Transco*, Lord Bingham confirmed that it was necessary to show that the defendant had brought on to or kept on his land an exceptionally dangerous or mischievous thing in extraordinary or unusual circumstances, which Delta has likely satisfied.[2]

Thus the houseowners could recover for damage to their paintwork but not the personal injury of their allergic reactions (*Rylands*; *Transco*). If any person suffered personal injury but had no interest in land, that lack of interest would itself rule out an action in *Rylands* (*McKenna v British Aluminium Ltd* (2002)). The local shopkeepers have suffered economic loss and, despite *Weller v Foot and Mouth Disease Research Institute* (1965), there seems to be no clear authority for recovery on their part, but the general tenor of *Cambridge Water Co* is against such recovery.

The house owners or tenants recovering for the damage to their paintwork could seek a claim in nuisance assuming they have an interest in the land affected (*Malone v Laskey* (1907)) though similarly they will be unable to claim for the allergic reactions as actions for personal injury should not be brought in nuisance. As this involves damage to property, the character of the neighbourhood is not a relevant factor in judging whether there is an unreasonable interference (*St Helen's Smelting Co v Tipping* (1865)).

An action in public nuisance may also lie against Delta. Here, the claimant will have to show that the nuisance affected a section of the public (*AG v PYA Quarries* (1957)) and that he suffered damage over and above that suffered by the public at large. The advantage to claimants in public nuisance is that no interest in land is required and both personal injury and economic loss are recoverable (*Rose v Miles* (1815)). Thus, those persons with no interest in land could sue in respect of the allergic reaction, which would constitute special damage, as could the shopkeepers.

Also, Delta may be liable in negligence. There would be no difficulty in showing the existence of a duty of care and causation, but breach may prove problematic, as we are told that the emission occurred for an unknown reason. If Delta could show that it had in place a proper system of inspection and control (*Henderson v Jenkins and Sons* (1970)), this could be sufficient to negate liability, perhaps in order to disprove a *res ipsa loquitur* assumption. If negligence could be proved against Delta, then of course any claimant who has suffered damage to property or to the person may sue, but the shopkeepers would be unable to recover for their economic loss, as the chances of a claimant now successfully relying on *Junior Books v Veitchi* (1983) seem non-existent.

If the factory had been operated under statutory authority, liability would not arise either under *Rylands* or nuisance unless negligence on the part of Delta could be shown

....

2　The key issue of a case on *Rylands v Fletcher* is often likely to be whether the use of the land is 'non-natural' or not 'ordinary'.

(*Green v Chelsea Waterworks* (1894); *Allen v Gulf Oil Refining* (1981)). However, in *Barr v Biffa Waste Services* (2012) the Court of Appeal held that, short of express or implied statutory authority to actually commit a nuisance, there is no basis for using a statutory scheme (here granting of a Waste Permit) to cut down private law rights, and the claimants did not have to demonstrate negligence. Carnworth LJ stated that the 'fundamental principles [of nuisance] were settled by the end of the 19th century and have remained resilient and effective since then'.

Finally, we must consider any causes of action that might arise under the **Human Rights Act 1998**. **Article 8** of the **European Convention on Human Rights**, brought into UK law by **s1** of the **1998 Act**, establishes the right to respect for private and family life. An action under the **Human Rights Act 1998** would raise no problems as regards interest and thus there would be scope for a greater range of persons to recover for both economic and personal injury losses, however the damages available are restricted (*Dobson v Thames Water (No 2)* (2011)).

In *López Ostra v Spain* (1995), it was held that the construction of a waste treatment plant next to the applicant's house, which had caused local pollution and health problems, was a violation of **Art 8**. In this case, the Spanish government did not own the plant, but it was held to be sufficient that the local authority had allowed it to be built on their land and the government had subsidised it. As **s6(1)** of the **1998 Act** makes it unlawful for a public authority to act in a way incompatible with a **Convention** right and by **s6(6)** an 'act' includes a failure to act, both the UK government and local authorities could be held liable for breaches of **Art 8**. **Article 8** has been held to cover toxic emissions from a factory (*Guerra v Italy* (1998)). Clearly therefore the emissions from Delta's factory could fall within **Art 8** and even **Art 2** if the emissions are sufficiently hazardous and if state authorities had not complied with their duty.

QUESTION 34

'Although the rule in *Rylands v Fletcher* has been subject to recent judicial scrutiny, there still remain areas of uncertainty and it is doubtful if it adds anything to existing English law.'

▶ Discuss the above statement.

How to read this Question

This is a general essay question in terms of wording insofar it provides a platform to discuss the uncertainty and difficulties in the interpretation of the rule and as reflected in the case law. The second half of the sentence is requiring you to consider what more the rule in *Rylands* adds, beyond the protection provided in nuisance. In this way you will need a firm grasp of the law and principles of each including a firm grasp of authorities such as *Northumbrian Water v Sir Robert McAlpine* (2014), *Hunter v Canary Wharf* (1997) and *Transco v Stockport Metropolitan Borough Council* (2004).

How to Answer this Question

The following aspects need to be discussed:

- ❖ the ingredients of an action in *Rylands*;
- ❖ the similarity with an action in nuisance;
- ❖ the problems raised by the requirement in *Rylands* for an escape and non-natural use;
- ❖ other actions that may reinforce *Rylands*, for example negligence.

Answer Structure

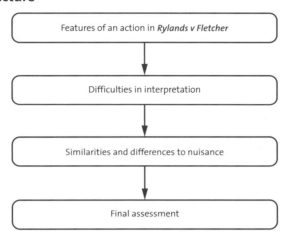

Features of an action in **Rylands v Fletcher**

↓

Difficulties in interpretation

↓

Similarities and differences to nuisance

↓

Final assessment

Up for Debate

Much of the uncertainty about the rule in *Rylands v Fletcher* is concerned with its origins, scope and the varied challenges that are created in either maintaining a clear distinction with the tort of private nuisance or as is the case now, seeing the rule subsumed within the broader umbrella of nuisance. D Nolan, 'The distinctiveness of Rylands v Fletcher' (2005) 121 Law Quarterly Review 421 is well worth reading for a range of perspectives on the debate.

ANSWER

The rule in *Rylands v Fletcher* (1868), states that a 'person who, for his own purposes, brings onto his lands and collects and keeps there anything likely to do mischief if it escapes must keep it in at his peril, and if he does not do so, he is *prima facie* answerable for all the damage which is the natural consequence of its escape'. In addition, the defendant must have made a 'non-natural' use of his land and the harm caused must be foreseeable (*Cambridge Water Co v Eastern Counties Leather plc* (1994) and *Northumbrian Water v Sir Robert McAlpine* (2014)). Some of the dispute lies within the interpretation of some of the terms.

For example the original meaning of the phrase 'natural use' was something that was there naturally or by nature, but gradually the courts interpreted it to mean 'ordinary' or 'usual'. In *Rickards v Lothian* (1913), Lord Moulton stated: 'It must be some special use bringing with it increased danger to others, and must not merely be the ordinary use of land or such use as is proper for the general benefit of the community.' Although this was described in *Read* by Viscount Simon as 'of the first importance', it was criticised by the House of Lords in *Cambridge Water Co*. Lord Goff stated that the phrase 'ordinary use of land' was lacking in precision and that the alternative criterion, 'or such as is proper for the general benefit of the community', introduced doubt and might not keep what is permitted within reasonable bounds. In *Transco*, the House of Lords considered in detail the non-natural requirement. Lord Bingham stated that the ordinary use test is to be preferred to the natural use test, as this makes it clear that *Rylands* only applies where the use of land is extraordinary and unusual. Lord Bingham doubted that a test of reasonable use was helpful since a use may be out of the ordinary but reasonable: for example, the storage of chemicals on industrial premises, as in *Cambridge Water*. It was also doubted that Lord Moulton's criterion of whether the use is proper for the general benefit of the community was helpful, echoing the criticism of this phrase by Lord Goff in *Cambridge*. Thus, Lord Bingham stated that it is necessary to show that the defendant had brought an exceptionally dangerous or mischievous thing in extraordinary or unusual circumstances.

The question of whether it adds anything to the existing state of the law, is dependent on its overlap with the law of nuisance; indeed, the House of Lords in *Cambridge Water Co v Eastern Counties Leather plc* (1994) held that the rule in *Rylands* is basically the law of nuisance extended to cover an isolated escape and thus the claimants must have a proprietary interest in the land affected (*McKenna v British Aluminium* (2002)).

Nuisance may be defined as an unreasonable interference with a person's use or enjoyment of land, or some right over it or in connection with it. It does not require an accumulation, as it applies, for example, to noise, and it applies to both dangerous and non-dangerous things. The relevance of the thing being dangerous is as to whether the defendant has made a reasonable use of his land. Nuisance differs from *Rylands*: in *Rylands*, there are defined ingredients to the tort; in nuisance, there are guidelines as to whether the interference with the claimant's land was unreasonable. Thus, in nuisance, the court will take into account the duration of the interference, whether it was of a temporary nature and whether it was an isolated event. It was held in *Bolton v Stone* (1951) that an isolated happening could not constitute a nuisance, whereas in *Cambridge Water Co*, it was held that such an isolated event could found an action under *Rylands*.

By the very nature of nuisance, the thing, be it noise or a physical thing, must escape from the defendant's land. Also in nuisance, there is no requirement that the defendant be the owner of the land, mere control being sufficient. There is no requirement in nuisance that there is a non-natural use of the land, only that it is unreasonable. It is, of course, possible that a natural use of land will be unreasonable due to (say) the presence of malice on the part of the defendant (*Hollywood Silver Fox Farm v Emmett* (1936)). In both torts, foreseeability of damage is required and neither of these torts covers personal injuries.

In many situations the two causes of action of Rylands and nuisance will coexist. *Rylands* does, however, fill one gap in the law, in that it does apply to an isolated event whereas nuisance does not. It has also been held that nuisance does not cover interference with purely recreational matters (*Bridlington Relay v Yorkshire Electricity Board* (1965)), whereas this restriction does not apply to *Rylands*.[3]

It could thus be said that, in practice, the majority of cases in which *Rylands* applies will also give rise to causes of action in nuisance and possibly other torts such as negligence. However, *Rylands* does cover some areas that other torts do not cover, such as the isolated event, which is not covered in nuisance, and the isolated event caused by the action of an independent contractor, which would be covered in neither nuisance nor negligence. In the case of *LMS International Ltd v Styrene Packaging Ltd* (2005), a *Rylands* action was successfully brought against a defendant in circumstances under which a fire spread from one industrial unit to another.

It can also be seen that recent cases have brought an element of certainty into the law regarding *Rylands*. It is now clear that foreseeability of damage is an essential ingredient, as is an interest in land, and that judicial opinion considers that *Rylands* is not applicable to personal injuries. However, the discussion of the phrase 'natural use' in *Transco* and the use of the phrase 'extraordinary and unusual' use has caused its own interpretation difficulties. It would appear to be more coherent to subsume *Rylands* under a broader nuisance legal umbrella, given the frequency with which they can be claimed together and allow for a more united incremental development of the law.[4]

QUESTION 35

One evening, Henry lights a bonfire in his garden in order to burn some garden rubbish. The smoke and smell from the bonfire annoy his neighbours, who are watching television with the windows open, and sparks from the fire damage some clothing that one of his neighbours has hung out in his garden to dry. The smoke from the bonfire drifts on to the road and is so thick that it obstructs the vision of a passing motorist who, as a result, runs into a lamp post. Henry goes indoors to listen to the radio and, some time later, the bonfire spreads to his neighbour's property, destroying a garden shed.

▶ **Advise Henry of his legal liability.**

How to Read this Question

This is another question demonstrating the relationship between nuisance, an action in *Rylands v Fletcher* (1868) and the liability Henry might incur in negligence as well as under the special rules that govern fires. Therefore ensure your answer adopts broad coverage of these areas.

---

3 When answering an essay question, the actual question set should be borne in mind and addressed throughout the answer, so here an emphasis on the unique properties of the tort addressing the issue of whether it 'add(s) anything to the existing law'.

4 This addresses the question set, as to how/why the situation is still uncertain thereby using similar terminology as used in the statement. It is important that conclusions to essays do that which will neatly tie up your arguments.

How to Answer this Question

The following points need to be discussed:

- ❖   liability in nuisance for the smoke and smell, and clothing;
- ❖   liability in negligence;
- ❖   the possibility of liability under *Rylands v Fletcher* (1868);
- ❖   liability for the fire damage.

Applying the Law

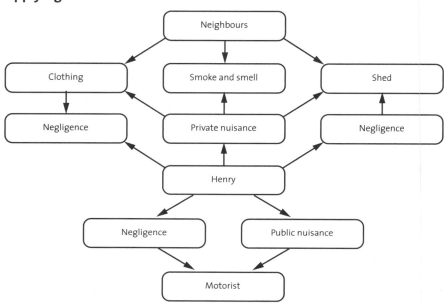

ANSWER

Concerning the smoke and the smell from the bonfire, an action may lie in nuisance which is an unreasonable interference with a person's use or enjoyment of land, or of some right over or in connection with it. However, not all interference will necessarily give rise to liability: the harm must be foreseeable (*Cambridge Water Co v Eastern Counties Leather plc* (1994); *Northumbrian Water v Sir Robert McAlpine* (2014)), and the interference must be substantial and not merely fanciful (*Walter v Selfe* (1851)). In deciding whether a particular interference is unreasonable or not, the court will rely on a series of guidelines. In Henry's case, the court would consider the duration of the interference, as the shorter the duration of the interference, the less likely it is to be unreasonable, as in *Harrison v Southwark and Vauxhall Water Co* (1891). In *Bolton v Stone* (1951), it was stated that a nuisance must be a state of affairs, however temporary, and not merely an isolated happening. Thus, although Henry might claim that the bonfire is an isolated event or it is lit on rare occasions, it does appear to be a temporary state of affairs and is capable in law of being a nuisance, and the fact that he may argue is a reasonable use of the land is not, of itself, a valid defence in nuisance (*AG v Cole* (1901); *Vanderpant v Mayfair Hotel* (1930)).

As regards any interference with health and comfort, or 'amenity' damage, the court will take into account the character of the neighbourhood, as 'what would be a nuisance in Belgravia Square would not necessarily be so in Bermondsey' (*Sturges v Bridgman* (1879)).[5] Thus, if Henry lives in a suburban or rural area, the occasional lighting of a bonfire might not constitute a nuisance, as there must be an element of give and take between neighbours. However, if Henry by his lack of care allowed an annoyance from the bonfire to become excessive, he would become liable in nuisance (*Andreae v Selfridge and Co* (1938)) and the overall judgment will depend on whether the interference is unreasonable. Note also the interference here is not purely recreational such as a television reception (*Bridlington Relay v Yorkshire Electricity Board* (1965)) but rather with their enjoyment of their property whilst merely sat with windows open and watching TV, and they cannot do this without the discomfort from the smoke and smell of Henry's bonfire.[6]

As nuisance protects a person's use or enjoyment of land, then traditionally only those neighbours with an interest in the land can sue (*Malone v Laskey* (1907)) and confirmed by *Hunter v Canary Wharf Ltd* (1997) in the House of Lords. Thus, only those neighbours with an interest in the property affected (for example, house owners or tenants) can sue, and not merely members of their families or guests, though there may be some more limited scope for them to claim under the **Human Rights Act 1998** for a breach of **Art 8**.

In relation to the physical damage to the clothing, the character of the neighbourhood is not relevant (*St Helen's Smelting Co v Tipping* (1865)) and a court would be far more likely to find that an interference is unreasonable where physical damage to property has occurred. Even if the bonfire did not originally constitute a nuisance, Henry's lack of care in allowing the interference to become unreasonable would make him liable (*Andreae*). It therefore seems likely that Henry would be liable for the damage to his neighbour's clothing.

Henry could also incur liability for the damage to his neighbour's clothing in negligence. Henry will owe his neighbour a duty of care under normal *Donoghue v Stevenson* (1932) principles and he has not acted as a reasonable person would and so could be in breach of his duty (*Blyth v Birmingham Waterworks* (1856)). The 'but for' test of Lord Denning in *Cork v Kirby MacLean* (1952) shows the required causal connection. Finally, the type of damage suffered by the neighbour is not too remote as it is reasonably foreseeable (*The Wagon Mound (No 1)* (1961)). Thus, Henry could be liable for the damage to the clothing in negligence.

As regards the passing motorist, he could not sue Henry in nuisance, as he has no interest in the land. He may be able to sue Henry in negligence, as the required elements of duty, breach and damage appear to be present. The motorist though may also have a cause of action in public nuisance, in that Henry has created a danger close to the highway (*Tarry v Ashton* (1876); *Castle v St Augustine's Links* (1922)).

....

5   Again this quote, adequately recalled, is almost always useful in a nuisance answer.
6   Noting this distinction allows you to express your understanding of both the scope of the ruling on TV reception interference and the interpretation of amenity rights. By the same process, it also demonstrates you have closely scrutinised the question and made appropriate legal conclusions.

In relation to the liability for the fire and the damage that it has caused to the garden shed liability is very difficult to found on the basis of *Rylands* because the 'thing' has not escaped from the defendant's land. This was confirmed in *Stannard v Robert Raymond Harvey Gore* (2012), and thus if the fire was accidental a defence under **s 86** of the **Fires Prevention (Metropolis) Act 1774** is provided. Instead, and as Henry started his fire deliberately, he may be liable only where it was a non-natural use, though starting a bonfire to burn rubbish is not instantly a non-natural use whereby he brought or kept on his land an exceptionally dangerous or mischievous thing in extraordinary or unusual circumstances (see further *Stannard* for a thorough review of *Rylands* in fire cases). There may be some liability under common law liability for fire, which is slightly adapted from the rule in *Rylands* as determined in *LMS International Ltd v Styrene Packaging Ltd* (2005).

In addition, Henry could also incur liability at common law in nuisance, as the fire has damaged his neighbour's property (*Goldman v Hargrave* (1967)), assuming that his neighbour has the necessary interest in the land. Liability could also attach in negligence, as there is no problem in establishing the key elements and, by leaving the fire to go indoors and listen to the radio, Henry has failed to take reasonable care to prevent the fire from causing damage (*Musgrove v Pandelis* (1919); *Ogwo v Taylor* (1987)).

Thus, Henry should be advised that he will be liable for the damage to the clothing and to the shed, and for the damage suffered by the motorist.

Aim Higher

Being aware of some of the recent debates *Rylands* will really develop your critical awareness of the law. The recent Court of Appeal decision in *Stannard v Robert Raymond Harvey Gore* (2012) is worth reading for its overview of the relationship between fire and the rule in *Rylands*, as is the article by J Steele and R Merkin 'Insurance between neighbours: Stannard v Gore and common law liability for fire' (2013) 25(2) Journal of Environmental Law 305. Similarly reading Lord Hoffmann's speech in *Transco* will help you fully grasp the interpretation of 'non-natural use'.

Common Pitfalls

One of the most challenging aspects of the rule in *Rylands* is the relationship between the rule and actions in both nuisance and negligence. It will often warrant very good exam technique in not over-developing your discussion and then running out of time. You must focus on developing the select and more important things and applying them as a result. Some of the rules can be quite technical so it is important to know precise and concise definitions.

11 Trespass to the Person, to Land and to Goods

INTRODUCTION

Trespass is an area that may be tested by the examiner either in its own right or as part of a question, mostly involving occupiers' liability or nuisance. They are contained torts and there have been a number of developments in the law of trespass, such as hostile touching, trespass to airspace and false imprisonment which may be worthy of discussion. This chapter contains, first, two problem questions followed by an essay question. Despite the overlap in principles a common mistake to be found is a confusing inclusion of criminal liability cases when discussing the torts. Please ensure that you do not do this unless such principles are directly applicable as in relation to 'arrest'.

Checklist
Students must be familiar with the following areas:
(a) the definition and elements of, and defences to, assault;
(b) the definition and elements of, and defences to, false imprisonment;
(c) the rule in *Wilkinson v Downton* (1897);
(d) the definition and elements of, and defences to, trespass to land and especially trespass to airspace;
(e) the definition and elements of, and defences to, trespass to goods, and in particular title to lost goods and the allowance for improvement of goods.

QUESTION 36

Arthur, who had been drinking heavily, entered Billie's pizzeria to buy a takeaway pizza. Billie took the order and requested payment. Arthur then discovered that he did not have the money to pay for the pizza and so Billie asked him to leave. Arthur picked up a chair and waved it above his head, shouting 'Give me the pizza'. Billie retreated to the back of the shop, scared and unable to escape. After five minutes or so of Arthur waving the chair and ranting, Chris the delivery driver returned, having made a delivery. Seeing Arthur, he said, 'Okay mate, put down the chair, eh?', and took a step towards him, holding out his hand. Arthur swung the chair at Chris, hitting him and cutting his arm. Chris wrestled the chair from Arthur, smashed it over Arthur's head and then ran out of the door to get help.

Hearing the commotion, Daisy, a passerby, assumed that the pizzeria was being robbed. She tripped Chris, who hit his head on the pavement and was knocked semi-conscious. Daisy then sat on Chris and called the police on her mobile phone. Billie, meanwhile, grabbed a pizza slicing wheel and approached Arthur. She said: 'If you don't leave now I'm going to slice you with this.' Arthur fled the pizzeria.

▶ Advise the parties as to their liabilities and remedies in tort.

How to Read this Question

The rather unfortunate set of circumstances involves many tort issues concerning assault, battery and false imprisonment. There are also potential discussions of defences that might apply, for example self-defence, or illegality. Ensure you have a clear structure that is coherent, and you consider the liability of the parties individually.

How to Answer this Question

The answer should contain, at least, a consideration of the following potential areas of liability:

❖ the status of Arthur as a trespasser;
❖ the assault by Arthur (and Billie);
❖ the battery by Arthur, Chris and Daisy;
❖ the false imprisonment by Arthur and Daisy;
❖ any possible defences?

Applying the Law

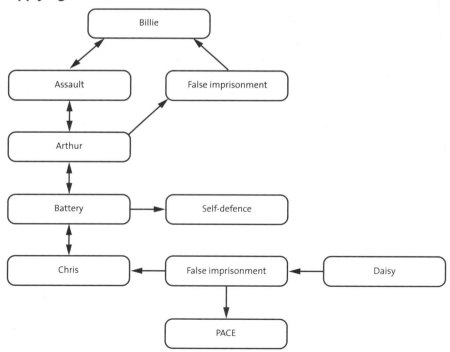

ANSWER[1]

Arthur

When Arthur entered the premises, he was a lawful visitor under a bare licence to enter, be on the premises to make a purchase or communicate (see, for example, *Robson v Hallett* (1967)), but at the point that Billie asked him to leave and he refused his licence to be present had been revoked (*Stone v Taffe* (1974)).

In picking up the chair and shouting at Billie, Arthur is clearly committing an assault. An assault can be defined as conduct that makes the claimant have reasonable apprehension of an immediate battery (application of force) or the threat to commit a battery. The immediacy of the threatened battery is relevant. Willes J in *Osborn v Veitch* (1858) noted that immediate in this context meant 'a present ability of doing the act threatened, for it can be done in an instant'.[2] Although the fear must be reasonably held, the claimant must also have a reasonable belief that the battery is able to be and will be committed (*Thomas v NUM (South Wales)* (1985)). In this case, while Arthur has not expressly stated that he will do anything to Billie, the threatening nature of his behaviour would suggest that Billie could reasonably believe that Arthur would apply some force to her and was sufficiently close for this to be an immediate application. It is highly probable in this situation that Arthur has committed an assault.

Arthur is also likely to have committed false imprisonment when Billie remained at the rear of the premises. False imprisonment requires that the defendant directly and intentionally confines the claimant without the claimant's consent or without other lawful excuse. It does not matter how long the confinement is, so long as it is total (*Bird v Jones* (1845)) (see also *R v Bournewood Community and Mental Health NHS Trust* (1998) and *HL v United Kingdom* (2005)). There is no lawful excuse that Arthur (including his intoxicated state) could rely on.

In relation to Arthur hitting Chris with the chair, it would appear that he has committed a battery. A battery is a direct (*Reynolds v Clarke* (1725)) and intentional (see *Letang v Cooper* (1964)) application of force to which the claimant does not consent and it can be committed indirectly for example throwing an object. Case law has suggested that the touching should be of a malicious or hostile character (*Wilson v Pringle* (1986); see also *F v West Berkshire Health Authority* (1989)), rather than, for example, constituting horseplay. Chris did not consent to being hit with the chair and Arthur's behaviour could not be described as anything other than hostile. The magnitude or full consequence of the injury suffered by Chris does not have to have been intended by Arthur, as battery requires only that the act itself was intentional.

Chris

The fact that Chris then responded with violence himself could similarly amount to a battery on Arthur. However on pleading self-defence he is entitled to use force to defend

---

1   This is a complex question that needs careful planning (see diagram). Time spent planning a problem question will not be wasted, as it will help to ensure a logical structure to the answer.

2   Use of a brief quote in an answer will add to the overall impression created that you have thorough and in depth knowledge of the law and are able to use such knowledge concisely to highlight principles or concepts.

himself, property or another person such as a response to a perceived threat of battery. The defence exists alongside s3 of the **Criminal Law Act 1967**. The person must honestly believe that force is necessary and then use only such force as is reasonable. The burden of proving the defence falls on the defendant who claims it, with the defendant having to prove an honest belief of a threat of imminent attack; and that the belief was reasonable (*Ashley v Chief Constable of Sussex Police* (2008)). In this case Chris would likely be able to satisfy this burden given the chair was being waved aggressively.

What is reasonable force will depend upon the circumstances but must be proportionate in relation to the threat (*Turner v MGM* (1950)). Given actual violence was perpetrated against Chris his response of wrestling and striking Arthur's head may be deemed reasonable and proportionate given the context of the facts (see comparatively *Cross v Kirkby* (2000) and *Lane v Holloway* (1968)). *Cross* also confirmed that the defence of *ex turpi causa* may also apply in cases of battery as a means to avoid any liability to Arthur for striking him with the chair.

Daisy

Daisy's actions in relation to Chris would almost certainly constitute battery. Her trip was a direct application of force and was unarguably of a hostile character. It is irrelevant that she made a mistake as to the nature of what Chris was doing. Daisy may also be liable for false imprisonment. She is undoubtedly restraining Chris's movement. Chris's imprisonment as such is both intentional and direct (see, for example, *Sayers v Harlow UDC* (1958)). Chris is described as being 'semi-conscious' and so may not be fully aware of the fact that his movement is being restricted but persons need not be aware of their 'confinement' for the tort to be made out (see Lord Atkin's statement in *Meering v Graham White Engineering* (1919) and *Murray v Ministry of Defence* (1988)). It is presumed, however, that if a person were unaware of their false imprisonment, any damages award would be nominal. Taking the above into consideration, it would seem that Daisy has falsely imprisoned Chris, and so he would be able to maintain an action against her for both battery and false imprisonment.

A defence does exist in limited circumstances under the **Police and Criminal Evidence Act (PACE) 1984**, which permits a citizen a limited power of arrest. **Section 24A** of that Act limits this power of arrest where a person knows or reasonably suspects that an indictable offence has been or is being committed. A further limitation restricts non-police action in arrests to situations in which the person reasonably believes that the intervention is necessary to prevent any of the situations in s24A(4) occurring. Daisy may claim that she reasonably suspected a robbery (an indictable offence) and that she reasonably believed that she was preventing Chris from absconding. This would be a determination for a court on the evidence.

Billie

The final consideration relates to Billie. By brandishing a weapon in the direction of Arthur and given the course of events to this point, it might well be that she is committing an assault. Arthur may well have a reasonable apprehension that he is about to be on the receiving end of a battery; however as Billie has made the threat conditional on Arthur leaving, by stating that, 'if you don't leave now', then such a conditional threat may nullify the threat of a battery, as in the classic case of *Tuberville v Savage* (1669).

Common Pitfalls

Do not forget that all trespasses require some 'direct' interference, but that trespass to the person and land differ in terms of whether they are capable of being able to be committed negligently. Ensure you fully grasp and apply any defences to your discussion.

QUESTION 37

Oliver is employed as a salesman. He is calling on Peter's shop to sell them some office stationery, when he sees a gold watch on the pavement outside. He picks it up and hands it to Peter, who takes his name and address. Some three months later, Oliver is passing Peter's shop, when he sees the watch in the window for sale. Oliver goes in and takes the watch from the window, but Peter grabs the watch from Oliver and there is a scuffle in which Oliver is injured.

▶ Advise Oliver. Would your advice differ if Oliver had found the watch behind the counter of Peter's shop?

How to Read this Question

This is a question of title to lost goods and also involves an element of trespass to the person. Notice the salient facts including where the watch is found originally and the distinction you are asked to draw if the watch is found behind the counter of Peter's shop.

How to Answer this Question

The following points need to be discussed:

❖ Oliver's right to the watch as against Peter's;
❖ rules regarding supervening possession;
❖ necessary intention present in non-public part of shop;
❖ any effect of Oliver being a trespasser.

Applying the Law

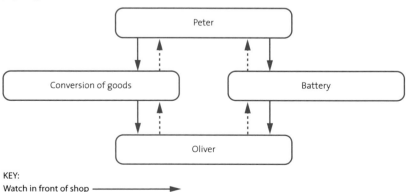

KEY:
Watch in front of shop ——————▶
Watch behind counter - - - - - - - - - - ▶

ANSWER

Oliver will wish to sue Peter for conversion of the watch and for trespass to the person.

Conversion has been defined as being 'committed wherever one person performs a positive wrongful act of dealing with goods in a manner inconsistent with the rights of the owner' (*Maynegrain v Campafina Bank* (1984), per Lord Templeman).[3] The tort is limited to tangible goods and does not apply to 'choses in action', as determined in *OBG Ltd v Allen* (2005). The tort is one of strict liability, in that, provided that the defendant intends to deal with the goods in a manner that is inconsistent with the rights of the owner (or someone with a superior right to the goods), the fact that the defendant is ignorant of these rights is no defence. So, for example, the innocent purchaser from a thief of stolen goods commits a conversion against the owner (*Moorgate Mercantile v Twitchings* (1977)). Hence, it follows that Peter has committed a conversion of the watch in offering it for sale, i.e. dealing with it as if holding the rights of the owner.

To sue in conversion, Oliver must show that he had the right to possession (*Marquess of Bute v Barclays Bank* (1955)). The owner of the watch, of course, remains the owner but, as he has not claimed his property, the normal rule is that the finder – that is, Oliver in our case – has a right to it against everyone except the true owner, if he has reduced the goods into his possession. Thus, in *Armory v Delamirie* (1721), the finder of a jewel was held to be able to recover it from a jeweller to whom it had been handed and who refused to return it.

All of this, however, assumes that the finder was the first person to reduce the goods into his possession and the possession counts as title (*The Winkfield* (1902)). However, we must decide whether someone other than Oliver had obtained earlier possession of the goods when Oliver found them, in which case, that person and not Oliver has the right to the goods. This can occur in two ways. First, if an employee finds goods in the course of his employment, the employee's possession is deemed to be that of his employer and the employee gains no possessory right against his employer (*Parker v British Airways Board* (1982)). The important element here is that the goods must be found in the course of employment – that is, the employment must be the cause of the finding of the goods and not merely the occasion of the finding of the goods (*Byrne v Hoare* (1965)). We are told that Oliver is a salesman and that he calls on Peter's shop to sell some stationery. Oliver was undoubtedly going about his employer's business when he found the watch, but it seems that Oliver's employment was the occasion of him finding the watch, rather than the cause, and so it is submitted that Oliver's employer does not have a right of possession to the watch.[4]

Second, if goods are found on land not occupied by the finder, in certain situations, the occupier's 'occupation' will confer upon him a possession of the lost goods, which is

---

3 It is always good practice to quote a definition supported with the use of legal authority, e.g. a judge and a case.

4 Although it is relatively easy to show that Peter is liable in conversion, it is more complex to argue in support of Oliver's right to the watch.

earlier in time than the finder and this previous possession can exist even though the occupier was unaware of the presence of the lost goods on his land. Such earlier possession will arise where the goods are buried on the land or attached to the land in such a manner as to suggest that the occupier is exerting exclusive control over the relevant area (*South Staffordshire Water Co v Sharman* (1896) and *Waverley BC v Fletcher* (1995)). Where the goods are found only lying on the premises and the public have access to the premises, the finder generally has a superior right to the occupier (*Bridges v Hawkesworth* (1851); *Hannah v Peel* (1945)), unless the occupier has 'manifested an intention to exercise control over the building and things which may be in or on it' (*Parker v British Airways Board* (1982), per Donaldson MR). In *Bridges*, the finder of some cash in a shop was held to be entitled to it as against the shop owner and the more modern case of *Parker* shows that the required intention is not easy to establish. In *Parker*, the finder of a bracelet in an airport lounge was held to be entitled to it as against the occupiers of the lounge. Thus, the weight of authority would allow Oliver a superior right to the watch as against Peter. By s3 of the **Torts (Interference with Goods) Act 1977**, Oliver may obtain a court order for the delivery of the watch, or the alternative of damages.

As Oliver is entitled to the watch, he is entitled to recover it from Peter using reasonable force if necessary to protect his property. As Peter has directly and intentionally applied hostile touching to Oliver's person, Oliver can sue Peter in battery (*Wilson v Pringle* (1987)) and in assault, if he was first put in reasonable fear of immediate physical contact.

If the watch was found behind the counter,[5] Peter will find it easier to establish the intention described in *Parker*, as it would be easier to show that Peter intended to exercise control of the area behind the counter and any things in it. In addition, if Oliver was trespassing when he went behind the counter, as it was not part of the premises to which he was invited (*The Calgarth* (1927)), then, as a trespasser, he would acquire no rights as against the occupier (*Parker*).

It seems likely that Peter did demonstrate the required intention in respect of the area behind the counter. Thus, he has a right to the goods as against Oliver and, when Oliver removed the watch from the window, Oliver was committing a conversion of the goods. Peter was entitled, therefore, to use reasonable force to protect his property, and he would be able to sue Oliver in battery and possibly assault as regards the ensuing struggle.

QUESTION 38

Critically assess the contribution made by the **Protection from Harassment Act 1997** to the existing common law landscape for trespass to the person.

---

5 When a question asks 'will your advice differ if …?' it almost always will, so do not overlook this part of the answer, as it gives you the opportunity to display further relevant knowledge.

How to Read this Question

This is a question that focuses on the effect of the 1997 statute to compensate for claims that were not recognised by the prior state of the common law. Due focus on the provision of the statute is required in outlining its effectiveness as well as the case law that underpins it. You should evaluate in which contexts the offence has been used, what it adds but also what it might limit or replace in the common law. Referring to the broad relationship the Act makes to the overall range of intentional torts would also be required so ensure you consider this, perhaps towards the end of your answer.

How to Answer this Question

The following points need to be discussed

- ❖ definition of harassment under the Act;
- ❖ flexibility of conduct;
- ❖ intention and the number of occasions;
- ❖ the rule in *Wilkinson v Downton*;
- ❖ overall assessment.

Answer Structure

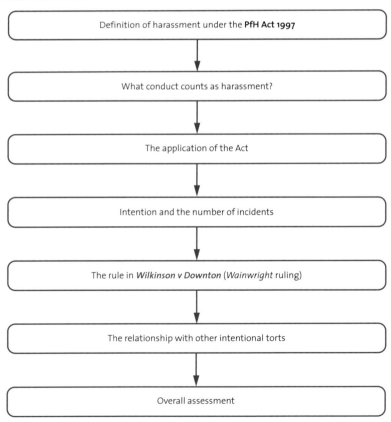

Definition of harassment under the **PfH Act 1997**

What conduct counts as harassment?

The application of the Act

Intention and the number of incidents

The rule in ***Wilkinson v Downton*** (*Wainwright* ruling)

The relationship with other intentional torts

Overall assessment

Up for Debate

Trespass to the person, land and to goods covers a very broad range of tortious conduct with statutory input as well as common law principles. Trespass to the person also shares some principles that would be found in the criminal law. Keeping with the torts of trespass to the person, recent debate has centred on the impact of the **Protection from Harassment Act 1997**, see for example K Patten, 'Defining harassment' (2010) 160 New Law Journal 331, and for a feminist critique see J Conaghan, 'Enhancing civil remedies for (sexual) harassment: s3 of the Protection from Harassment Act 1997' (1999) 7 Feminist Legal Studies 203. For early coverage of the broad principles of the intentional torts see FA Trindale, 'Intentional torts: some thoughts on assault or battery' (1982) 2 Oxford Journal of Legal Studies 211.

ANSWER

The **Protection from Harassment Act 1997** was introduced to tackle a broad range of conduct in particular stalking that may amount to harassment. The Act confirms it is a criminal offence, where an individual pursues a harassing course of conduct (including alarming the person or causing distress) which he knows or ought to know amounts to harassment of the other, and this is judged objectively (**s1**, **s2**, **s7**). Where harassment is made out it can confer a civil remedy of damages or an injunction as available under **s3** of the Act.

Despite the reference to alarm or distress in the Act, it is clear also from Lord Nicholls' comments in *Majrowski v Guy's and St Thomas's NHS Trust* (2007) that merely annoying, frustrating or upsetting behaviour cannot be sustained as harassment, but it must be of a sufficiently oppressive and unacceptable character. This is evidently done on a case by case basis as Baroness Hale confirmed in the same case that the definition of such harassment is not fixed and the courts are left to 'draw sensible lines between the ordinary banter and badinage of life and genuinely offensive and unacceptable behaviour'. Its flexibility is an advantage to claimants who may argue that they have been unduly victimised, however as academics like *Conaghan* argue a disproportionate focus on the conduct detracts from the focus that should be placed on the effect on the claimant's disposition.[6]

That the conduct is broad can also be seen in the case of *Thomas v News Group Newspapers* (2002) where persistent newspaper articles could amount to harassment, though where conduct is used to further freedom of expression, e.g. under **Art 10** of the **ECHR**, it is likely that a defendant would be able to offer a defence under **s1(3)** of the Act, that their conduct was reasonable, alongside other persons who may have legitimate reasons, e.g. debt collectors or salespersons. Similarly the Act has been stretched to apply in cases of workplace harassment, though it was confined to extraordinary circumstances in *Veakins*

6 Highlighting academic opinion is a good way of enhancing the critical analysis of your response and conveying wider reading to an examiner.

v Kier Islington (2009), and that the Act would not ordinarily sustain a claim, where negligence (despite the high threshold set in *Hatton v Sutherland* (2002)) would be the most appropriate cause of action.

Similarly the scope of the offence demonstrates that it imposes on the one hand a greater burden on the defendant than the other intentional torts such as battery and assault. Whereas the latter offences require intention (notwithstanding the difficulties posed in defining it in all cases, e.g. *Gibbon v Pepper* (1695)), or the acceptance of subjective recklessness as amounting to the necessary intent (*Iqbal v Prison Officers Association* (2009)), the necessary mental state for harassment can be identified through actual knowledge or knowledge objectively based on what a reasonable person would think, irrespective of what the defendant would think. In this sense the protection offered to claimants is far greater and onerous on the defendant. By contrast, there is some retained discretion by the court to judge the number of incidents of harassing conduct, whether they are of a similar type and the time apart they are (*James v DPP* (2009)). Such factors influence whether they can amount to a course of conduct, so the claimants cannot unduly claim harassment for isolated or one-off events

The effect of the Act may have been to enhance protection, but its introduction also appears to have finally put the nail in the coffin for the rule in *Wilkinson v Downton* (1897) which was expansive in its scope and was namely where the defendant had wilfully done an act calculated to cause physical harm to the claimant. This original rule, which would allow recovery for psychiatric injury, also carried uncertainty as to whether there was a need for express intent to cause such harm. The rule has now been somewhat relegated as an outdated precedent after *Wainwright v Home Office* (2003), where it was confirmed that at the very least negligence should be required to cause such harm, but, even if intention was present not all, intentionally caused psychiatric harm could give rise to liability. As Lord Hoffmann reasoned in *Wainwright* in workplaces people constantly say things with the intention of causing distress but litigation was not the answer. The requirement of a course of conduct (under the **Protection from Harassment Act 1997**) shows that isolated incidents need not require the law's intervention. As Lord Hoffmann made clear the scope of the rule in *Wilkinson* is even further limited given that the tort of negligence (though with restricted circumstances) now allows for the recovery for negligent infliction of psychiatric illness and given the judicial antipathy shown to the rule in *A v Hoare* (2006) and the effect of the **Protection from Harassment Act 1997**, the opportunity to revive this rule looks highly unlikely.

It is clear therefore that the **Protection from Harassment Act 1997** has added to the landscape of recovery in the law of trespass to the person. Where assault and battery are confined to instances of direct apprehension or application of immediate and direct force (see generally *Collins v Wilcock* (1984)) it was the effect of cases such as *R v Ireland* (1997) which created some legal and social impetus for the creation and justification of the Act, as such conduct as unwanted and harassing telephone calls was falling within legal loopholes and leaving the claimant without a remedy. Indeed recent debate suggests the Act could even be used to provide protection in cases of sustained cyber abuse or bullying via social media websites like Twitter. Though the Act has drawn criticism, it has recently been amended to introduce two new stalking related offences as found in the **Protection of Freedoms Act 2012**, demonstrating that the stricter rules of statutory interpretation will not always be adequate, and that different types of offending behaviour will require new legislation. The broad scope of the Act to cover a wide range of conduct and behaviour might be problematic for those arguing for greater coherence and certainty, at least in the criminal law. However in the civil courts it is likely that claimants will be likely to rely on its provisions, as in the workplace cases, to seek a remedy.

12 Defamation, Privacy and Human Rights

INTRODUCTION

The law on both defamation and privacy are arguably the most controversial and atten-tion-grabbing areas of tort, often fuelled by a series of high profile celebrity cases. It is an area of law perhaps inconsistently shaped by human rights considerations that seek a balance between freedom of expression and the respect for private and family life. The common law that previously developed in the law of defamation has regularly been labelled as the most draconian, with the persistent risk of a 'chilling effect' on democratic freedom of expression. Coupled with concerns of how to sue online pub-lishers, given the problem of internet archiving, as well as tackling the phenomenon that English law encouraged 'libel tourism', the law has now been transformed by the **Defamation Act 2013**. This chapter reflects the new Act through a problem question and one essay question. However given the Act has only recently been enforced, only time will tell how the courts interpret its provisions, with much of the previous common law still being relevant and at the very least highly persuasive. *To help with your under-standing of this area of law, there is an additional example of a problem question avail-able online.*

The impact of **Art 8** of the **ECHR** has also been present in non-defamatory contexts, con-cerning the publication of private information. The question of whether there is an emerging tort of privacy in English law, has been posed as the common law has grappled with finding a way to protect those harmed through the development of the equitable remedy of breach of confidence. All the while salacious celebrity scandals occupy news-paper columns, the desire to keep information private through super-injunctions, the effect of the internet and social media as well as developments such as the Leveson Inquiry all mingle to paint a complex legal and social picture of free expression, privacy and the limits of each. There is similarly both an essay question and a problem question which provides coverage of this area.

Finally both defamation and the law of privacy are perhaps the most prominent examples where the **Human Rights Act 1998** has had significant impact. The last essay question surveys some of its overall impact on tort common law.

QUESTION 39

Ian is a sports commentator for Eastland Television. He decides to make a programme on Eastleith Rovers, a local amateur football team that has reached a regional cup final. In the programme, there is a shot of the team in a public house with the comment from Ian: 'This is how the team prepares on Friday night for its cup final match on Saturday.' In fact, the scene was shot on a Saturday night after a previous game. This film also shows John, the centre-forward, eating a hamburger with the comment from Ian: 'As John is single, he has to do his own cooking so he eats out a lot.' John is in fact married to Jane, who is most upset at this comment.

Eastleith Rovers lose their cup final and Ian, in his post-match summary, states: 'They played appallingly badly, even by the standards of an amateur team.' The *Eastland Gazette* reviews the programme and match, repeats Ian's comments regarding the team playing badly and wonders whether this was due to John's poor diet.

▸ Advise John, Jane and Eastleith Rovers of any action they might have in defamation.

How to Read this Question

This is a wide-ranging question that covers some elements of innuendo, references to the claimant and republication. Always be sure to look closely at the content of what has been said and ask yourself questions such as who it has been said about, has it been published, is it true, is it fact or opinion etc. Follow a systematic structure using the **Defamation Act 2013** as a guide and apply the principles in a logical fashion. You need to be aware of the key sections of the statute to apply them concisely to the facts.

How to Answer this Question

The following points need to be discussed:

❖ whether the statement is libel or slander and actionable as likely to cause serious harm;
❖ whether the statement is defamatory, referred to the claimant and published;
❖ the defences of honest opinion, matter of public interest, or offer of amends;
❖ the republication by *Eastland Gazette*.

Applying the Law

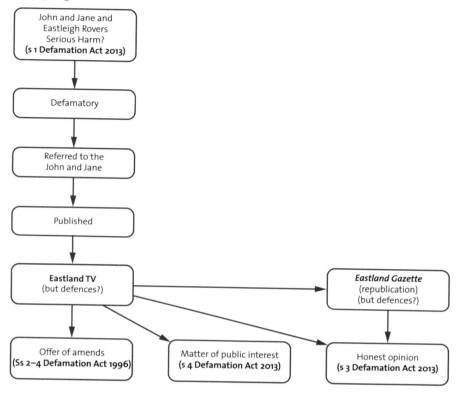

ANSWER

First, the statements made by Ian in the television programme are deemed to be publication in a permanent form by s1 of the **Defamation Act 1952**. They may constitute libel, however, under the provision of s1 of the **Defamation Act 2013**; a statement is only defamatory if the statement caused or is likely to cause serious harm. Being labelled as single when married and eating out a lot is not the most damning, thus it would be up to the judge to determine.[1]

Though the statement that John is single is not prima facie defamatory, when coupled with the true innuendo that John is married to Jane, the statement that he is single might lead people who know that he lives with Jane to assume that they are not in fact married (*Cassidy v Daily Mirror* (1929)). Thus, the statement could lower John in the estimation of right-thinking members of society generally (*Sim v Stretch* (1936); *Byrne v Deane* (1937)) or to expose him to hatred, contempt or ridicule (*Parmiter v Coupland* (1840)), though this would be a stretch.

....

1   The introductory paragraph identifies and introduces the relevant law which will be applied to the problem's facts.

Ian's statement concerning John obviously also carries the suggestion that Jane is living with John without being married to him, and thus defamatory to her. The fact that Jane not being referred to by Ian is no bar to her suing (*Morgan v Odhams Press* (1971)). In both John's and Jane's case, there would be no problem in showing that the statement referred to them and had been published to a third party.

In respect of John and Jane, no defences seem available to Ian or his employer. It is not true (s 2 **Defamation Act 2013**) and it is likely that s 3 of the new Act, the honest opinion defence cannot be made out either. Under this defence, the statement must be an opinion (s 3(1)) and here the statement of being single and eating out as a result is presented as fact. This is provable as not true. Nonetheless, even if taken as an opinion of his apathy for cooking, indicated by him having meals out on the basis of being single (s 3(2)) it must be honestly held (s 3(4); *Slim v Daily Telegraph* (1968); *British Chiropractic Association v Singh* (2010)) rather than a reasonable person agreeing with the opinion (*Silkin v Beaverbrook Newspapers* (1958)). Whether Ian honestly held this opinion is somewhat questionable; however critically it must be an opinion on the basis of a fact which existed at the time the statement was published (s 3(4)(a) and *Spiller v Joseph* (2010)). No such fact exists in the present scenario therefore honest opinion is unlikely to be made out.

The scope of any application of it being a publication on a matter of public interest is perhaps more likely, as outlined in s 4 of the Act. Even using the broad tests as in *London Artists v Littler* (1969) (see *Lord Phillips in Flood v Times Newspapers* (2012)) and the reluctance to found something not in the public interest (*Jameel v Wall Street Europe (No 2)* (2005)), Ian must reasonably believe that he was publishing it in the public interest (s 4(1)(a)(b)). With an allowance for editorial judgment, the circumstances would have to be considered, including reference to the criteria of responsible journalism, *Reynolds v Times Newspapers*. There is insufficient information to draw any firm conclusions, but there is some doubt here given the lack of what would be simple steps to check whether the footballer was married or not.[2]

If a strong case is made, Ian and the television company may make use of the offer to make amends contained within ss 2–4 of the **Defamation Act 1996**. By s 2(4), such an offer must be to make and publish a suitable correction and apology, and to pay compensation.

The next question is whether the team, Eastleith Rovers, can sue in defamation. It would still need to demonstrate serious harm which might be more difficult, given such comments are often made about football performances by which journalists are free to comment to the broader public. Similarly as a profit-making body unless there were some consequential financial losses, it is likely the club could not pass the first threshold. If it could however the statement that the team prepares for a cup final by drinking the night before and the statement concerning how badly they played are both prima facie defamatory, and these statements were published to third parties with arguably it being a class

---

2   You must give broad coverage of the range of defences in defamation answers, including specific references to the new section in the Act.

so small that the words must refer to each member of it, allowing an individual member of the team to sue (*Knupffer v London Express Newspapers* (1944)).

There seems to be no defence to the allegations regarding drinking, and public interest may be defeated on the same basis as prior given the lack of responsible journalism demonstrated by Ian's embellishment of the facts, or not taking reasonable steps (see *Galloway v Telegraph Newspapers Ltd* (2006)). As regards the allegation that they played appallingly badly, the most applicable defence is honest opinion. In our case, the comment is an opinion based on the loss and he does not have to set out all the relevant facts in detail before he gives his opinion (*McQuire v Western Morning News* (1903)). Although Ian's comment may be honest in this respect, the defence can be rebutted by showing that the defendant acted out of malice (*Thomas v Bradbury Agnew* (1906)). The burden of proving malice will be on the claimant (*Telnikoff v Matusevich* (1991)). However, the defendant will still have to show that the facts on which the comment was based were true and the comment was objectively fair, in that anyone, however prejudiced or obstinate, could honestly have held the views expressed. Overall it would seem that a defence of honest comment would be likely to succeed.

The review in the *Eastland Gazette* constitutes a republication of the comments regarding the team and, by implication, republishes the statement regarding John and Jane. It is clear therefore that an action could still lie against the *Gazette* as they would satisfy the position of editor (given the *Gazette*'s editorial control of content) or as a commercial publisher under **s 10** of the **Defamation Act**. Therefore they will not have the defence of innocent publication available to them (**s 1 Defamation Act 1996**).[3] The question of whether Eastland Television's liability would extend to the republication is likely to be answered positively. Not only is it a natural consequence that such coverage would be repeated (*Slipper v BBC* (1991)) and, as in *McManus v Beckham* (2002), if the TV station knew what he or she said was likely to be repeated or a reasonable person in such a position would have known of such a risk, it would make them liable for the repeats. Even if this was not the case, again the scope of the honest opinion defence would be applicable to cover opinions based on facts.

QUESTION 40

Evaluate the ability of the **Defamation Act 2013** to tackle the criticisms that were made of the state of the common law prior to its enactment.

How to Read this Question

This essay requires a discussion of the key provisions of the new Act, with justification and references to the previous state of the common law, thus you must have a firm grasp of both. Taking a systematic approach that structures analysis around the key sections of the Act would be a valuable approach to have to organise your information. Take relevant sections in turn and place it in the context of how it develops and remedies old inadequacies or problems with the law.

---

3   Section 10 of the Defamation Act is an important provision of the new law on who can be sued for libel.

How to Answer this Question

The following points need to be considered:

- ❖ the definition of defamation;
- ❖ s1 and the serious harm requirement;
- ❖ s2 and the truth defence;
- ❖ s3 and honest opinion;
- ❖ s4 public interest defence;
- ❖ s5 website operators;
- ❖ s8 and the single publication rule;
- ❖ s11 and the use of juries.

Answer Structure

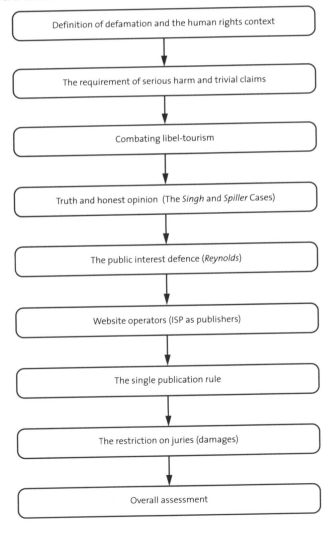

Definition of defamation and the human rights context

↓

The requirement of serious harm and trivial claims

↓

Combating libel-tourism

↓

Truth and honest opinion (The *Singh* and *Spiller* Cases)

↓

The public interest defence (*Reynolds*)

↓

Website operators (ISP as publishers)

↓

The single publication rule

↓

The restriction on juries (damages)

↓

Overall assessment

Up for Debate

The newly established **Defamation Act 2013** has transformed the landscape of the tort of defamation. Only with the passing of time and case law, will the effects of the Act be truly measured. Many of the sections of the new Act have been specifically targeted to resolve previous uncertainties or features of defamation that were seen to be unfair, curbing free expression or not in keeping with technological developments. For a very readable overview of the Act see Farrer and Co 'A quick guide to the Defamation Act 2013' (2014) 25(2) Entertainment Law Review 55, and for an appraisal of the merit of the sections in the Act read D Hooper, O Murphy and K Waite, 'Defamation Act 2013: what difference will it really make?' (2013) 24(6) Entertainment Law Review 199, or for a more expansive version see A Mullis, 'Tilting at the Windmills: the Defamation Act 2013' (2014) 77(1) Modern Law Review 87.

ANSWER

Defamation is premised on protecting a person's reputation against untrue statements published in either permanent form (libel) or non-permanent form (slander) (see, for example, *McManus v Beckham* (2002)). It is a tort that has strong democratic implications in so far as it involves the striking of a fair balance between freedom of expression (as protected by **Art 10** of the **European Convention on Human Rights** (**ECHR**)) and the individual interest in reputation which is somewhat less directly protected by **Art 8** of the **ECHR**.

Section 1 of the Act requires the statement to cause serious harm to the reputation of the claimant. This was presumably to tackle the previous phenomenon of libel (which was actionable per se, without proof of damage) being used for even trivial remarks with only a minimal risk of reputational damage (for example, the facts in *Spiller v Joseph* (2010) were described as 'a storm in a tea cup'). This is perhaps reflected in the relative ease with which the interpretation of defamatory can be satisfied: that the statement must tend to lower the claimant in the estimation of right-thinking members of society generally, which leads to them being shunned, avoided or subject to ridicule (Lord Atkin in *Sim v Stretch* (1936)). It is commonly understood that mere insults or abuse are not defamatory, although in the case *of Berkoff v Burchill* (1996) the Court of Appeal held that reputation should be applied to situations of contempt, scorn or ridicule even if it did not question professional competence. A principal issue affecting freedom of expression is that all that is required is for a person to demonstrate the statement made people think less of them, which is relatively easy to establish.

The same section requires there to be proof of financial loss in the case of profit-making bodies. This is presumably to avoid the type of long-running saga that was seen in *Steel and Morris v United Kingdom* (2005), and to avoid what are still seen as companies with deep pockets, using libel laws to curb the criticisms of dissenters, who endure restrictions to public funds.

The previous perception was that the law was stacked in favour of the claimant. Commentators have argued that defamation has a so-called 'chilling' effect because threatened legal action can prevent free expression or public debate (see Baroness Hale in *Jameel v Wall St Journal Europe* (2007)). This is further enhanced in an era of international communication facilitated by the internet. This allowed a person to claim defamation in a legal system outside the country in which they normally reside, to take advantage of more favourable libel laws. This phenomenon, termed libel-tourism has made defendants liable in England where an action would fail elsewhere. However **s 9** makes changes to the law with the burden on claimants to demonstrate that England and Wales is the most appropriate jurisdiction to hear the case.

Section 2 of the Act replaces the old common law defence of justification with an equivalent defence of truth. All that was required to trigger the common law defence was that the publication be true, and not to confuse the issue with reasonable deserts; however the position that it is for the defendant to prove that it was substantially true (in spite of the claimant being best placed to disprove it) remains.

Section 3 of the Act replaces the common law defence of honest comment with a very similar defence of honest opinion. The scope of this defence adopts some of the changes made to the common law defence by *Spiller v Joseph* (2010), which in itself was based on the decision in *British Chiropractic Association v Singh* (2010) where the spirit of the defence was surmised as the 'bulwark of free speech'. A danger in the fact that the legislature has proceeded in this way – by substantially restating the common law – is that it is unclear whether the legislature actually meant to change the law in some respect.

Section 4 replaces the *Reynolds* defence with a statutory defence of 'publication on a matter of public interest'. One change that this section makes, the defence in **s 4**, requires that the 'defendant reasonably believe that publishing the statement complained of was in the public interest'. As the explanatory notes suggests the spirit of *Reynolds* is found within the section. However it is likely that some degree of indecision and discretion will remain about its scope and the interpretation of public interest balanced against the responsible journalism criteria in *Reynolds*. This was confirmed in *Flood v Times Newspapers* (2012) where the Supreme Court held the application of *Reynolds* is to be approached on a case by case and fact sensitive basis, bearing in mind its overall purpose: to allow the press to publish stories of genuine public interest.

Website operators are given a defence by **s 5**, where it can be shown they did not post the defamatory statement. This section is largely in response to the previous state of the law where the common law has been playing catch-up in determining the publisher status of internet service providers (ISP) as outlined in *Godfrey v Demon Internet* (2001) and more recently in *Payam Tamiz v Google Inc* (2013), which generally reflects how the law should respond to a technological and social media age.

An important change is made by **s 8** which asserts a new single publication rule, for the purpose of limitation periods. Where a statement is republished by its original author, and the republication is essentially the same as the original publication, a new cause of action will not be triggered thus protecting online or archived material as shown in the case of *Loutchansky v Times Newspapers (No 2)* (2002) (confirmed by the European Court of Human Rights (ECtHR) in *Times Newspapers Ltd v UK* (2009)). However there are many unanswered questions about this rule including determining the relevant first publication date, and the extent to which material differences, e.g. presentation and prominence, will be sufficient to trigger a new publication.

Jury trials are effectively eliminated by s11 of the Act. Therefore what is seen as the punitive and disproportionate level of damages awarded for reputational loss (compared with say personal injury) may be curtailed. Instances where an original award is reduced by 50 per cent as seen in *Rantzen v Mirror Group Newspapers* (1993) will arguably become less frequent.

The Act no doubt broadly falls in favour of free speech advocates. Some of the changes introduced in the Act, seem to be logical, focused and common sense provisions to resolve prior concerns. However it is only with further judicial application in the case law, will judgments about the effectiveness of the Act be fully justified.[4]

Aim Higher

The law on this area is very new. Being aware of the policy aims of the new Act requires a wide-ranging breadth of understanding of the previous state of the law. This is an area where reference and discussion of academic opinion and the political and social contexts of the development of law will be very important to draw additional credit. Draw on topical and recent examples to highlight your discussion but do not be tempted to rant or reduce your answer to a narrative or a stream of consciousness. Ensure that examples and the policy or social arguments are rooted in your legal analysis. An interesting area of the law is the development of internet based publications with Justice Eady in the first-instance High Court decision of *Tamiz v Google* (2012) admitting that 'It is probably fair to say that none of the decisions so far relating to the role of Internet service providers (ISPs) has definitively established, in general terms, exactly how such entities fit into the traditional framework of common law principles.'

Common Pitfalls

For defamation you must give time and coverage for a proper appraisal of the defences, as it is often reasonably straightforward to make out the defamatory statement exists, insofar as the elements can be applied reasonably quickly. Having good timing and an effective exam technique here is critical. Also be wary of not to being too dismissive by arguing that a defence does not apply, in some cases where there is at least some doubt you should justify why it does not apply.

---

4 Note the structure in the essay which focused on key sections and discussed the provisions in terms of its improvement on the old law.

QUESTION 41

Consider the extent to which tort law is able to offer protection for a person's right to privacy.

How to Read this Question

This essay requires you to consider the development of the law in relation to the protection of 'privacy', particularly given the interest in the area as a result of the **Human Rights Act 1998** and recent developments in the common law.

How to Answer this Question

The following points require discussion:

❖ how privacy is protected in tort law;
❖ the influence of the **Human Rights Act 1998**;
❖ breach of confidence;
❖ the *Campbell* case and the concept of misuse of personal information;
❖ super-injunctions and the wider political context.

Answer Structure

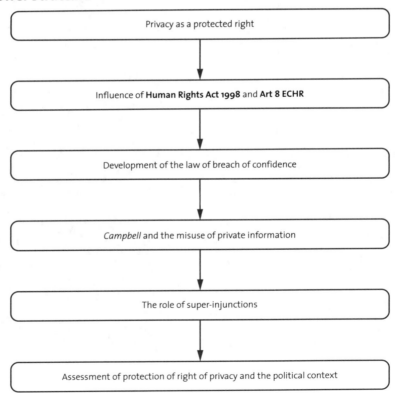

Privacy as a protected right

↓

Influence of **Human Rights Act 1998** and **Art 8 ECHR**

↓

Development of the law of breach of confidence

↓

Campbell and the misuse of private information

↓

The role of super-injunctions

↓

Assessment of protection of right of privacy and the political context

Up for Debate

Action for invasions of privacy have continued to be fuelled by celebrity cases against newspapers and with the foundations of both the law of breach of confidence and human rights, the common law has developed at a considerable pace in developing what some argue is a new tort for the invasion of privacy. Case law is fascinating, highly topical and current, and there are many case comments which are always worth reading as they provide good analysis of the judgments and the state of the law, see for example S Foster, 'Balancing privacy with freedom of speech: press censorship, the European Convention on Human Rights and the decision in *Mosley v United Kingdom*' (2011) 16(3) Communications Law 100, and S Foster, 'Football, private lives and the public interest: McClaren v News Group Newspapers Limited' (2012) 17(4) Communications Law 131. For a more thorough and academic overview of the jurisprudence of leading cases and the effect on the development of tort law see P Giliker, 'English tort law and the "tort" of breach of confidence' (2014) 1 Juridical Review 15.

ANSWER

Privacy is not explicitly recognised as a tort in its own right as shown in the very different cases of *Wainwright v Home Office* (2004) and *Kaye v Robertson* (1991), and recently confirmed in *Browne v Associated Newspapers* (2007). However rapid and regular developments in the common law have extended protection to unjustifiable invasions of a person's privacy in limited circumstances, largely due to the impact of the **Human Rights Act 1998**.[5]

Privacy in terms of a protected right consideration is based on **Art 8** of the **European Convention on Human Rights (ECHR)** which protects a person's private and family life, though it is not absolute and a balance has to be drawn with **Art 10** where there may be interference with freedom of expression. Similarly through **Art 10(2)** freedom of expression is qualified for the necessary protection of reputations and disclosure of information received in confidence. The common law has developed due to **s 6** of the **HRA** which requires public authorities (of which courts are one) to positively protect **Convention** rights and thus judges are required to develop the common law in a way that is consistent with the **ECHR** (including the effect of **s 2** which is to take into account European jurisprudence, e.g. *Von Hannover v Germany* (2004)).

Instead of developing a free-standing tort of privacy, which according to Lord Hoffmann in *Wainwright* would be better undertaken by Parliament, the courts have attempted to absorb the balance of **Art 8** and **Art 10 Convention** rights by developing the law of breach of confidence (*A v B plc* (2002)). A breach of confidence seeks to protect an individual against the wrongful disclosure of confidential information. The basic elements of the

5   Careful explanation is needed here of the background to the development of the law relating to privacy. It is still not a clearly defined area and the law is evolving quickly.

tort, prior to recent developments, require that there should be information that would be considered private and that the defendant disclosed the information when that would involve a breach of confidentiality owed to the owner of the information. In *A v B plc* (2002), it was stated that a duty of confidentiality would arise when a party subject to a duty knew or ought to know that the other party could reasonably expect his privacy to be protected.

One of the prominent cases in the development of privacy was *Douglas v Hello!* (2005), where though the claimant's argument that the HRA had created a new tort of privacy, a breach of confidence was upheld by virtue of photographs being inherently private as amongst other reasons it was known they were exclusive for commercial reasons. In *Campbell v MGN* (2004) Lord Nicholls attempted (though did not succeed in the long term) to develop the law to a language of a 'misuse of private information'. Therefore, in circumstances under which a person received information that they should know is reasonably regarded as confidential (private), a duty not to misuse that information was owed, regardless of any pre-existing relationships. The House of Lords held by a majority that the photograph and details of her treatment were a breach as any reasonable person would (or should) realise that the details of a person's medical treatment were the kind of information that would attract the obligation of confidence.

For a breach of confidence to become actionable there must be some disclosure of private information. What constitutes this is understood by reference to Lord Nicholls' definition in *Campbell*, and which has been approved in *McKennitt v Ash* (2006). It was also suggested in *Campbell* that private information would generally be obvious but, where it was not, a question of whether disclosure of the material would give substantial offence to the person to whom it related arose. There must also be some reasonable expectation on the part of the person to whom it relates that the information should be kept private.

A further area not yet conclusively determined is what amounts to an *unjustified* disclosure of private information. Baroness Hale in *Campbell* seemed to suggest that there could be a difference in circumstances under which the information related to public figures, justified through Art 10 of the ECHR and given special consideration in s 12 of the HRA. This would especially be the case in relation to celebrities who might court publicity, although in no way does this mean that they are not entitled to privacy. This would particularly be the case where, as in *Campbell*, a person had lied about information that was in the public interest to correct. This approach has been confirmed in *Browne* where the details of the start of the claimant's meeting with his partner had been lied about.

It appears to largely depend on the subject-matter at hand and whether a claimant pursues it, often creating the very publicity they were keen to avoid in the first place. In *Mosley v News Group Newspapers* (2008), the claimant was awarded £60,000 in damages for unauthorised publication of his participation in a sado-masochistic 'orgy' with a number of prostitutes with the cost to the defendant exceeding £1 million. The decision was aggressively criticised in the media with comment that the judiciary was creating a law of privacy unaccountably.

The context of the development of the law has also occurred with the backdrop of the use of super-injunctions by celebrities seeking to suppress publication. In *LNS v Persons Unknown* (2010) Justice Tugendhat refused the injunction, noting that the principal reason for suppressing the story was the effect it would have on the applicant's sponsorship deals. Given the profile of the claimant, it was difficult to argue that an injunction would be in the public interest. However, an injunction was granted in the case of *ETK v News Group Newspapers* (2011) because of the effect that publication of their father's affair would have on his children and that the public interest was not advanced in the publication. More lately and famously the remedy has proved to have its limitation as in the case of *Giggs v News Group Newspapers and Imogen Thomas* (2012) for its lack of effectiveness in relation to social media, particularly Twitter.

To conclude, it would appear that recent case law has started to establish some clear parameters as to the types of personal information that a person may be entitled to keep from disclosure to the public. The balance of opinion though generally in favour of freedom of expression has perhaps been swayed after the phone-hacking scandal at the *News of the World* triggered wider examination of press practices. The aftermath of the scandal received considerable public attention and the outcome of the 2011 Leveson Inquiry on Culture, Practice and Ethics of the Press will be the establishment of a new independent regulator to replace the current Press Complaints Commission, and which after much political debate will be underpinned by a new Royal Charter. Whether in future this will reduce the number of cases and thus the development of the law remains to be seen, but so long as public demand to read such stories remains, the tension between those in the public eye and those publishing information about them, will be likely to continue.[6]

Aim Higher

Privacy is a fast-moving and highly topical area of the law. The best advice is to stay as current as you can. This area has grown beyond recognition in ten years and there is more space for evolution. Much of the litigation occurs initially in the High Court and remains there, so have a look at the range of cases (with many celebrities who you would identify) claiming invasions of privacy. Consider also the wider impact of the Leveson Inquiry and the debate around the rights of victims and those defending freedom of expression. The development of law here has political and social implications which the judges themselves are all too aware of.

---

6   Essay questions are often set on topics which are controversial and/or newsworthy, so any up to date contextual, e.g. policy material that can be introduced will add to the quality of the answer. Even when the events have occurred after the end of the relevant lecture programme, inclusion of them in the answer will show that the context is thoroughly appreciated.

Common Pitfalls

If you're writing an essay on this area of law, ensure you are aware of the key cases and be clear on the relationship between human rights, breach of confidence and the surrounding debate on how privacy can be best protected. Ensure you have a clear chronology of the development of privacy, perhaps drawing your own timeline of the essential cases and the incremental changes to the law.

QUESTION 42

Nancy, an Olympic athlete, and Ron, a famous singer, employed Kate as a nanny to look after their two young children. Nancy was a high-profile campaigner against drugs in sport and Ron undertook a considerable amount of work for charities that protected children working in unfavourable conditions in the developing world. The couple held an invitation-only charity fund-raising party at their property and sold the exclusive reporting rights to a Sunday newspaper. Kate sold a story about the couple and a set of secretly taken photographs of the party to *Slur* magazine. The story alleged that Ron used his charity work to spend time away from home because the couple's marriage was not solid. It also promised details of intimate conversations with Nancy revealing her bulimia and stating that she used cocaine in her struggle to stay fit for competition. Finally, *Slur* promised 'shocking insight into the personal and emotional frailties' of Ron, based on bullying that he had suffered as a child. The story was to be serialised over three weeks and was previewed in the edition prior to the serialisation under the headline 'Things they wouldn't want you to know', along with the photographs of the party.

▶ Advise Nancy and Ron, assuming that this information is largely true.

How to Read this Question

The question involves the consideration and application of various legal principles relating to the protection of a person's privacy. As this area of law is still evolving, there are elements of uncertainty that require a discussion of recent case law and the impact of the **Human Rights Act 1998**. It is always important in such discussions to draw some factual distinctions with any well known cases, which may be triggered here in relation to the exclusive photographs being sold to *Slur*, as well as the nature of the private information in its publication.

How to Answer this Question

The following points would require discussion:

❖   how privacy is protected in tort law;
❖   the influence of the **Human Rights Act**;
❖   breach of confidence and the emergence of the concept of misuse of personal information;
❖   whether Nancy and Ron can protect their personal information.

Applying the Law

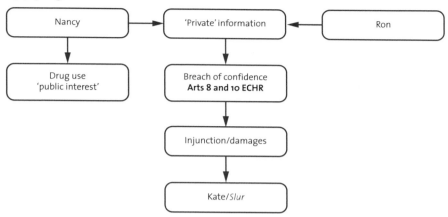

ANSWER

While there is no specific tort of privacy at Nancy and Ron's publication (*Wainwright v Home Office* (2004); *Kaye v Robertson* (1991); *Browne v Associated Newspapers* (2007)), the courts have developed rights to permit the protection of private information which they can use against both Kate and *Slur* in relation to the publication.

Privacy in terms of a protected right consideration is based on **Art 8** of the **European Convention on Human Rights (ECHR)** which protects a person's private and family life, though it is not absolute and a balance has to be drawn with **Art 10** where there may be interference with freedom of expression. Similarly through **Art 10(2)** freedom of expression is qualified for the necessary protection of reputations and disclosure of information received in confidence.

In *McKennitt v Ash* (2006), the Court of Appeal noted that cases in the English courts and in the European Court of Human Rights (*Campbell v MGN* (2004); *Douglas v Hello!* (2006); *Von Hannover v Germany* (2005)) have 'wrestled with the problem of identifying the basis for claiming privacy or confidence in respect of unauthorised or purloined information'. The tort is satisfied if information about a person's private life is obtained by the defendant and the defendant discloses the information when that would involve a breach of a duty of confidentiality owed to the owner of the information (*A v B plc* (2002)). In *McKennitt*, it was observed that some of the difficulties with the use of the breach of confidence concept had been overcome by Lord Nicholls in *Campbell* renaming the tort as one of misuse of private information. Indeed, in that case, Lord Hoffmann stated that an action for breach of confidence was also concerned with the protection of 'human autonomy and dignity', and continued that a person had a right to 'control the dissemination of information about one's private life'.[7]

---

7   Use of direct quotes, as in this paragraph, add quality to an answer.

A duty of confidentiality would arise when a party subject to a duty knew or ought to know that the other party could reasonably expect his privacy to be protected. There is no longer any requirement for a pre-existing relationship of confidence between the parties (*Campbell* (2004)), although such a relationship does exist in relation to Kate as a nanny to the family and is not limited to a commercial context (*Argyll v Argyll* (1967)). So far as both Kate and *Slur* are concerned, the duty would arise if they knew or ought to have known that the information they had received was of a private nature. Given the circumstances, it is apparent that they should have been aware of this fact. In determining the meaning of what constitutes 'information of a private nature', Lord Nicholls stated in *Campbell* that 'the touchstone of private life is whether in respect of the disclosed acts the person in question had a reasonable expectation of privacy'. In *McKennitt*, further elaborating on this concept, it was determined that intimate relationship details, intimate conversations between the claimant and defendant in that case, which were understood to be private and which would never be held in public, revelations about the state of a person's health and even trivial details about how somebody behaved at home might fall into the definition (see also *Mosley v News Group Newspapers Ltd* (2008)).

Given the intensely personal nature of some of the revelations, such as Nancy's bulimia, the apparently fragile state of the couple's relationship and Ron's character flaws, it is submitted that Nancy and Ron would face little problem in convincing the court that the information was fully within the category of private information.[8] The fact that the couple are famous should not have a bearing on their entitlement to some privacy, as was noted by Lindsay J in *Douglas v Hello!* (2001) when he observed that even a public figure was entitled to a private life, although he might expect and accept that his circumstances would be scrutinised more carefully by the media. This would be more likely in a situation in which a person courted publicity, but, again, did not mean that there was no entitlement to a private life.

So far as the photographs are concerned, the case of *Douglas v Hello!* (2001), which held that unauthorised photographs of a wedding were private information, is helpful. In that case, the exclusive nature of the picture deal was known to the defendant photographer and a breach of confidence was found. It would be difficult for either Kate or *Slur* to avoid liability for the publication of the photographs on this authority, as there was an invited guest list and an exclusive publication deal in place.

Nancy may face a problem in relation to the revelation that she used cocaine in order to help her to remain fit for competition. Because of the balance that must be struck between a person's right to a private life under **Art 8** of the **ECHR** and the equally important freedom of expression protected by virtue of **Art 10**, there is a tension that arises, as both cannot be protected in respect of the same information. In this circumstance, particularly where the 'flip-side' of the fact that celebrities should expect some level of greater scrutiny of their lives is concerned, it may be felt that there is a genuine

---

8   This is illustrative of the vital process of applying the stated law to the facts given.

public interest in the revelation (*Theakston v MGN* (2002); *A v B* (2002)). As a result, *Slur* might well be permitted to publish the details. *Slur* could also take comfort from the decision in *Campbell*. In that case, the claimant, a world-famous 'supermodel', had limited success against the defendant newspaper that had published pictures of her leaving a meeting of Narcotics Anonymous, as well as details of her treatment. The House of Lords held that although the photograph and treatment details were an invasion of her privacy, details of her previously denied drug addiction were permitted to be published as a means of setting the record straight. This approach was recently confirmed in the Court of Appeal's decision in *Browne v Associated Newspapers* (2007), in which the details of the circumstances surrounding the way in which the claimant had met his former partner had been lied about. Although the courts have not explicitly set out the conditions under which a claim of public interest would be able to defeat an action for the misuse of personal information, the fact that Nancy had been a high-profile campaigner against drugs in sport might well be fatal to any attempt that she may make to restrain publication of that aspect of the serialisation.[9]

Beyond the potential for publication of the information in relation to Nancy's drug use, it would appear that Nancy and Ron would be able to claim damages against Kate and *Slur* in relation to the publication of the unauthorised photographs, and would be able to restrain publication of the additional details through applying for an injunction.

QUESTION 43

Comment upon the influence of the **Human Rights Act 1998** on the development of English tort law.

How to Read this Question

The **Human Rights Act (HRA)** is increasingly a feature of modern tort law, and thus is now becoming a feature of some examiners' questions. This question requires a broad view of the impact of the **Human Rights Act** on tort law, while at the same time necessitating a recognition and assessment of areas in which examples can be provided of the impact. You can draw analysis from any area of the law that has had interactions with human rights, but it is obviously not possible to cover absolutely everything. Nuisance and the law on privacy are two such examples where human rights implications can be found.

How to Answer this Question

The following points require explanation and discussion:

❖ the basic duty of the courts in relation to human rights compatibility;
❖ nuisance and human rights;
❖ 'privacy' and human rights;
❖ overall assesment.

---

9 As this is a relatively new and fast developing field of law, considerable detail about the cases will be necessary.

Answer Structure

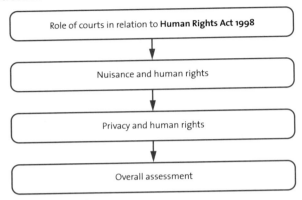

Up for Debate

The **Human Rights Act 1998** was a highly constitutionally significant development in the law, and though the Act was traditionally seen to apply to the vertical relationship between the state and the individual, the consequences for the law of tort has been through its possible horizontal effect between individuals. This has most prominently been seen in privacy and defamation contexts, and is a fascinating feature of the development of both areas of the law. For reading on this debate see M Arden, 'Human rights and civil wrongs: tort law under the spotlight' (2010) Jan Public Law 140, T Bennett, 'Horizontality's new horizons: re-examining horizontal effect: privacy, defamation and the Human Rights Act: part 1' (2010) 21(3) Entertainment Law Review 96, T Bennett, 'Horizontality's new horizons: re-examining horizontal effect: privacy, defamation and the Human Rights Act: part 2' (2010) 21(4) Entertainment Law Review 145.

ANSWER

The **Human Rights Act 1998 (HRA)** has undoubtedly had profound effects on the structure and practice of law in the UK since it came into force in 2000. The **HRA** has made the majority of the rights contained in the **European Convention on Human Rights (ECHR)** (so-called 'Convention rights' – s 1) available as remedies in the UK courts and requires public authorities to act compatibly with the **Convention** rights (s 6), subject to limited exceptions. The **HRA**'s implication for private law was, initially, less obvious. However, as the definition of public authorities, according to s 6(3), includes courts and tribunals, it would be unlawful for either to act inconsistently with a **Convention** right, and thus the law of tort has developed indirectly through the horizontal effect of the **HRA**. There is no automatic need to create new causes of action in tort but this has minimally been interpreted against a background of what **Convention** rights demand.

For example the courts have been required to decide a number of cases in private nuisance by reference to questions of breaches of **Convention** rights. The principal **Convention** rights that have been called into question have been **Art 8**, which contains the right to respect for private and family life, and **Art 1** of the **First Protocol** to the **ECHR**, which entitles a person to peaceful enjoyment of property. Prior to the **HRA** coming into force, the European Court of Human Rights had held that certain interferences with a person's ability to enjoy their property as they wished, and which would more than likely amount to a nuisance in English law, would fall within the protection offered by **Art 8** and **Art 1** of the **First Protocol** (*López Ostra v Spain* (1995); *Guerra v Italy* (1998)). However, **Art 8** is not absolute and by virtue of **Art 8(2)** permits interference by a public authority with the right in circumstances where it is necessary in a democratic society, in the interests of national security, public safety or the economic well-being of the country amongst others. A similar qualification attaches to **Art 1** of the **First Protocol**. Examples in English law have included the decision in *Dennis v MOD* (2003), which was concerned with noise nuisance created by low-flying military aircraft but an injunction on the basis of an **Art 8** breach was overridden by the public interest in maintaining a trained air force.

The House of Lords' decision in *Marcic v Thames Water Utilities* (2004) demonstrates some of the limits of the **HRA** in nuisance cases. The essential question was whether a statutory system that prevented the claimant from bringing an action in nuisance was **Convention**-compliant. They held that it was, because Parliament had considered that there should be a balance based on costs and the defendant's system of priorities was permitted to reflect that. That finding was based on *Hatton v UK* (2003), which was concerned with night flights from Heathrow Airport. It was confirmed that the national authorities were best placed to make decisions on the policy around night flying as they had 'direct democratic legitimation' and that they had a broad margin of discretion in balancing the various competing factors, of which the economic well-being of the country was one. The impact of the **HRA** would seem to therefore accord greater consideration of a balancing exercise between private and wider public interests than the tort of nuisance alone may have done, and this effect is critical for the development of tort law.

A further consideration is the requirement that a successful action in nuisance requires that the claimant has an interest in land (*Hunter v Canary Wharf* (1997)). The compatibility of that requirement with **Convention** rights was called into question, by Neuberger J in *McKenna v British Aluminium* (2002) (see also *Dobson v Thames Water Utilities* (2009)). In *Dobson v Thames Water No 2* (2011), a declaration of the breach of all the occupants' **Art 8** rights was made by the court, but having awarded damages in nuisance to the legal occupiers of homes no independent rights to compensation would be created. So the effect of the **HRA** in the tort of nuisance has clearly been felt but not so significantly to displace or transform the common law.

With respect to privacy, at the heart of the issue is the **Art 8** right to respect for private and family life, set against the **Art 10** right to freedom of expression. Of crucial importance here is *Von Hannover v Germany* (2004) where the court confirmed that **Art 8** imposes a positive obligation upon states to make sure that due protection is given to privacy rights meaning that such rights should be protected as between private parties. This represents a further example of the *horizontal* application of the **Convention** rights.

Section 12 of the **HRA** specifically requires that regard is to be paid to **Art 10** in any case in which there is the possibility that granted remedy might interfere with the right to freedom of expression, and **Art 10(2)** provides inherent qualifications on the right, including considerations of reputations and disclosure of information received in confidence. That would mean that any case brought on the basis of **Art 8** or the tort of breach of confidence would automatically involve consideration of **Art 10**, and so the law has developed on this basis. In the area of 'privacy' and in the now-leading case of *Campbell v MGN* (2004), Lord Nicholls has gone so far as to say that the 'values enshrined in **Articles 8** and **10** are now part of the cause of action for breach of confidence'.

As **Art 10** protects freedom of expression, not all information will be protected. Publication might be in the public interest and may disclose wrongdoing or hypocrisy. In *Campbell* details of the claimant's previously denied drug addiction were permitted to be published as a means of setting the record straight. This approach was confirmed in the Court of Appeal's decision in *Browne v Associated Newspapers* (2007). Although the courts have not explicitly set out the conditions under which a claim of public interest would be able to defeat an action for the misuse of personal information, it is clear that it is something to be determined in the balancing exercise of a claimant's **Art 8** and **Art 10** rights; see, for example, *Ferdinand v Mirror News Group* (2011). The debate was drawn into sharp focus by the cases of *Mosley v News Group Newspapers* (2008) and *LNS v Persons Unknown* (2010) which clearly set out the considerations undertaken by the courts.

Therefore it can be seen from a brief analysis of private nuisance and 'privacy', that the **HRA** is clearly having an impact in these, as well as other, areas within the law of tort. To quote Neuberger J in *McKenna*, 'we are in the early days of the **Human Rights Act 1998** and of its application to the common law'. How the continuing development of human rights and common law principles will develop is difficult to predict, although the courts are setting boundaries incrementally through the case law.

Aim Higher

In a human rights context, being able to refer to the jurisprudence of the ECtHR insofar as it relates to tort law will give your answers greater authority and legitimacy.

Common Pitfalls

A common assumption is that a recourse to 'human rights' will mean that a claimant is compensated. That won't always be the case. Most of the rights engaged in tort law are qualified rights rather than absolute rights and so will generally need to be balanced against competing considerations. In other cases **Convention** rights are already well protected through the existing common law, and in cases where a breach of a **Convention** right is established, it will not necessarily affect the extent or create additional remedies where the common law adequately provides them.

13

INTRODUCTION

This final chapter concerns a topic that many students often ignore. All claimants in tort are seeking a remedy. The most important remedy in tort is damages and questions involving a discussion of damages for personal injury or death can often be set by examiners. Such questions may take the form of a general essay question requiring a critical discussion, or a problem question and this chapter provides one of each. Problem questions may typically contain details such as a claimant's salary and other personal circumstances that will help you determine the amount of losses incurred. You would not necessarily be expected to produce detailed calculations of them but rather to discuss the particular heads of damage that are recoverable and how they would be calculated.

Checklist
Students must be familiar with the following areas:
(a) types of damages – nominal, contemptuous, general, special damages, special damage (that is, actual loss, which must be proved if the tort is not actionable per se), aggravated and exemplary;
(b) damages for personal injury – pecuniary and non-pecuniary loss;
(c) damages for death (*though discussion of this is not included in the problem question*).

QUESTION 44

James is crossing the road when he is injured due to the negligent driving of Ken. As a result of this accident, James, who is married with two young children, will be confined to a wheelchair for the rest of his life.

▶ **Explain how a court would assess what damages James should receive from Ken?**

How to Read this Question

Although this is written in the form of a problem, it is in fact a directed question on the calculation of damages for personal injury and death. The first line indicates negligence and therefore liability has already been established, and thus requires no discussion. Instead the question requires a consideration of the various heads of damages under which James could recover, and notice key features in the question such as being confined to a wheelchair, his marriage and how he has dependants. As mentioned previously, estimates would not be necessary and, indeed, given the facts are brief, they would be difficult to derive in any case.

How to Answer this Question

The following points need to be discussed:

- ❖ the object of damages;
- ❖ how the claimant's damages are calculated, including the various heads of pecuniary loss;
- ❖ any potential deductions, e.g. for double recovery;
- ❖ any non-pecuniary losses.

Applying the Law

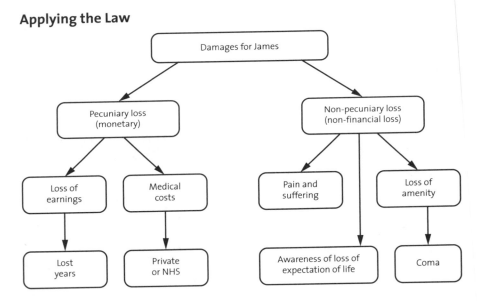

ANSWER

The object of awarding damages in tort is to put the claimant, as far as money can do so, in the position he or she would have been had the tort not happened. Thus, as a general rule, if, as a result of the accident, James has lost money or will have to spend money that he otherwise would not have had to spend, he can recover in respect of these sums.[1]

If we apply this general principle to the pecuniary loss that James has suffered, we can see that the first thing James has lost is wages, as he is now confined to a wheelchair (assuming for the present that James ceases to be paid any salary by his employer from the date of the accident). James will have lost a certain amount of wages up to the date of trial and

---

1   It is not necessary to establish the liability of Ken, because the question states that he is negligent.

this is calculated using his net wages as a basis, as James has only lost his take-home pay, not his gross pay. For further loss, the problem is more difficult, due to uncertainties of future income, life expectancy etc. The court will calculate James's net annual loss and multiply that by a figure based on the number of years the loss is likely to last (the multiplier). The multiplier is not simply the duration of the disability, but a lower figure with a maximum value of around 25 (see *Wells v Wells* (1998)) to take account of the fact that James has received the money as a lump sum, rather than over a period of years. The multiplier is also designed to take account of the 'general vicissitudes of life'. It should also be noted that any award will be final and, should James's condition worsen, he will not normally be able to go back to court to claim any added sums (*Fitter v Veal* (1701)). Thus, it is essential to wait until James's medical condition stabilises before any trial. **Section 32A** of the **Senior Courts Act 1981** does allow a provisional award to be made with the right to additional compensation (once only) should the condition worsen, but s32A has been given a somewhat restrictive interpretation by the High Court in *Willson v Ministry of Defence* (1991).

An obvious problem for James is the effect of future inflation if he receives a lump sum. No especial protection is given in respect of this (*Lim Poh Choo v Camden Health Authority* (1980)), but recently courts have begun to approve 'structured settlements', in which part of the sum payable to the claimant is invested by the defendants in an annuity that can provide an index-linked annual sum for the rest of the claimant's life (*Kelley v Dawes* (1990); s2(1) of the **Damages Act 1996**, as amended by the **Courts Act 2003**). The court now has a duty to consider whether periodical payments are appropriate.

It may be that, as a result of the accident, James has a reduced expectation of life. If so, James can recover the earnings that he would have received during the years he has lost due to his reduced expectation of life (*Pickett v British Rail Engineering* (1980)), although, following the general principle of damages in tort, James's living expenses must be deducted (*Harris v Empress Motors* (1983)).

James will also be compensated for any loss of pension rights that accompanies his loss of salary.

James can claim in respect of any future expenses which he will incur as a result of the accident. Thus, James can recover for nursing care and this may be obtained privately even if it is available under the NHS (s2(4) of the **Law Reform (Personal Injuries) Act 1948**). He may also recover the reasonable value of gratuitous services rendered to him by way of voluntary care by a member of his family (*Hunt v Severs* (1994)), or free hospice care (*Drake & Starkey v Foster Wheeler Ltd* (2010)).

James can also claim for any changes necessary to his accommodation: for example, the provision of wheelchair ramps, additional costs of lighting or heating and future costs of a gardener, tradesmen, etc., if James did these jobs himself and now cannot do so (see, for example, *Willson*).

It may well be the case that James already receives compensation from a person other than the tortfeasor[2] and deduction from previous amounts may have to be made to prevent double recovery.

The **Social Security (Recovery of Benefits) Act 1997** provides that no deduction for social security benefits is to be made against awards for pain and suffering, and that specified benefits only may be deducted from awards for loss of earnings, cost of care and loss of mobility.

For other benefits, the general rule is that a benefit received by the claimant is only deducted where it truly reduces the loss suffered (*Parry v Cleaver* (1970)). Hence, sick pay or wages paid during the period following the accident are deducted, but not any insurance sums that James receives (*Bradburn v Great Western Railway* (1874)) or charitable donations, ill health awards or higher pension benefits (*Smoker v London Fire and Civil Defence Authority* (1991)).

James will, of course, also suffer non-pecuniary loss. First, there will be the pain and suffering that James has endured and will suffer in the future. Also, if, as a result of the accident, James has suffered a loss of expectation of life and is aware of this, then by **s1(1)(b)** of the **Administration of Justice Act 1982**, the court is required to take this into account when assessing damages. Next, James will be compensated for any loss of amenity – that is, his capacity to engage in pre-accident activities – and this award may be made even if he is in a coma (*West v Shepherd* (1964); *Lim Poh Choo*). James will also be compensated for the injury itself using practitioner quantum guidelines. James should be advised that the Court of Appeal held in *Heil v Rankin* (2000) that awards for non-pecuniary loss were too low and that, for the most severe injuries, the awards should be increased by about one-third.

Finally, James will be awarded interest on his damages in respect of losses up to the date of trial under **s35A** of the **Senior Courts Act 1981**.[3]

QUESTION 45
It is a general rule of law that damages are awarded to compensate the claimant, rather than to punish the defendant. Are there any situations in which a claimant could make a profit out of the damages awarded to him?[4]

How to Read this Question
This is an essay question on the topic of damages in the law, asking for a peculiar focus on the concern that damages might lead to the claimant acquiring a profit. Ensure that you do not engage in a lengthy descriptive discussion and that you adequately address instances where the law has either limited or allowed the possibility of drawing a 'profit' with sufficient analysis.

....

2   Note the tortfeasor is Ken, but in fact his insurance company will be paying, as it is obligatory to have third-party motor insurance (or the Motor Insurers' Bureau will pay if the driver is uninsured).

3   Note that the majority of claims will be settled out of court before trial, but with damages assessed on the principles stated here.

4   This question will take considerable thought and planning to extract relevant information from your knowledge of remedies (see diagram).

How to Answer this Question

This question calls for a discussion of the following aspects of the law of damages:

- ❖ the purpose of damages;
- ❖ general and special damages;
- ❖ aggravated damages;
- ❖ exemplary damages;
- ❖ non-deduction of insurance sums;
- ❖ possible double compensation under the **Fatal Accidents Act 1976**;
- ❖ damages in defamation.

Answer Structure

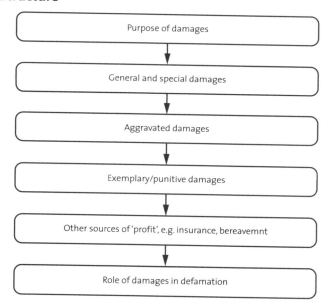

Purpose of damages

↓

General and special damages

↓

Aggravated damages

↓

Exemplary/punitive damages

↓

Other sources of 'profit', e.g. insurance, bereavemnt

↓

Role of damages in defamation

Up for Debate

Damages are the primary remedy for those making a claim in tort but the question of who is to blame and who pays are not always the same person. Thus the rules on damages can intertwine with broader philosophical considerations of corrective and distributive justice. It can also be a highly technical and complicated part of the law and there is a large range of discretion, and much of the literature is concerned with only specific aspects of the rule. For example for a discussion that argues for the abolishment of exemplary damages see A Beever, 'The structure of aggravated and exemplary damages' (2003) 23 Oxford Journal of Legal Studies 87, and for a comparison between damages in tort and the **Human Rights Act** see J Steele, 'Damages in tort and under the Human Rights Act: remedial or functional separation?' (2008) 67 Cambridge Law Journal 607.

ANSWER

The general principle governing an award of damages in tort is to put the claimant in the position in which he would have been had the tort not occurred, as far as this can be done by an award of money. In many situations, this will not be possible. For example, in personal injury cases the loss of wages suffered by the claimant can be calculated exactly, but such a calculation is difficult as regards a broken leg that causes an absence from work. A claimant must expressly plead any quantifiable special damage that he has suffered, for example, medical expenses or loss of wages, and will in addition be awarded general damages that are not quantified in and assessed by the court. By definition, therefore, these general plus special damages, together with any interest awarded, should match the loss suffered by the claimant.

However, in certain circumstances, the court may make an award of aggravated damages. Aggravated damages may be awarded where the defendant's conduct caused injury to the feelings or pride of the claimant: see, for example, *Harsford v Bird* (2006), a claim in trespass in which the Privy Council, refusing an award of aggravated damages, stated that there would be a requirement of 'high-handed, insulting or oppressive conduct' before such a claim would succeed. In *Archer v Brown* (1985), it was stated that sums awarded in respect of aggravated damages should be moderate (see also *W v Meah* (1986)). An example of circumstances that might justify an award of aggravated damages can be seen in *Marks v Chief Constable of Greater Manchester* (1992).

Both of these types of damages are compensatory in nature and that a claimant will not make a profit out of them. Although greater sums may be awarded in the case of aggravated damages, these increased sums only reflect the increased loss or suffering to which the defendant has subjected the claimant. Where truly moderate sums are awarded for aggravated damages, this rationale is unexceptionable, but where much larger sums are awarded, it may be difficult to distinguish between aggravated damages and exemplary damages, as Lord Wilberforce pointed out in *Cassell v Broome* (1972). The distinction is important, because the function of exemplary damages is to punish the defendant and it is in such situations that one might suggest that the claimant is making a profit out of the damages awarded.

In *Rookes v Barnard* (1964), the House of Lords described those circumstances in which exemplary, or punitive, damages could be recovered in tort.[5] Lord Devlin held that such damages could be awarded in three situations only: where authorised by statute; in the case of oppressive, arbitrary or unconstitutional acts by a government servant; or where the defendant has calculated that he will make a profit out of the tort, even if normal compensatory damages are awarded.

---

5   Note that exemplary or punitive damages are much more widely used in other common law systems, notably the USA, which partly accounts for the much higher levels of damages paid out in such a jurisdiction.

These categories have been strictly adhered to. Thus, in *Cassell*, Lord Reid stated that the oppressive, arbitrary or unconstitutional categories did not extend to oppressive action by a company. However, in *Holden v Chief Constable of Lancashire* (1987), it was held that exemplary damages could be awarded for unlawful arrest even if there had been no oppressive behaviour by the arresting officer, since the category contemplated that the action be oppressive, arbitrary *or* unconstitutional.

In *Cassell*, it was held that exemplary damages are only available in those categories described in *Rookes*, and this whole area has more recently been considered in *Kuddus v Chief Constable of Leicestershire Constabulary* (2001). In *Kuddus*, the House of Lords emphasised that the question was whether the facts fell within the Lord Devlin's categories in *Rookes*. (See also *Mosley v News Group Newspapers* (2008) where exemplary damages were refused, and *Ramzan v Brookwide Ltd* (2010) where they were granted in a case of trespass where a profit had been made.)

Thus there are limitations to the prospect of profit for the claimant and indeed the fear that claimants may profit from exemplary damages was stated in *Thompson v Commissioner of Police of the Metropolis* (1997). Here, the Court of Appeal held that limits should be placed on exemplary damages awarded for unlawful and violent conduct by the police, and set an 'absolute maximum' figure.

Another way in which a claimant may profit from an award of damages is where he or she sues in respect of a consequence of the defendant's conduct for which he or she is already insured. In such situations, the original rule is that insurance benefits are ignored for the purpose of assessing damages (*Bradburn v Great Western Railway* (1874)). Though note in *Gaca v Pirelli General plc* (2004), it was held that insurance benefits received by an employee after an accident at work were no longer to be disregarded unless the employee had contributed to the insurance premium.

Another area where double recovery is allowed by statute is in the award of damages under the **Fatal Accidents Act 1976**. By s4 of the **1976 Act**, any benefits that accrue to the dependants as a result of the death of the deceased are to be disregarded. Thus, in *Pidduck v Eastern Scottish Omnibus* (1990), a widow's pension that was paid to a widow following the death of her husband was held to be non-deductible. The **1976 Act** also provides, in s3(3), that in assessing damages for a fatal accident, the chances of the widow remarrying are to be disregarded. In *Martin v Owen* (1992), it was held that the chance that the parties might have divorced should be taken into account. This conclusion seems rather surprising at first but, when one realises that s4 of the **1976 Act** expressly contemplates double recovery, it will be interpreted strictly to restrict any such double recovery to that stated in the Act. So, a widow who remarried after being awarded damages for loss of dependency could make a profit out of those damages. It could also be argued that as, by s1(A) of the **Fatal Accidents Act 1976**, a sum of £11,800 is paid for loss of a spouse or minor child, the sum could represent a disproportionately high figure amounting to double recovery. Alternatively, it has been argued that this figure is insultingly small.

Finally, one might consider the position of successful claimants in defamation action where traditionally juries have inconsistently awarded very large damages against newspapers. However s 11 of the new **Defamation Act 2013** will severely restrict the use of juries by removing the assumption that they will be used, and therefore instances where original jury awards are reduced by 50 per cent as seen in *Rantzen v Mirror Group Newspapers* (1993) will become less frequent.

Index